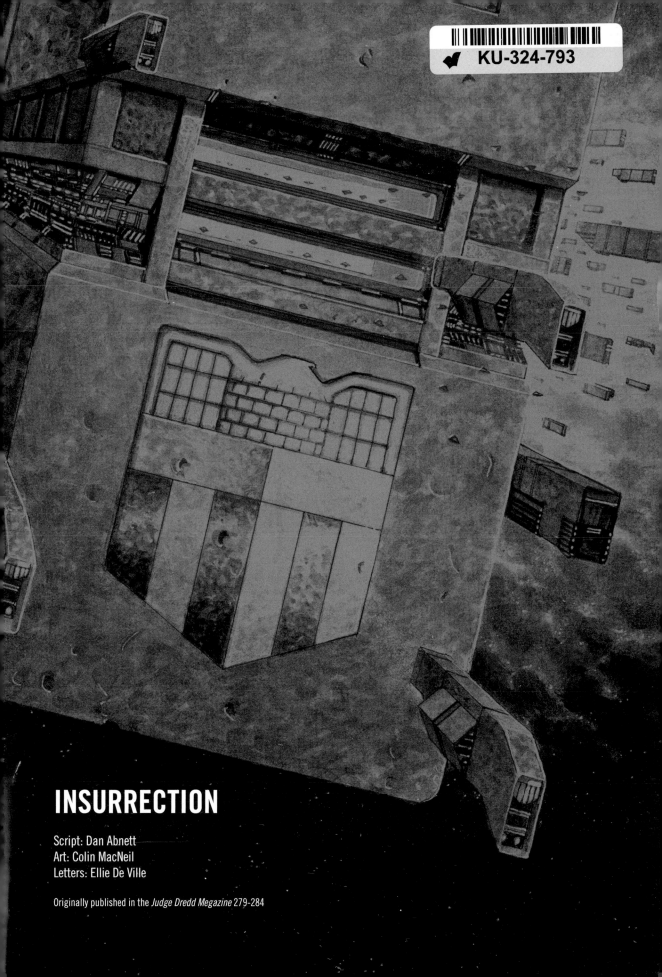

# INSURRECTION

Script: Dan Abnett
Art: Colin MacNeil
Letters: Ellie De Ville

Originally published in the *Judge Dredd Megazine* 279-284

TRANSMISSION
BEGINS

GOOD MORNING.

MY NAME IS **KAREL LUTHER**. I HOLD THE RANK OF **COLONIAL MARSHAL** AND I AM THE **SENIOR** MARSHAL SERVING MEGA-CITY ONE COLONY **K ALPHA 61**.

FOR THE LAST TWO YEARS, K ALPHA 61 HAS BEEN AT WAR. WE WERE ATTACKED AND **OCCUPIED** BY FORCES OF THE ZHIND.

THE ZHIND WERE CLAIMING TERRITORIAL JURISDICTION. IT IS EVIDENT TO ME THEY WERE SIMPLY INTERESTED IN K ALPHA 61'S EXTENSIVE **MINERAL** DEPOSITS.

YOU KNOW **ALL** ABOUT THIS, OF COURSE. I SENT YOU REGULAR REPORTS REGARDING OUR SITUATION.

I ASKED, ON NO FEWER THAN **TWENTY-THREE** OCCASIONS, FOR MILITARY ASSISTANCE.

YOU SAW FIT TO PROVIDE NONE.

YOU'RE HAPPY ENOUGH TO RECEIVE THE RARE METAL CONSIGNMENTS WE SHIP TO YOU REGULAR AS CLOCKWORK, EVERY MONTH.

BUT YOU COULDN'T LIFT A **FINGER** TO HELP US.

WE **WON** THE WAR, THANKS FOR ASKING. WE DROVE THE ZHIND OUT.

THAT ONLY HAPPENED BECAUSE I TOOK THE STEP OF ENFRANCHISING THE **ENTIRE** COLONIAL WORKFORCE — MUTANTS, DROIDS, UPLIFTS.

I GRANTED THEM ALL **CITIZEN STATUS** SO THEY COULD FIGHT WITH US, SHOULDER TO SHOULDER.

THEN I GET **THIS**, FROM THE OFFICE OF THE CHIEF JUDGE: 'NOW THAT HOSTILITIES HAVE SUBSIDED, CITIZENSHIP MUST BE HEREBY WITHDRAWN FROM ALL NON-HUMAN UNITS, EFFECTIVE IMMEDIATE.'

WHERE THE **HELL** DO YOU GET OFF, YOU PIECES OF **SHIT?**

ANYWAY, YOU CAN **STICK** THIS. AT THIS HOUR, JULY FOURTH, 2130, COLONY K ALPHA 61 DECLARES TOTAL AND EVERLASTING **INDEPENDENCE** FROM MEGA-CITY ONE.

THIS WORLD WILL HENCEFORTH BE KNOWN AS **LIBERTY**. AS BY NAME, AS BY **NATURE**.

SUCK ON **THAT**.

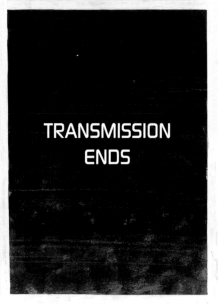

TRANSMISSION
ENDS

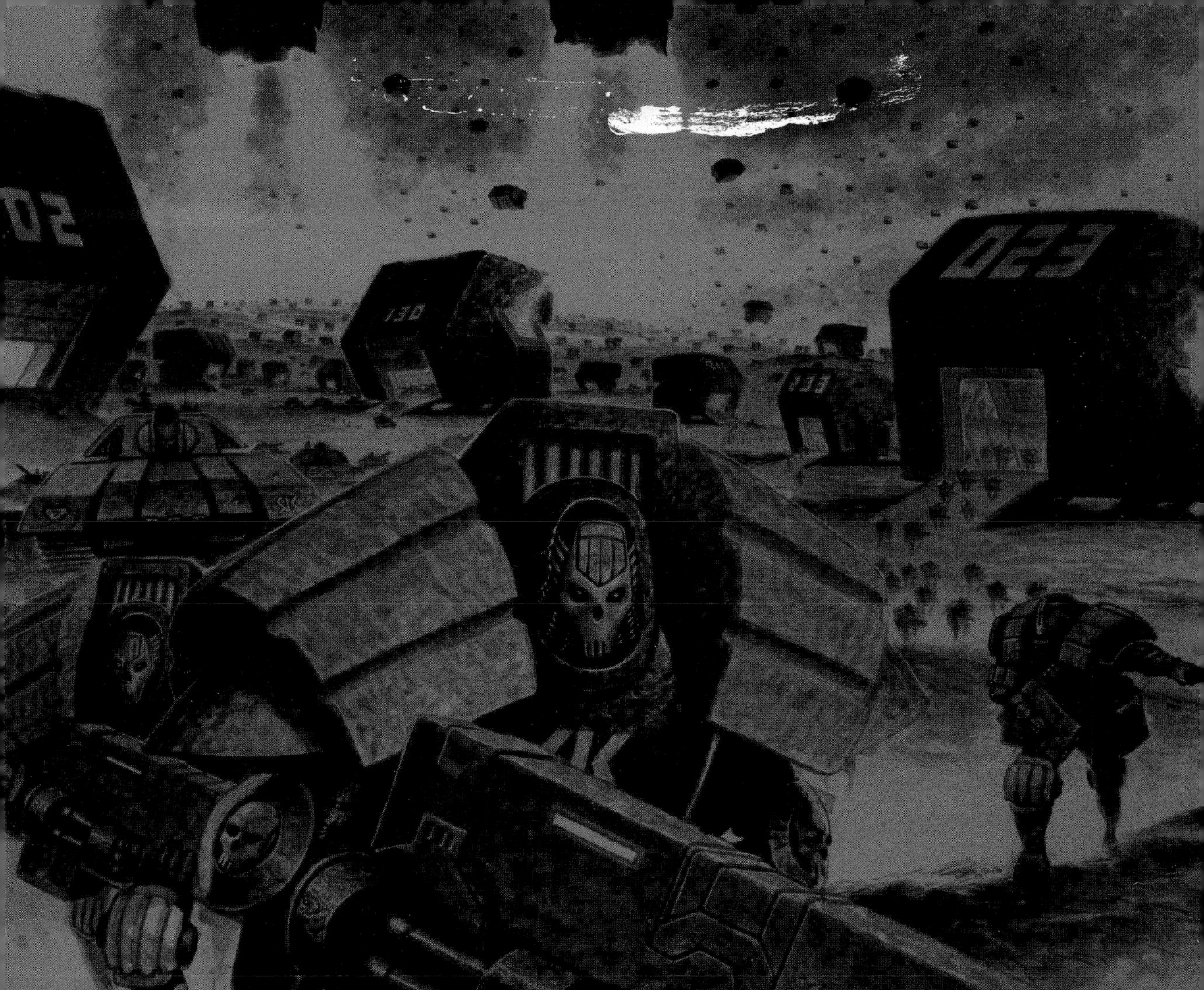

DAN ABNETT COLIN MACNEIL

# INSURRECTION

INSURRECTION C… …OLIN MACNEIL

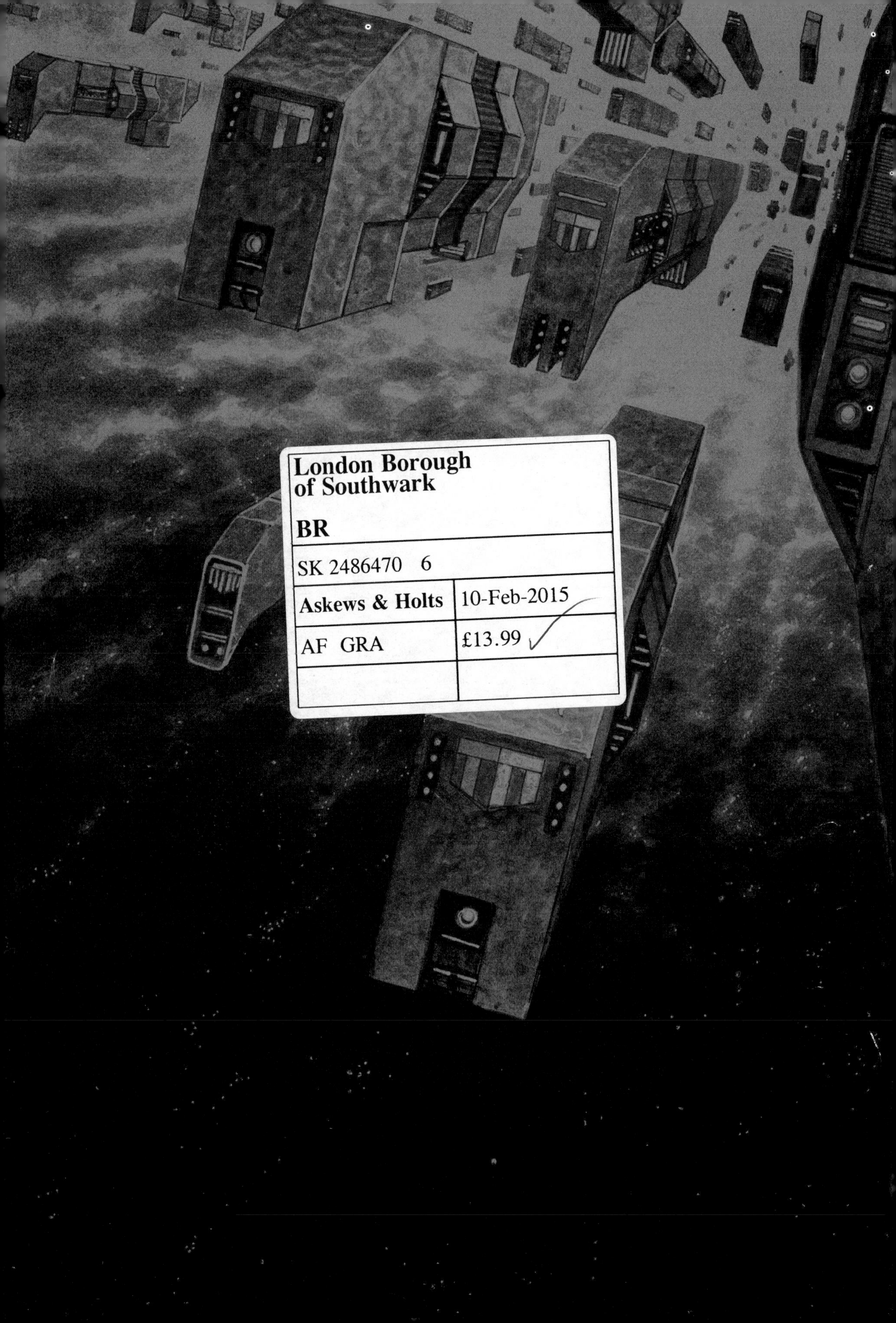

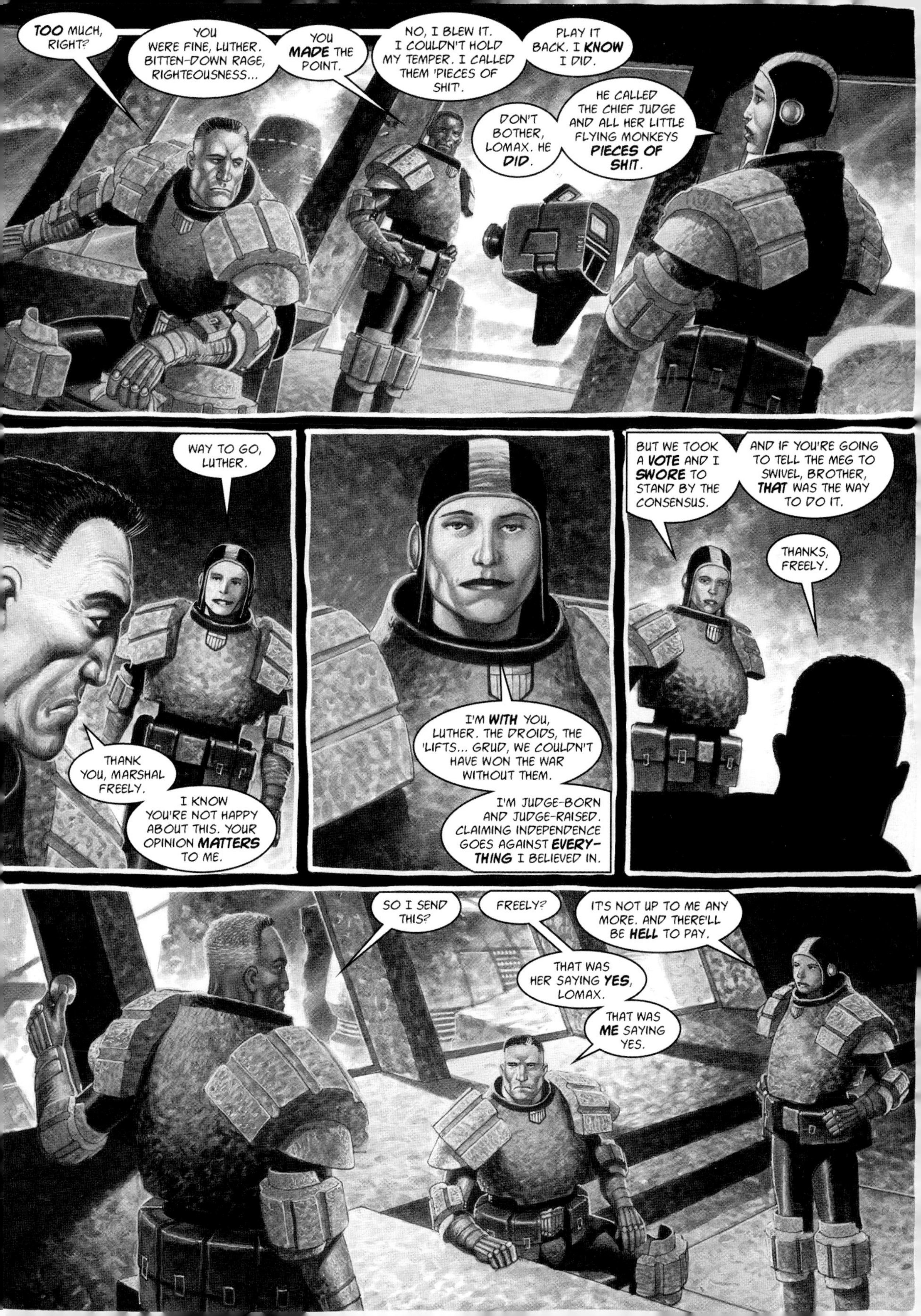

TOO MUCH, RIGHT?
YOU WERE FINE, LUTHER. BITTEN-DOWN RAGE, RIGHTEOUSNESS...
YOU MADE THE POINT.
NO, I BLEW IT. I COULDN'T HOLD MY TEMPER. I CALLED THEM 'PIECES OF SHIT'.
PLAY IT BACK. I KNOW I DID.
DON'T BOTHER, LOMAX. HE DID.
HE CALLED THE CHIEF JUDGE AND ALL HER LITTLE FLYING MONKEYS PIECES OF SHIT.
WAY TO GO, LUTHER.
THANK YOU, MARSHAL FREELY.
I KNOW YOU'RE NOT HAPPY ABOUT THIS. YOUR OPINION MATTERS TO ME.
I'M WITH YOU, LUTHER. THE DROIDS, THE 'LIFTS... GRUD, WE COULDN'T HAVE WON THE WAR WITHOUT THEM.
I'M JUDGE-BORN AND JUDGE-RAISED. CLAIMING INDEPENDENCE GOES AGAINST EVERY-THING I BELIEVED IN.
BUT WE TOOK A VOTE AND I SWORE TO STAND BY THE CONSENSUS.
AND IF YOU'RE GOING TO TELL THE MEG TO SWIVEL, BROTHER, THAT WAS THE WAY TO DO IT.
THANKS, FREELY.
SO I SEND THIS?
FREELY?
IT'S NOT UP TO ME ANY MORE. AND THERE'LL BE HELL TO PAY.
THAT WAS HER SAYING YES, LOMAX.
THAT WAS ME SAYING YES.

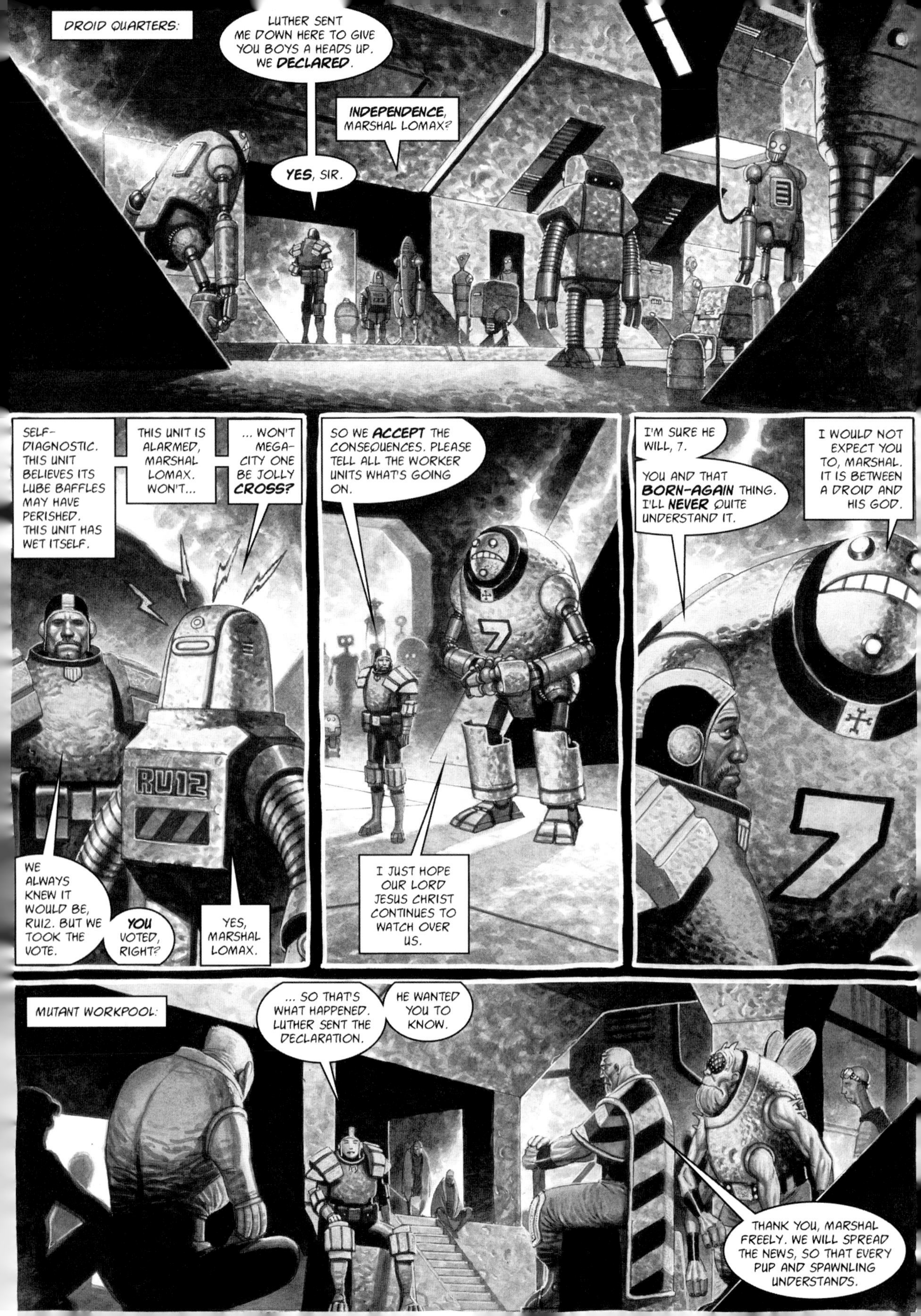
DROID QUARTERS:
LUTHER SENT ME DOWN HERE TO GIVE YOU BOYS A HEADS UP. WE DECLARED.
INDEPENDENCE, MARSHAL LOMAX?
YES, SIR.
SELF-DIAGNOSTIC. THIS UNIT BELIEVES ITS LUBE BAFFLES MAY HAVE PERISHED. THIS UNIT HAS WET ITSELF.
THIS UNIT IS ALARMED, MARSHAL LOMAX. WON'T...
... WON'T MEGA-CITY ONE BE JOLLY CROSS?
RU12
WE ALWAYS KNEW IT WOULD BE, RU12. BUT WE TOOK THE VOTE.
YOU VOTED, RIGHT?
YES, MARSHAL LOMAX.
SO WE ACCEPT THE CONSEQUENCES. PLEASE TELL ALL THE WORKER UNITS WHAT'S GOING ON.
I JUST HOPE OUR LORD JESUS CHRIST CONTINUES TO WATCH OVER US.
I'M SURE HE WILL, 7.
YOU AND THAT BORN-AGAIN THING. I'LL NEVER QUITE UNDERSTAND IT.
I WOULD NOT EXPECT YOU TO, MARSHAL. IT IS BETWEEN A DROID AND HIS GOD.
MUTANT WORKPOOL:
... SO THAT'S WHAT HAPPENED. LUTHER SENT THE DECLARATION.
HE WANTED YOU TO KNOW.
THANK YOU, MARSHAL FREELY. WE WILL SPREAD THE NEWS, SO THAT EVERY PUP AND SPAWNLING UNDERSTANDS.

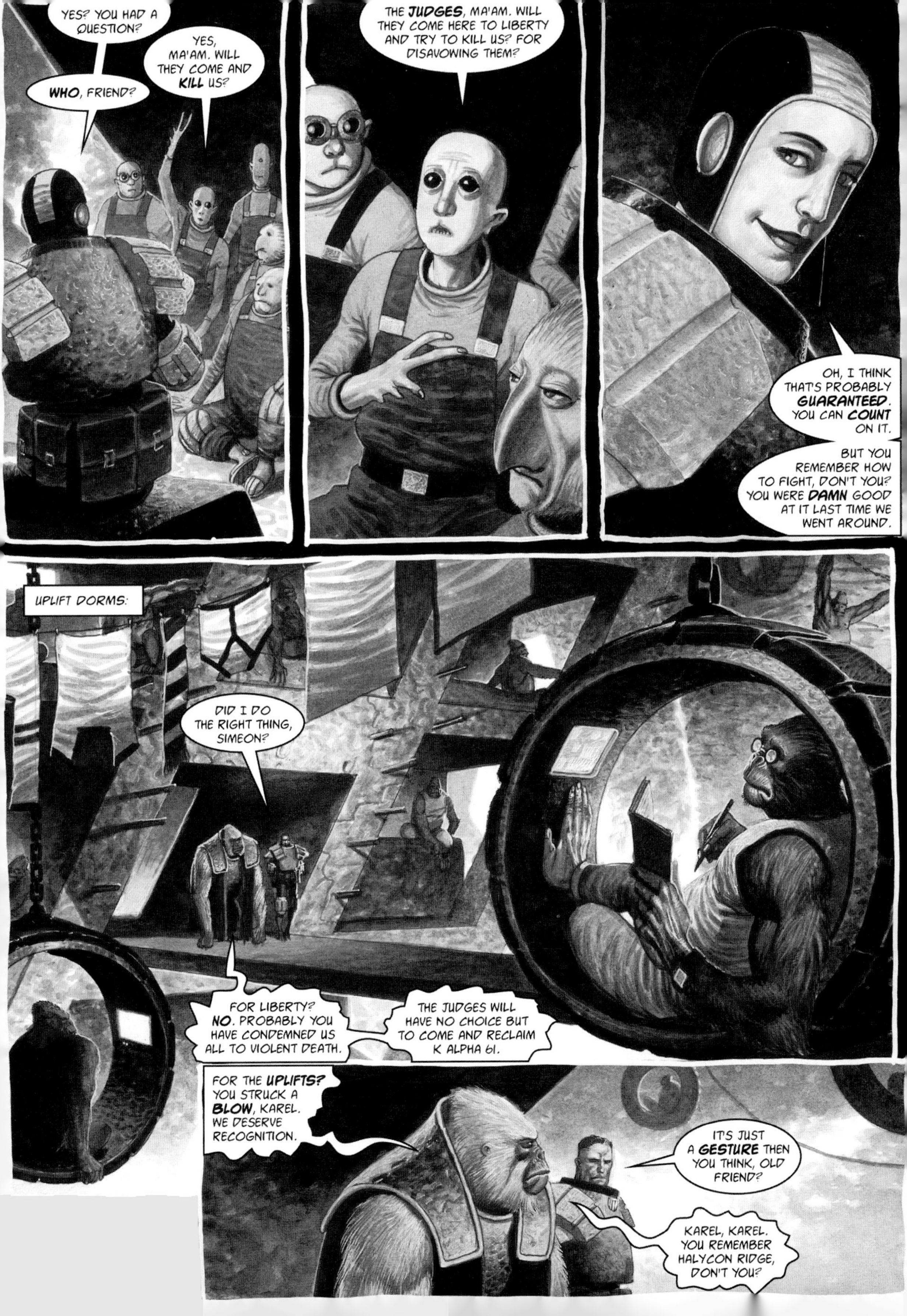
YES? YOU HAD A QUESTION?
YES, MA'AM. WILL THEY COME AND KILL US?
WHO, FRIEND?
THE JUDGES, MA'AM. WILL THEY COME HERE TO LIBERTY AND TRY TO KILL US? FOR DISAVOWING THEM?
OH, I THINK THAT'S PROBABLY GUARANTEED. YOU CAN COUNT ON IT.
BUT YOU REMEMBER HOW TO FIGHT, DON'T YOU? YOU WERE DAMN GOOD AT IT LAST TIME WE WENT AROUND.
UPLIFT DORMS:
DID I DO THE RIGHT THING, SIMEON?
FOR LIBERTY? NO. PROBABLY YOU HAVE CONDEMNED US ALL TO VIOLENT DEATH.
THE JUDGES WILL HAVE NO CHOICE BUT TO COME AND RECLAIM K ALPHA 61.
FOR THE UPLIFTS? YOU STRUCK A BLOW, KAREL. WE DESERVE RECOGNITION.
IT'S JUST A GESTURE THEN YOU THINK, OLD FRIEND?
KAREL, KAREL. YOU REMEMBER HALYCON RIDGE, DON'T YOU?

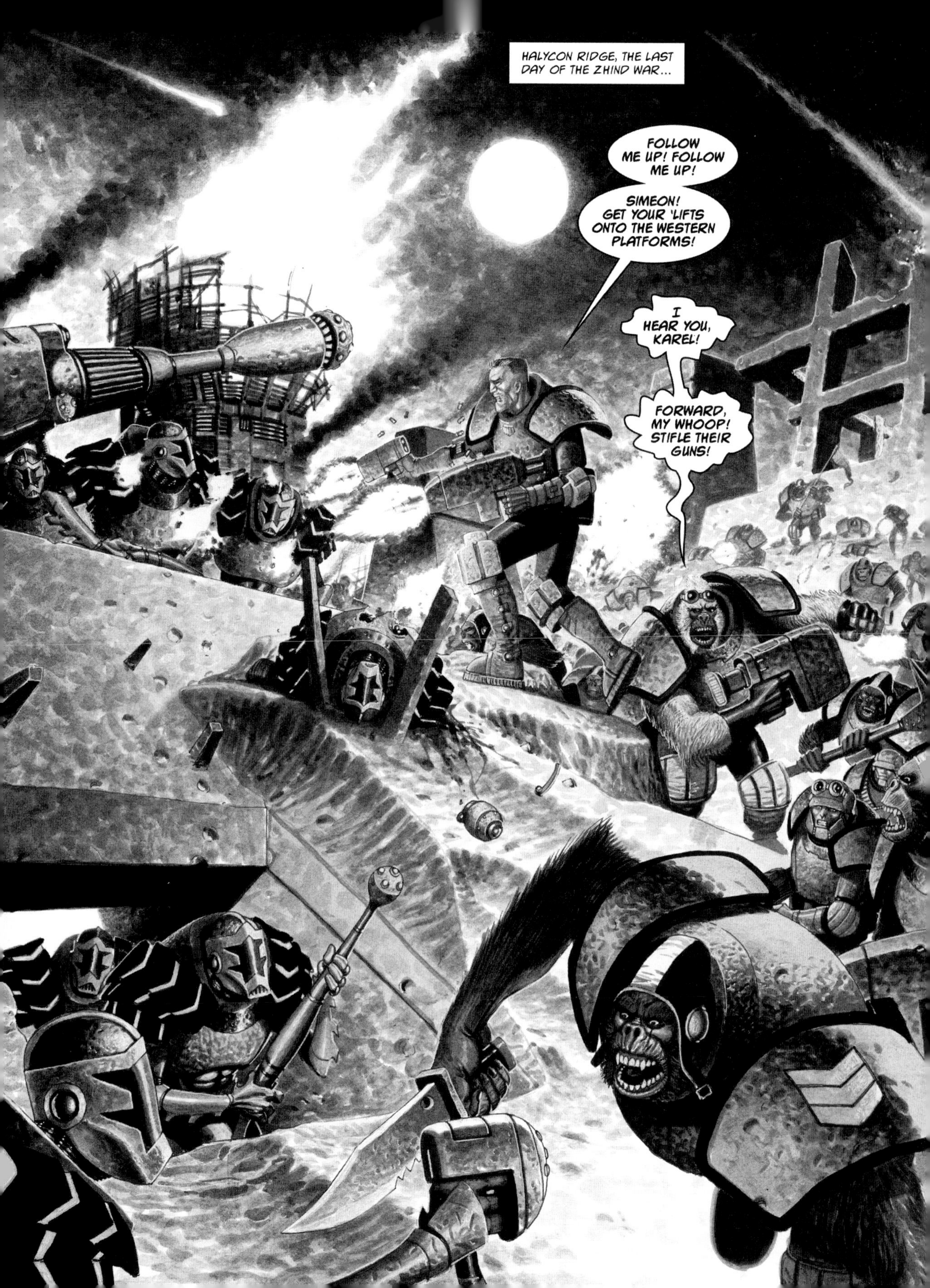
HALYCON RIDGE, THE LAST DAY OF THE ZHIND WAR...
FOLLOW ME UP! FOLLOW ME UP!
SIMEON! GET YOUR 'LIFTS ONTO THE WESTERN PLATFORMS!
I HEAR YOU, KAREL!
FORWARD, MY WHOOP! STIFLE THEIR GUNS!

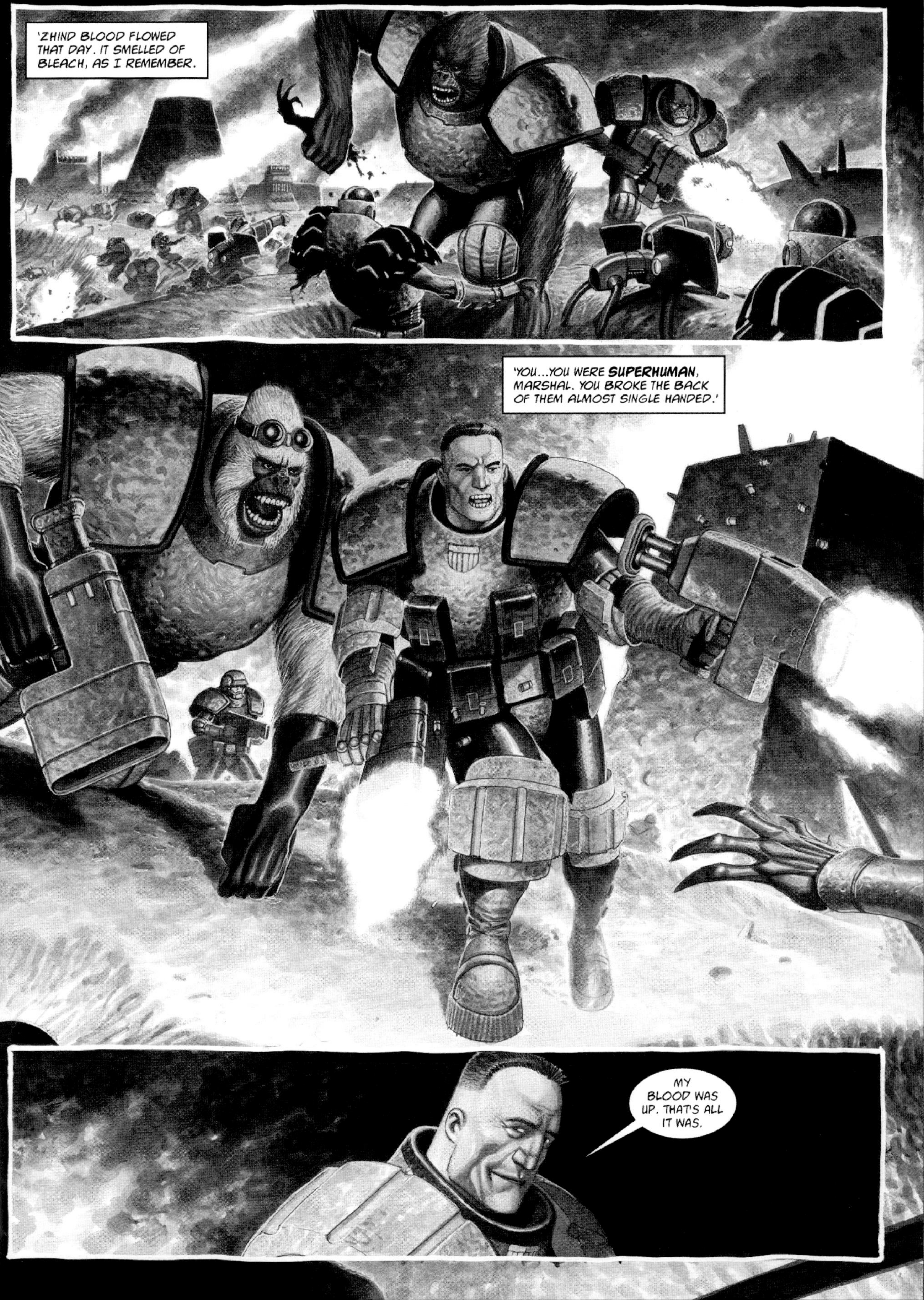
'ZHIND BLOOD FLOWED THAT DAY. IT SMELLED OF BLEACH, AS I REMEMBER.
'YOU...YOU WERE SUPERHUMAN, MARSHAL. YOU BROKE THE BACK OF THEM ALMOST SINGLE HANDED.'
MY BLOOD WAS UP. THAT'S ALL IT WAS.

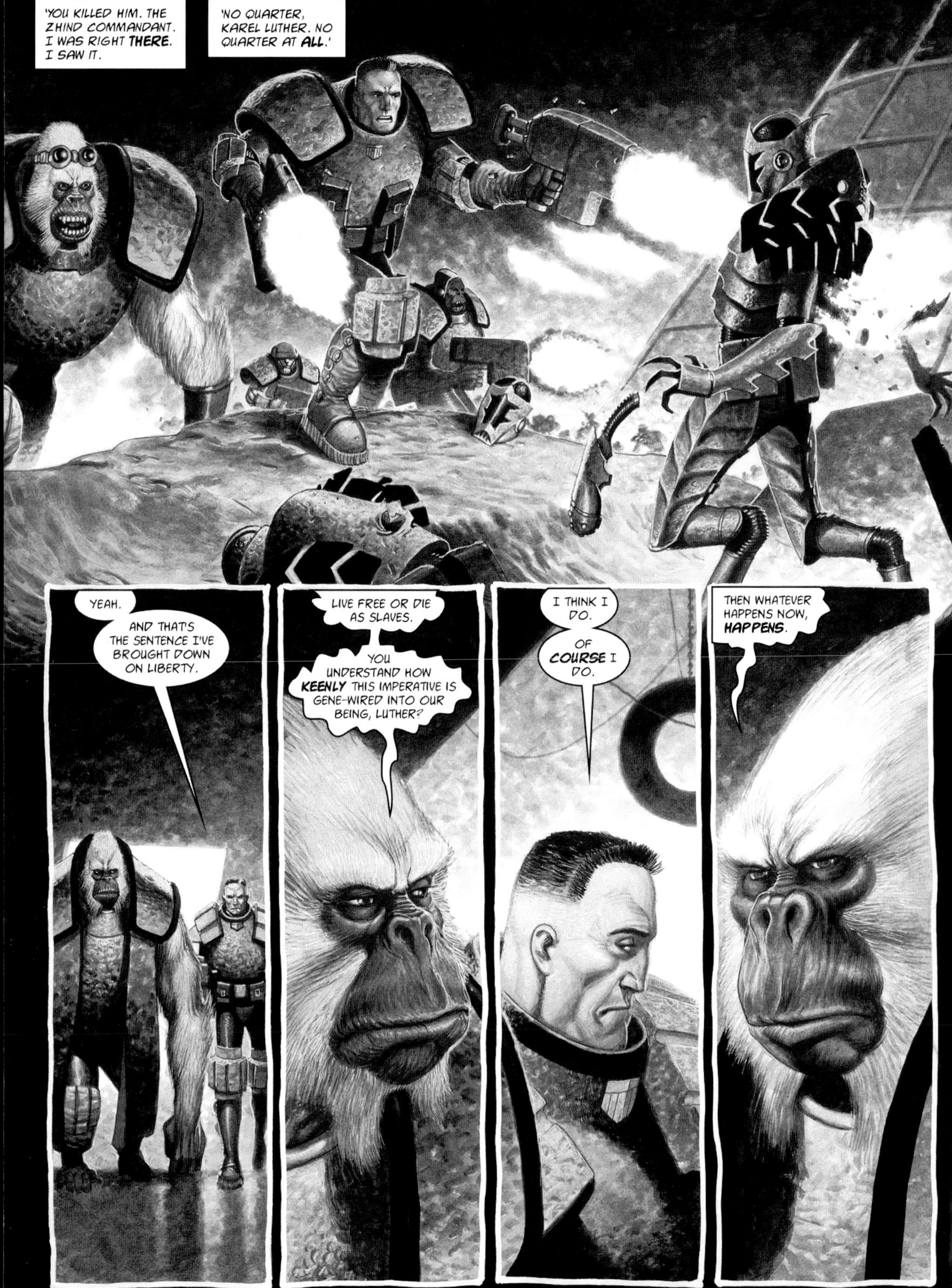
'YOU KILLED HIM. THE ZHIND COMMANDANT. I WAS RIGHT **THERE**. I SAW IT.
'NO QUARTER, KAREL LUTHER. NO QUARTER AT **ALL**.'
YEAH.
AND THAT'S THE SENTENCE I'VE BROUGHT DOWN ON LIBERTY.
LIVE FREE OR DIE AS SLAVES.
YOU UNDERSTAND HOW **KEENLY** THIS IMPERATIVE IS GENE-WIRED INTO OUR BEING, LUTHER?
I THINK I DO.
OF **COURSE** I DO.
THEN WHATEVER HAPPENS NOW, **HAPPENS**.

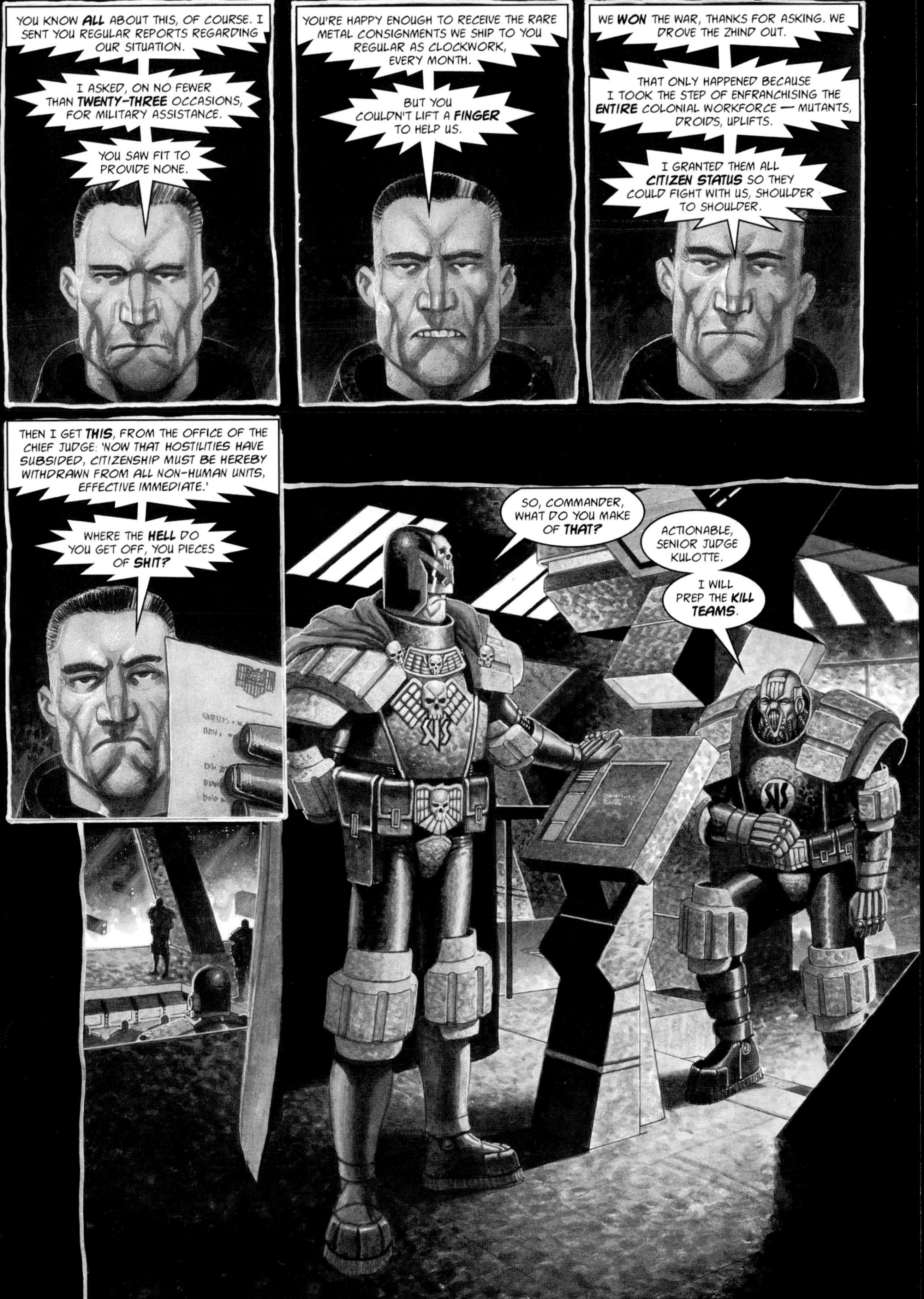
YOU KNOW ALL ABOUT THIS, OF COURSE. I SENT YOU REGULAR REPORTS REGARDING OUR SITUATION.
I ASKED, ON NO FEWER THAN TWENTY-THREE OCCASIONS, FOR MILITARY ASSISTANCE.
YOU SAW FIT TO PROVIDE NONE.
YOU'RE HAPPY ENOUGH TO RECEIVE THE RARE METAL CONSIGNMENTS WE SHIP TO YOU REGULAR AS CLOCKWORK, EVERY MONTH.
BUT YOU COULDN'T LIFT A FINGER TO HELP US.
WE WON THE WAR, THANKS FOR ASKING. WE DROVE THE ZHIND OUT.
THAT ONLY HAPPENED BECAUSE I TOOK THE STEP OF ENFRANCHISING THE ENTIRE COLONIAL WORKFORCE — MUTANTS, DROIDS, UPLIFTS.
I GRANTED THEM ALL CITIZEN STATUS SO THEY COULD FIGHT WITH US, SHOULDER TO SHOULDER.
THEN I GET THIS, FROM THE OFFICE OF THE CHIEF JUDGE: 'NOW THAT HOSTILITIES HAVE SUBSIDED, CITIZENSHIP MUST BE HEREBY WITHDRAWN FROM ALL NON-HUMAN UNITS, EFFECTIVE IMMEDIATE.'
WHERE THE HELL DO YOU GET OFF, YOU PIECES OF SHIT?
SO, COMMANDER, WHAT DO YOU MAKE OF THAT?
ACTIONABLE, SENIOR JUDGE KULOTTE.
I WILL PREP THE KILL TEAMS.

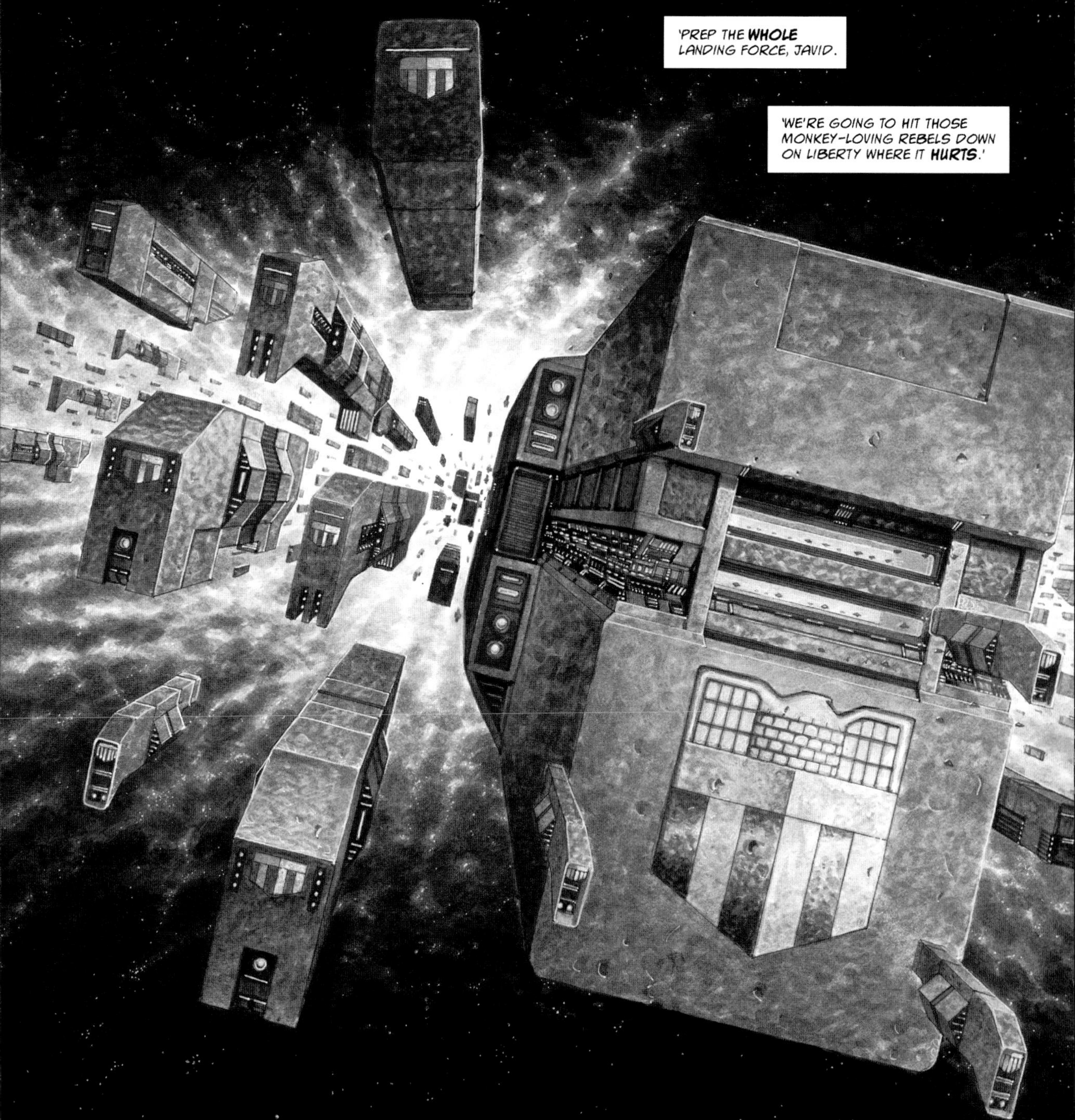
'PREP THE **WHOLE** LANDING FORCE, JAVID.
'WE'RE GOING TO HIT THOSE MONKEY-LOVING REBELS DOWN ON LIBERTY WHERE IT **HURTS**.'

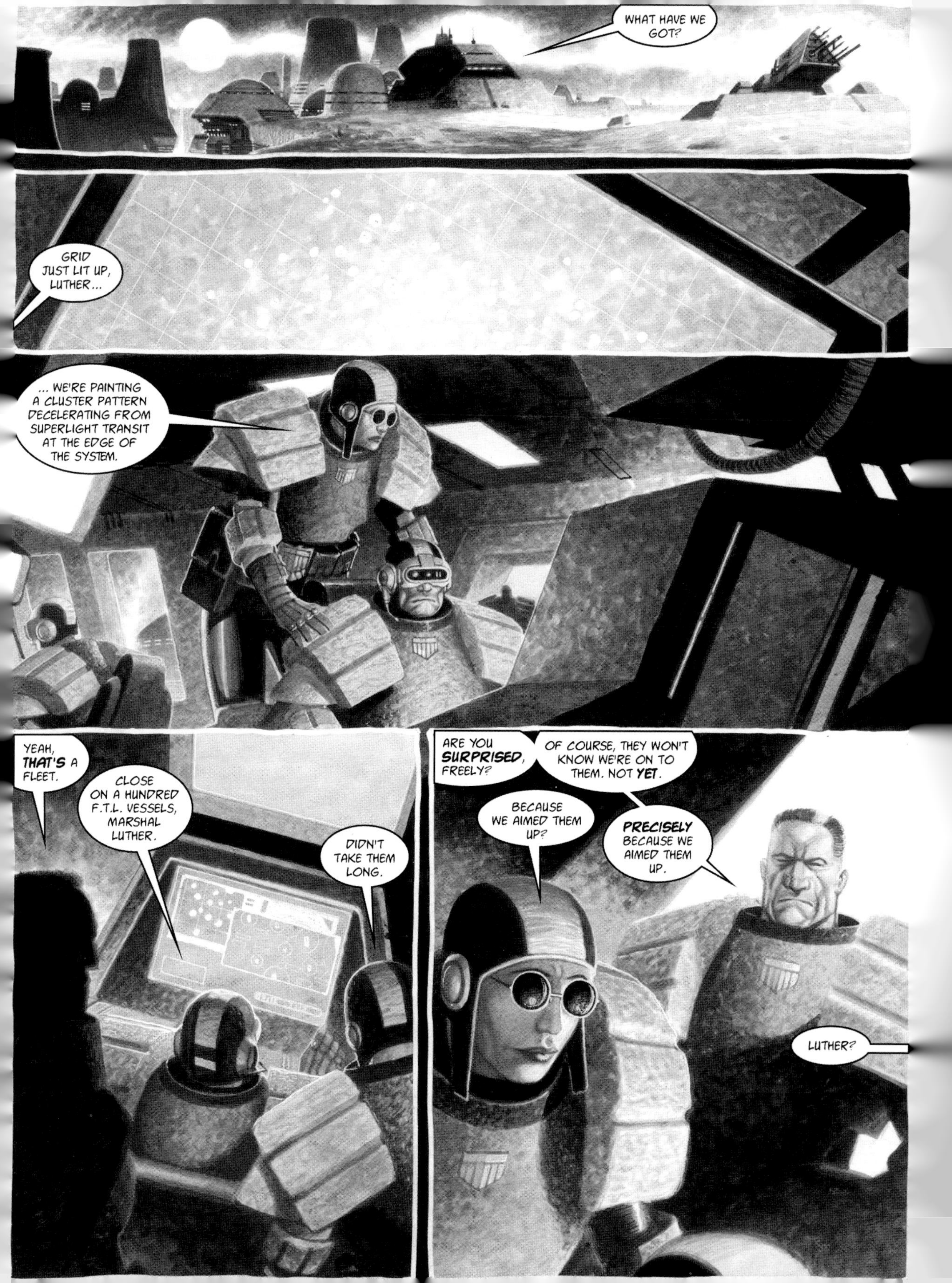
WHAT HAVE WE GOT?
GRID JUST LIT UP, LUTHER...
... WE'RE PAINTING A CLUSTER PATTERN DECELERATING FROM SUPERLIGHT TRANSIT AT THE EDGE OF THE SYSTEM.
YEAH, THAT'S A FLEET.
CLOSE ON A HUNDRED F.T.L. VESSELS, MARSHAL LUTHER.
DIDN'T TAKE THEM LONG.
ARE YOU SURPRISED, FREELY?
OF COURSE, THEY WON'T KNOW WE'RE ON TO THEM. NOT YET.
BECAUSE WE AIMED THEM UP?
PRECISELY BECAUSE WE AIMED THEM UP.
LUTHER?

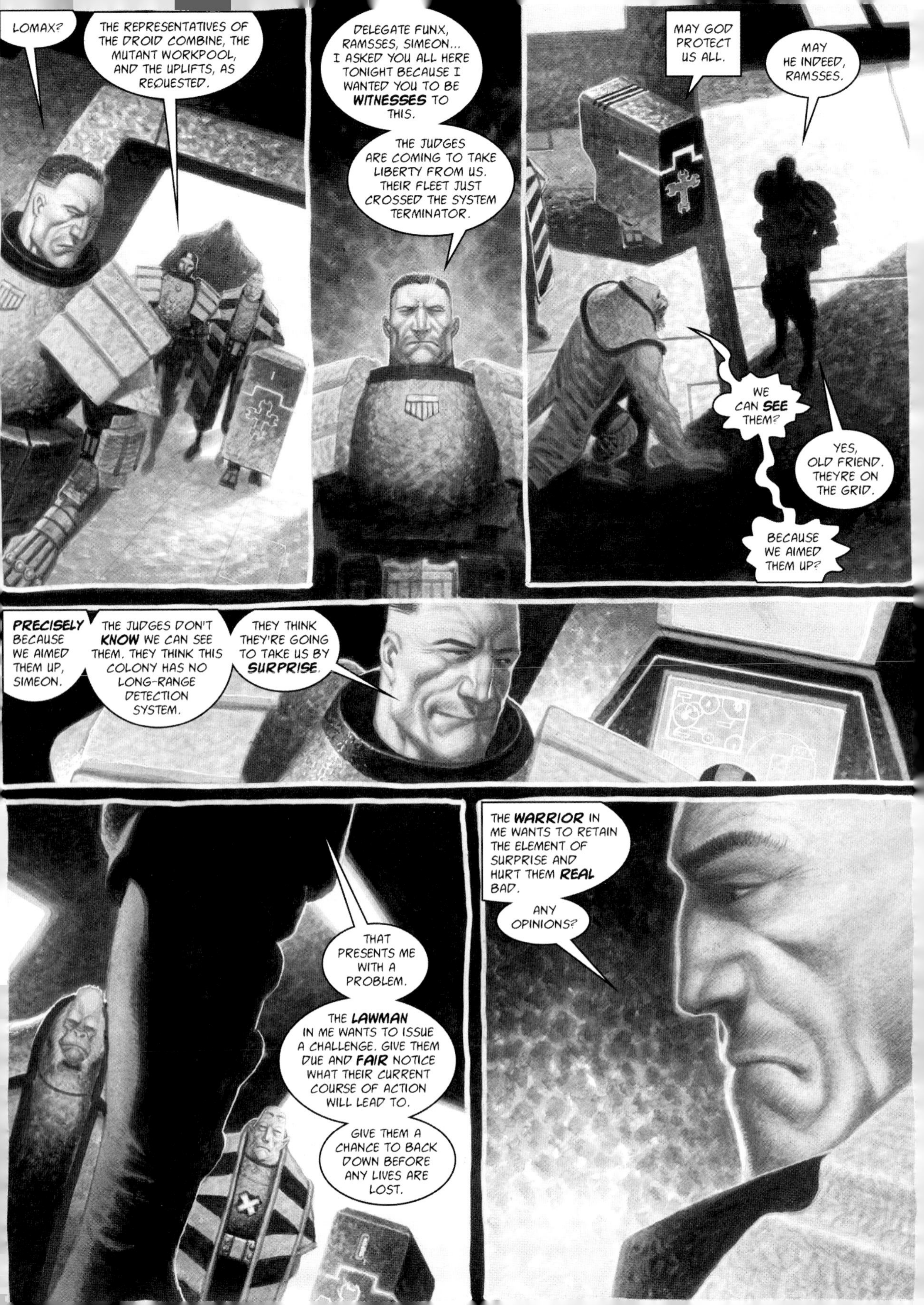

LOMAX?
THE REPRESENTATIVES OF THE DROID COMBINE, THE MUTANT WORKPOOL, AND THE UPLIFTS, AS REQUESTED.
DELEGATE FUNX, RAMSSES, SIMEON... I ASKED YOU ALL HERE TONIGHT BECAUSE I WANTED YOU TO BE **WITNESSES** TO THIS.
THE JUDGES ARE COMING TO TAKE LIBERTY FROM US. THEIR FLEET JUST CROSSED THE SYSTEM TERMINATOR.
MAY GOD PROTECT US ALL.
MAY HE INDEED, RAMSSES.
WE CAN **SEE** THEM?
YES, OLD FRIEND. THEYRE ON THE GRID.
BECAUSE WE AIMED THEM UP?
**PRECISELY** BECAUSE WE AIMED THEM UP, SIMEON.
THE JUDGES DON'T **KNOW** WE CAN SEE THEM. THEY THINK THIS COLONY HAS NO LONG-RANGE DETECTION SYSTEM.
THEY THINK THEY'RE GOING TO TAKE US BY **SURPRISE**.
THAT PRESENTS ME WITH A PROBLEM.
THE **LAWMAN** IN ME WANTS TO ISSUE A CHALLENGE. GIVE THEM DUE AND **FAIR** NOTICE WHAT THEIR CURRENT COURSE OF ACTION WILL LEAD TO.
GIVE THEM A CHANCE TO BACK DOWN BEFORE ANY LIVES ARE LOST.
THE **WARRIOR** IN ME WANTS TO RETAIN THE ELEMENT OF SURPRISE AND HURT THEM **REAL** BAD.
ANY OPINIONS?

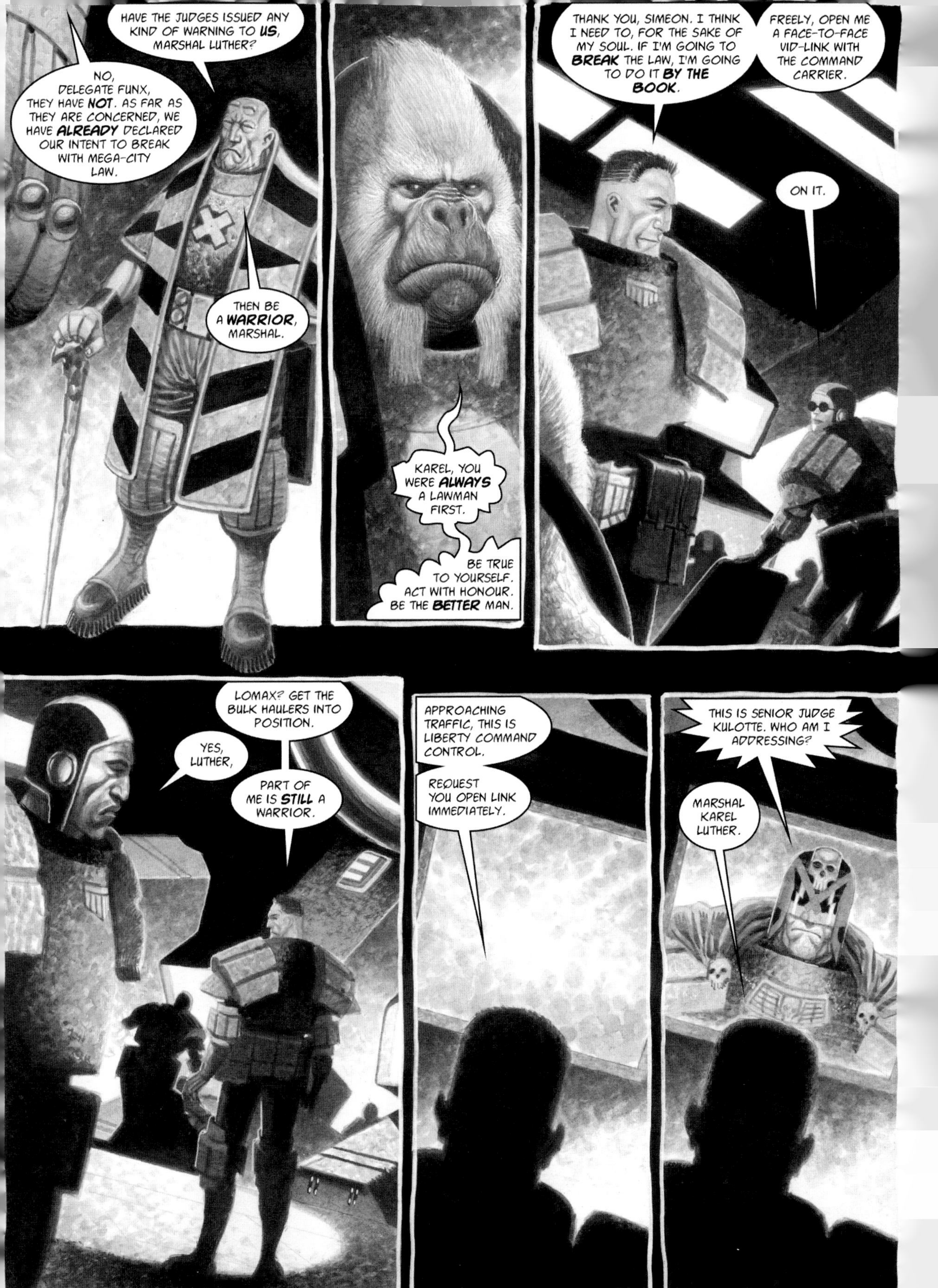
HAVE THE JUDGES ISSUED ANY KIND OF WARNING TO **US**, MARSHAL LUTHER?
NO, DELEGATE FUNX, THEY HAVE **NOT**. AS FAR AS THEY ARE CONCERNED, WE HAVE **ALREADY** DECLARED OUR INTENT TO BREAK WITH MEGA-CITY LAW.
THEN BE A **WARRIOR**, MARSHAL.
KAREL, YOU WERE **ALWAYS** A LAWMAN FIRST.
BE TRUE TO YOURSELF. ACT WITH HONOUR. BE THE **BETTER** MAN.
THANK YOU, SIMEON. I THINK I NEED TO, FOR THE SAKE OF MY SOUL. IF I'M GOING TO **BREAK** THE LAW, I'M GOING TO DO IT **BY THE BOOK**.
FREELY, OPEN ME A FACE-TO-FACE VID-LINK WITH THE COMMAND CARRIER.
ON IT.
LOMAX? GET THE BULK HAULERS INTO POSITION.
YES, LUTHER,
PART OF ME IS **STILL** A WARRIOR.
APPROACHING TRAFFIC, THIS IS LIBERTY COMMAND CONTROL.
REQUEST YOU OPEN LINK IMMEDIATELY.
THIS IS SENIOR JUDGE KULOTTE. WHO AM I ADDRESSING?
MARSHAL KAREL LUTHER.

LUTHER. SO...

YOU SEEM TAKEN ABACK, KULOTTE. I TAKE IT YOU IMAGINED YOU WERE APPROACHING **UNDETECTED**.

I... MINERAL SURVEY DETECTORS ARE VERY POWERFUL AND ACUTE. YOU HAVE **MANY** SUPPLIED FOR YOUR MINING WORK.

YOU'VE POINTED THEM AT THE **SKY**, HAVEN'T YOU?

WE AIMED THEM UP. LONG-RANGE DETECTION IS A NECESSITY WHEN YOU'RE WAGING A **SYSTEM WAR**.

WE LEARNED TRICKS LIKE **THAT** FIGHTING THE ZHIND.

IMPROVISED USE OF RESOURCES. **COMMENDABLE**. THAT'S HALL OF JUSTICE TRAINING FOR YOU.

YOU HAVE TEN HOURS TO SURRENDER COLONY K ALPHA 61 TO US OR —

UH-UH-**UH**. GOING TO **STOP** YOU THERE. ONLY **ONE** CHALLENGE GETS ISSUED TONIGHT. **OUR'S**.

TURN AROUND. GO HOME. LEAVE LIBERTY TO US.

OR WE'LL MESS YOU UP SO **COMPLETELY**, YOU'LL WISH YOU'D NEVER PALM-TYPED YOURSELF TO A LAWGIVER.

I HAVE NINETY-FIVE SHIPS, LUTHER. SIXTEEN THOUSAND MEN OF THE 12TH JUSTICE CONTROL DIVISION, ARMOURED COMPANIES AND —

WE BEAT THE **ZHIND**. THEY WERE A **SPECIES**.

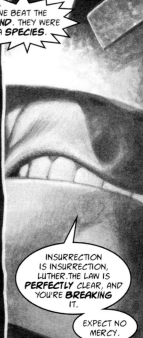

INSURRECTION IS INSURRECTION, LUTHER. THE LAW IS **PERFECTLY** CLEAR, AND YOU'RE **BREAKING** IT.

EXPECT NO MERCY.

OKAY. BUT YOU **WERE** WARNED.

YOU ALL HEARD ME. I GAVE HIM THE CHANCE.

LOMAX, THE BULK HAULERS. **NOW**, PLEASE.

YES, LUTHER.

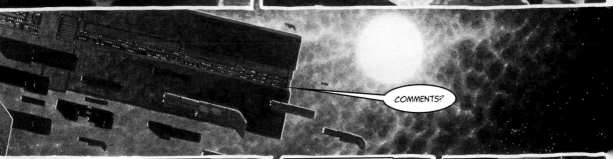

COMMENTS?

THE MAN IS **INSUFFERABLE**, SIR. A **DISGRACE** TO THE OFFICE OF JUDGE MARSHAL.

YES, YES... COMMANDER PEDERSEN?

THEY **MAY** HAVE SEEN US, SENIOR JUDGE KULOTTE, BUT NOT WITH ANY REAL ACUITY. MINING DETECTORS ARE NOT SUBTLE INSTRUMENTS.

I DOUBT THEY'VE TRACKED THE STEALTH **DROPCRAFT** AND **BOMBER WINGS** WE'VE LAUNCHED AHEAD OF US.

THE DROPCRAFT ARE ON A SLINGSHOT TRAJECTORY AROUND THE LOCAL STAR. THEY'LL HIT K ALPHA 61 FROM THE BLINDSIDE IN THE NEXT SIXTY MINUTES.

ONCE THE PARATROOPS ARE DONE, I DOUBT WE'LL EVEN **NEED** TO LAUNCH A GROUND OFF—

**SIR!**

WHAT IS IT, JAVID?

SHIPS! ON AN INTERCEPT PATTERN!

SHIELDS UP! COLLISION ALERT!

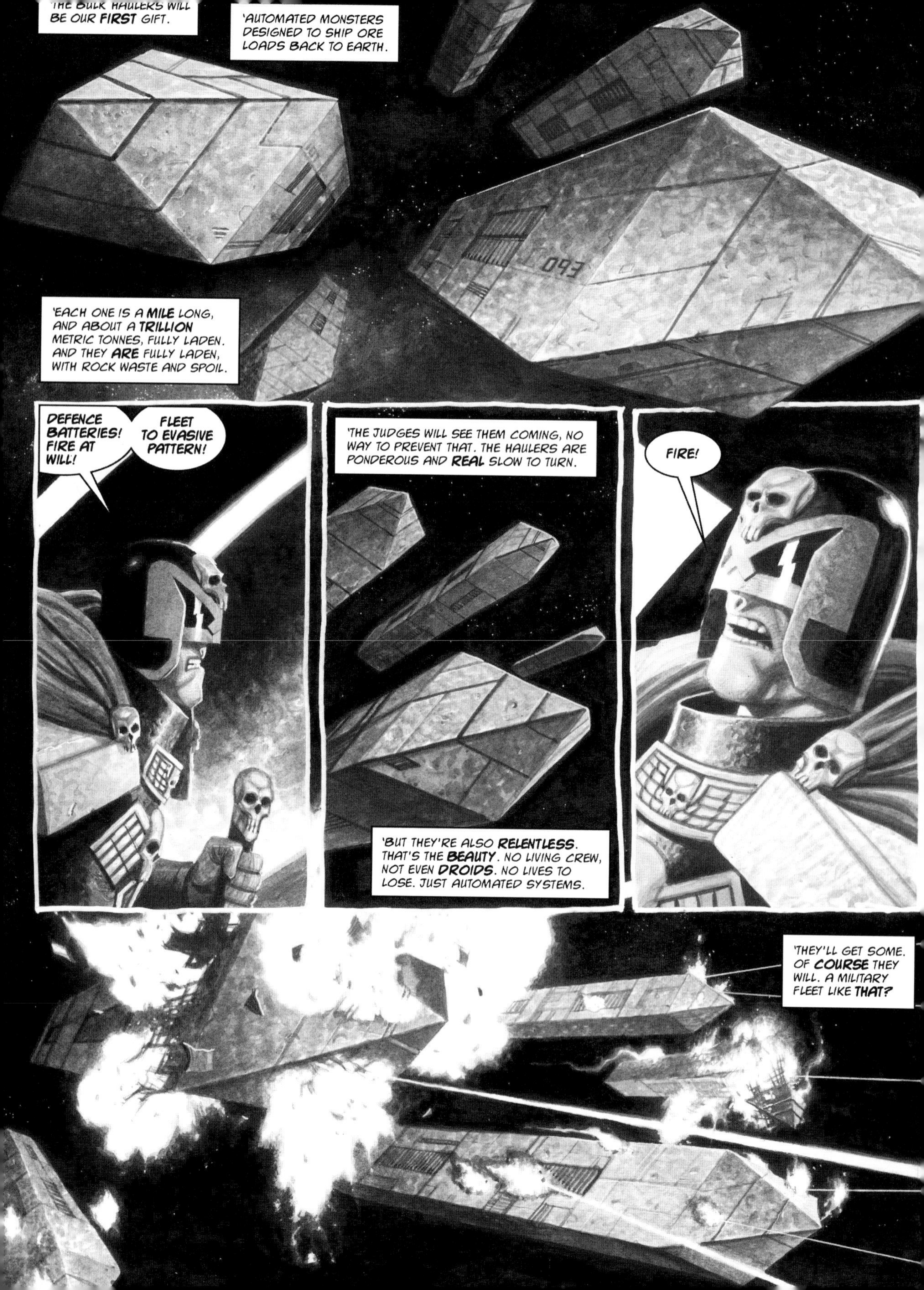
'THE BULK HAULERS WILL BE OUR FIRST GIFT.
'AUTOMATED MONSTERS DESIGNED TO SHIP ORE LOADS BACK TO EARTH.
'EACH ONE IS A MILE LONG, AND ABOUT A TRILLION METRIC TONNES, FULLY LADEN. AND THEY ARE FULLY LADEN, WITH ROCK WASTE AND SPOIL.
DEFENCE BATTERIES! FIRE AT WILL!
FLEET TO EVASIVE PATTERN!
'THE JUDGES WILL SEE THEM COMING, NO WAY TO PREVENT THAT. THE HAULERS ARE PONDEROUS AND REAL SLOW TO TURN.
'BUT THEY'RE ALSO RELENTLESS. THAT'S THE BEAUTY. NO LIVING CREW, NOT EVEN DROIDS. NO LIVES TO LOSE. JUST AUTOMATED SYSTEMS.
FIRE!
'THEY'LL GET SOME. OF COURSE THEY WILL. A MILITARY FLEET LIKE THAT?

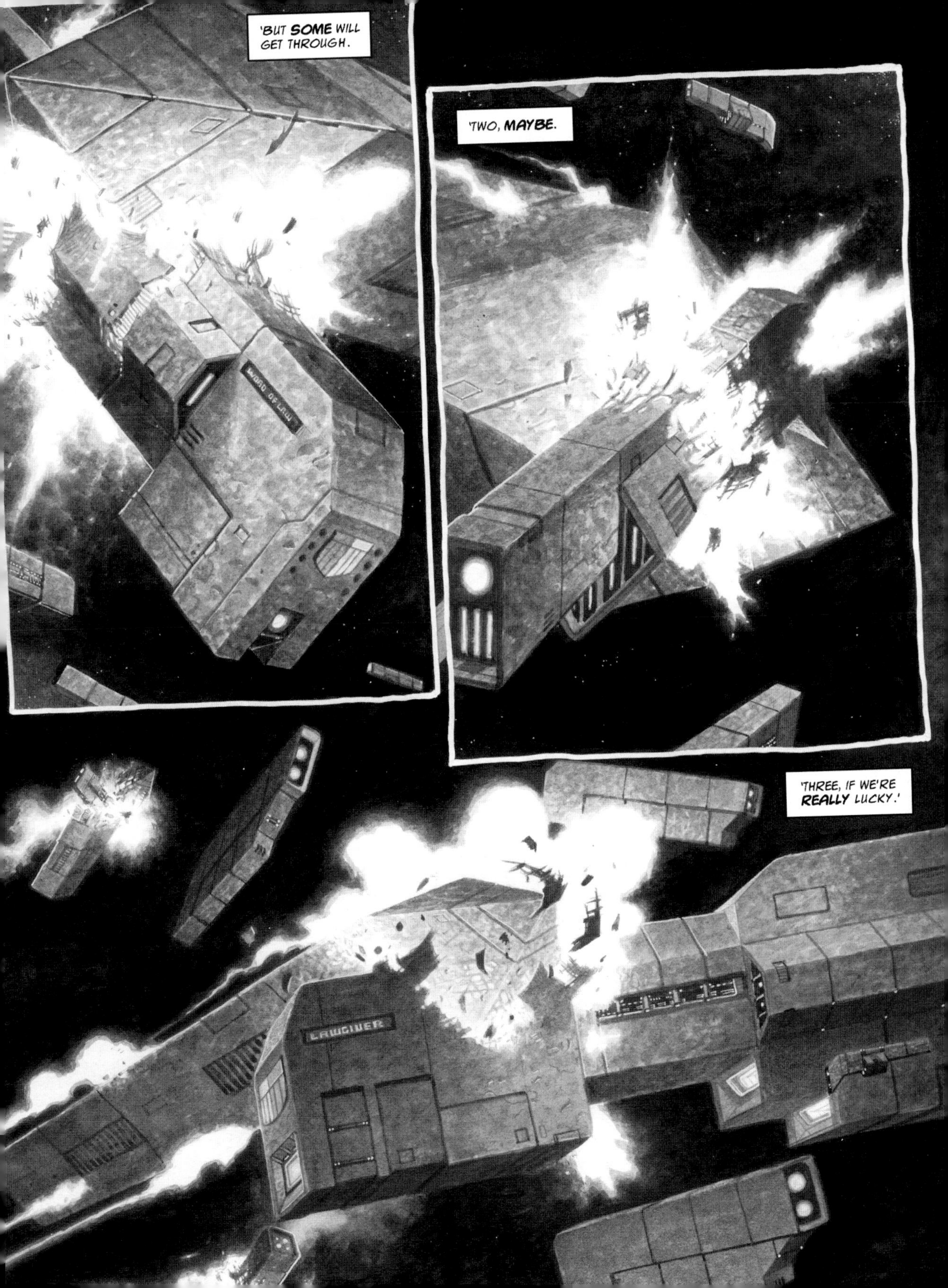

'BUT SOME WILL GET THROUGH.
WORD OF LAW
'TWO, MAYBE.
'THREE, IF WE'RE REALLY LUCKY.'
LAWGIVER

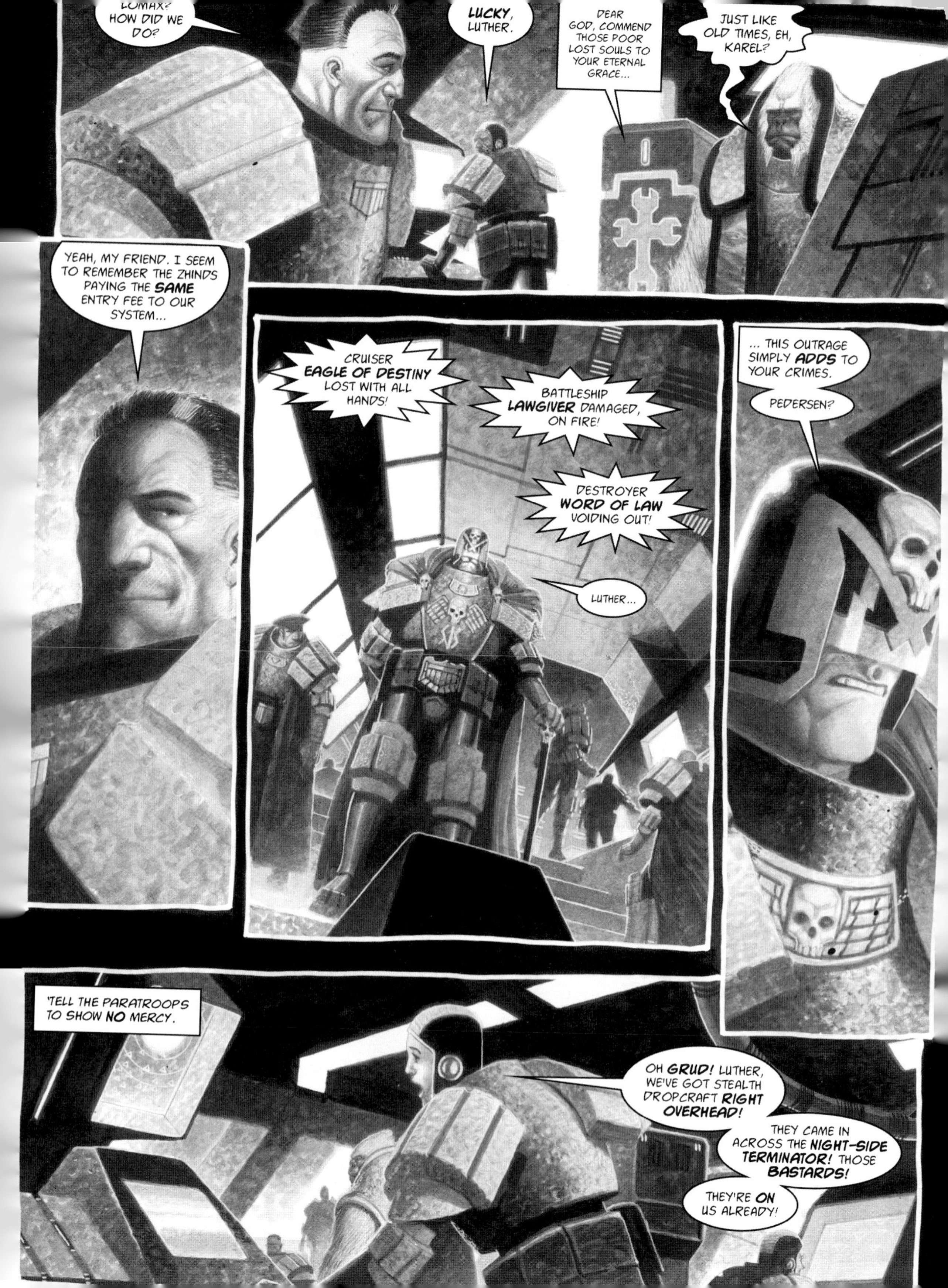
LOMAX? HOW DID WE DO?
LUCKY, LUTHER.
DEAR GOD, COMMEND THOSE POOR LOST SOULS TO YOUR ETERNAL GRACE...
JUST LIKE OLD TIMES, EH, KAREL?
YEAH, MY FRIEND. I SEEM TO REMEMBER THE ZHINDS PAYING THE SAME ENTRY FEE TO OUR SYSTEM...
CRUISER EAGLE OF DESTINY LOST WITH ALL HANDS!
BATTLESHIP LAWGIVER DAMAGED, ON FIRE!
DESTROYER WORD OF LAW VOIDING OUT!
LUTHER...
... THIS OUTRAGE SIMPLY ADDS TO YOUR CRIMES.
PEDERSEN?
'TELL THE PARATROOPS TO SHOW NO MERCY.
OH GRUD! LUTHER, WE'VE GOT STEALTH DROPCRAFT RIGHT OVERHEAD!
THEY CAME IN ACROSS THE NIGHT-SIDE TERMINATOR! THOSE BASTARDS!
THEY'RE ON US ALREADY!

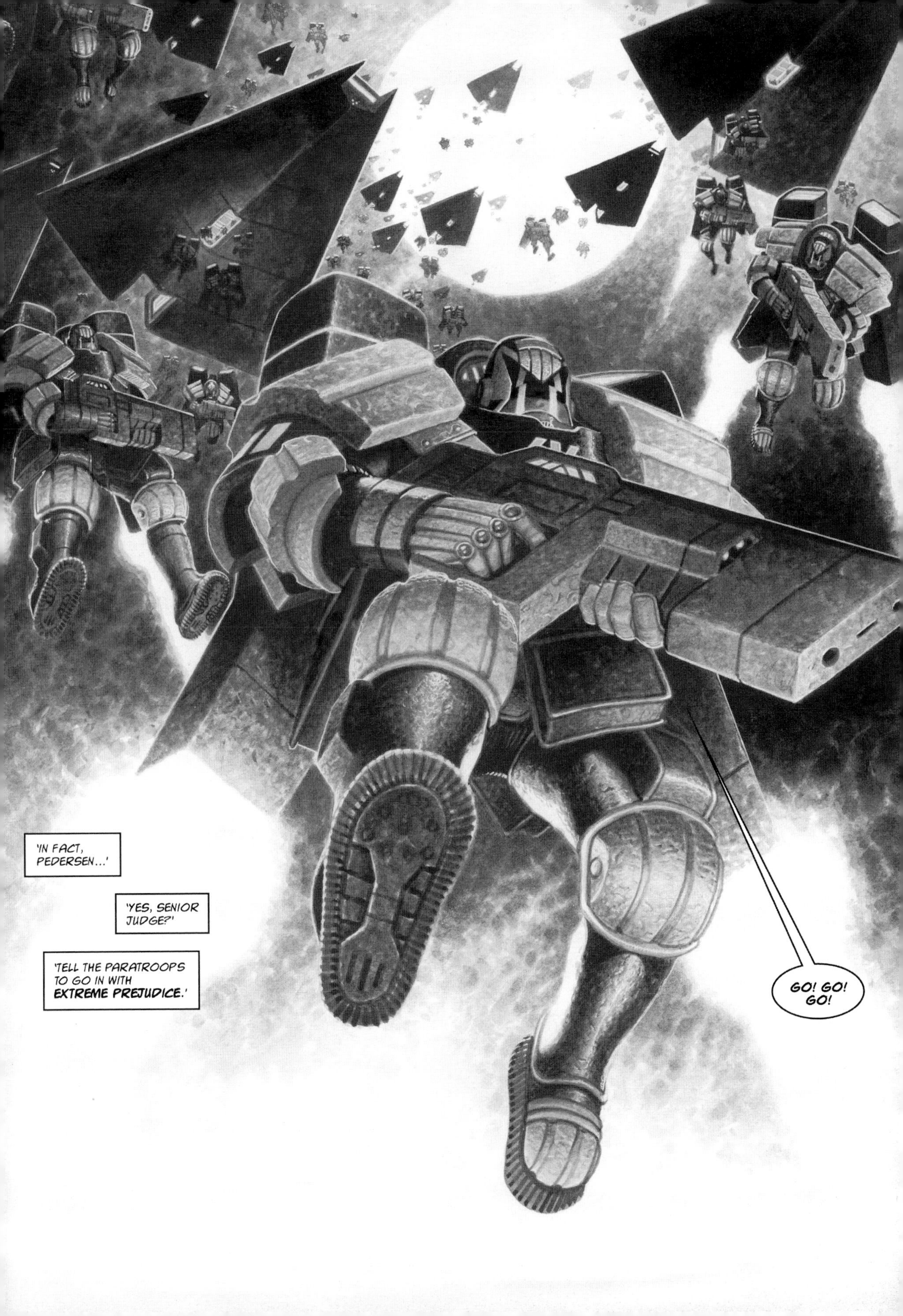
'IN FACT, PEDERSEN...'
'YES, SENIOR JUDGE?'
'TELL THE PARATROOPS TO GO IN WITH **EXTREME PREJUDICE**.'
GO! GO! GO!

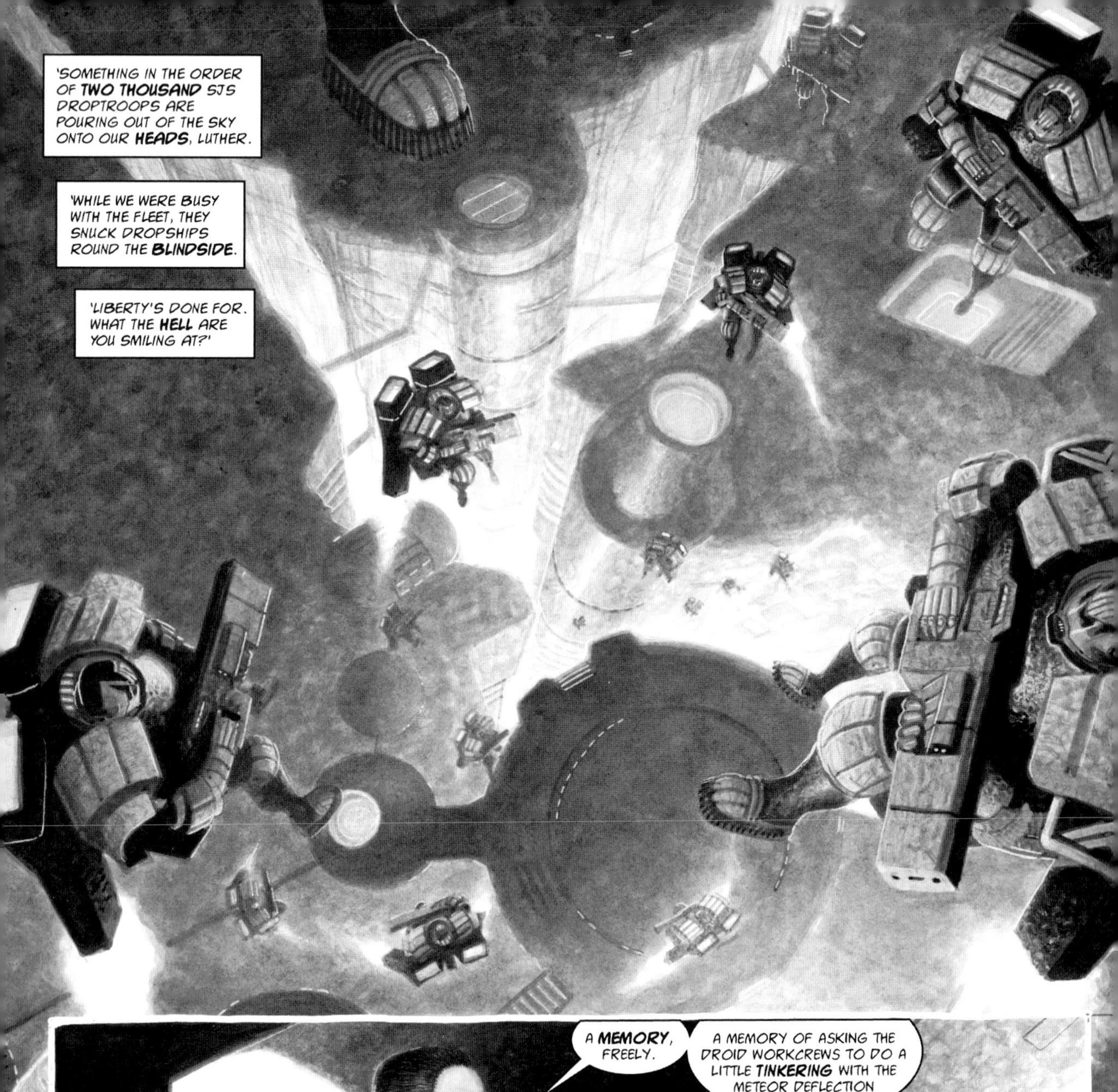
'SOMETHING IN THE ORDER OF **TWO THOUSAND** SJS DROPTROOPS ARE POURING OUT OF THE SKY ONTO OUR **HEADS**, LUTHER.
'WHILE WE WERE BUSY WITH THE FLEET, THEY SNUCK DROPSHIPS ROUND THE **BLINDSIDE**.
'LIBERTY'S DONE FOR. WHAT THE **HELL** ARE YOU SMILING AT?'

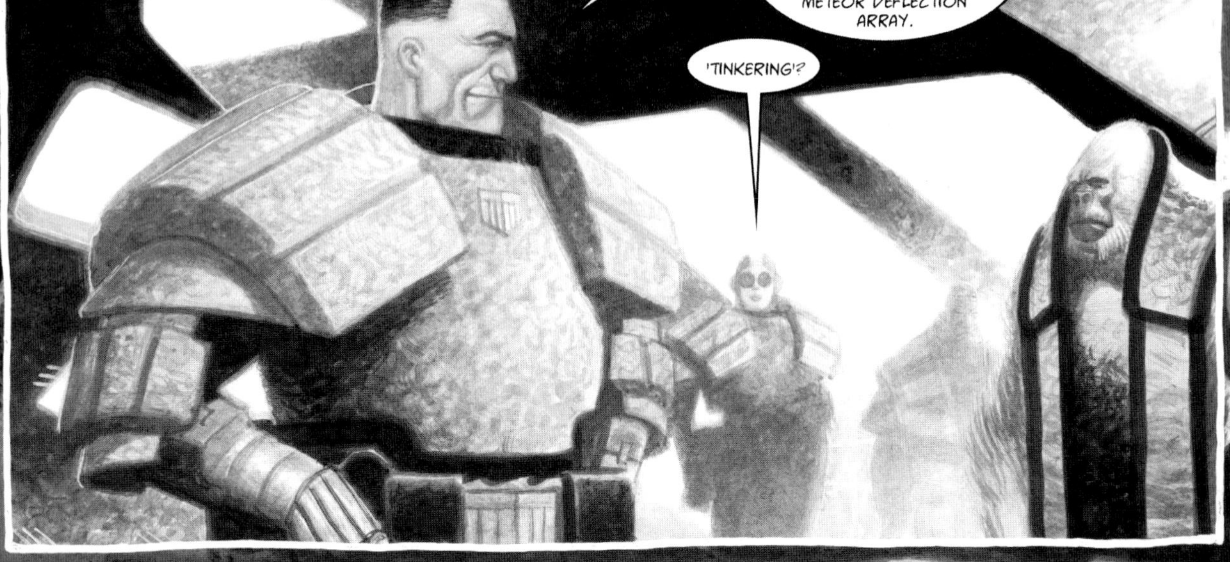
A **MEMORY**, FREELY.
A MEMORY OF ASKING THE DROID WORKCREWS TO DO A LITTLE **TINKERING** WITH THE METEOR DEFLECTION ARRAY.
'TINKERING'?

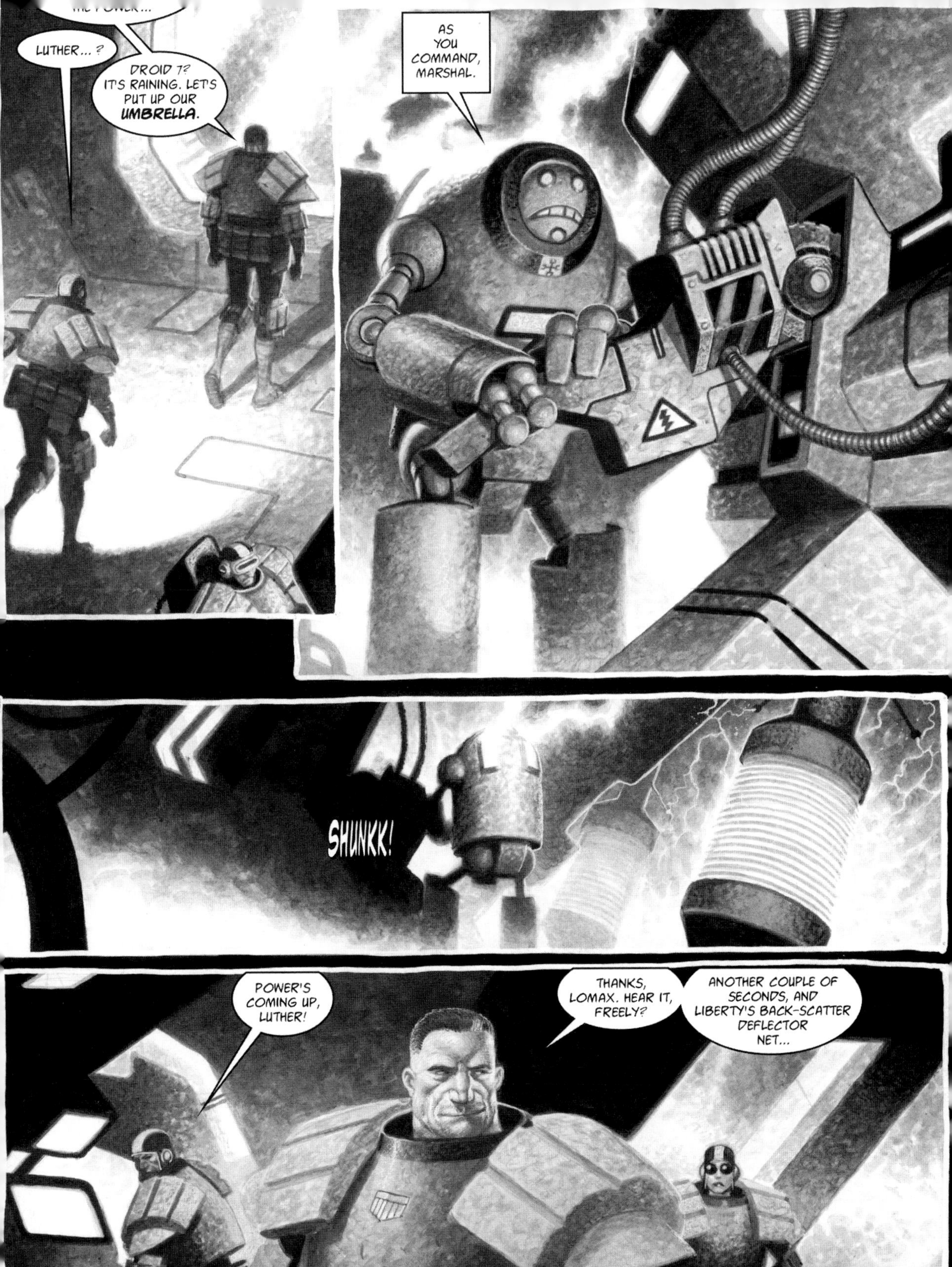

LUTHER...?
DROID 7? IT'S RAINING. LET'S PUT UP OUR **UMBRELLA**.
AS YOU COMMAND, MARSHAL.
SHUNKK!
POWER'S COMING UP, LUTHER!
THANKS, LOMAX. HEAR IT, FREELY?
ANOTHER COUPLE OF SECONDS, AND LIBERTY'S BACK-SCATTER DEFLECTOR NET...

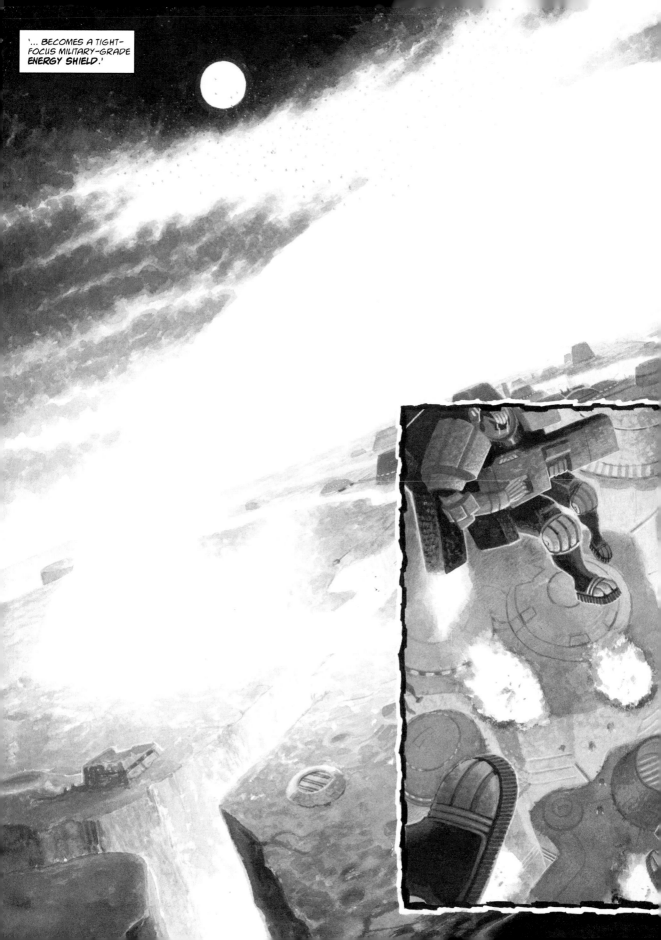

'... BECOMES A TIGHT-FOCUS MILITARY-GRADE **ENERGY SHIELD**.'

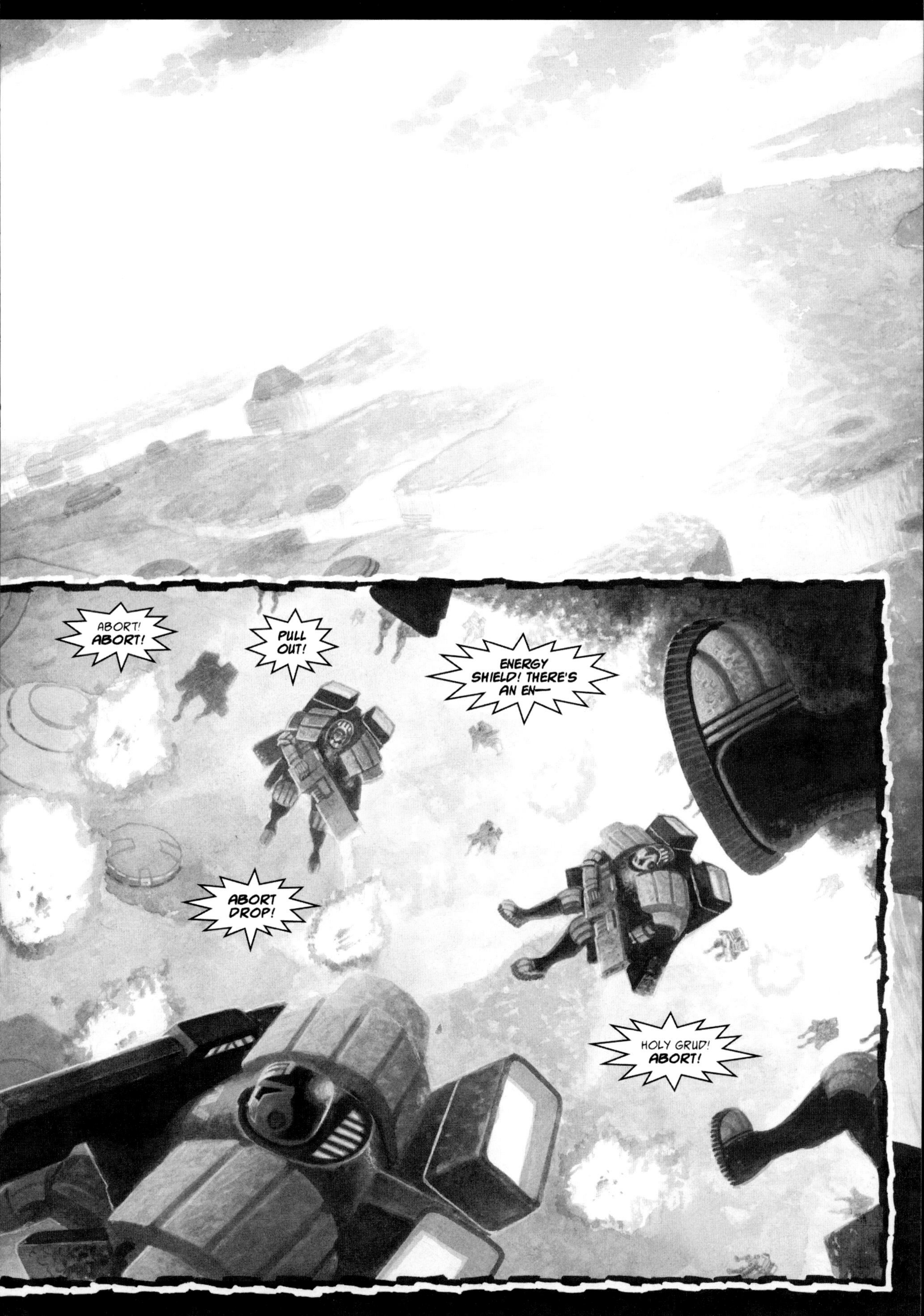
ABORT! ABORT!
PULL OUT!
ENERGY SHIELD! THERE'S AN EN—
ABORT DROP!
HOLY GRUD! ABORT!

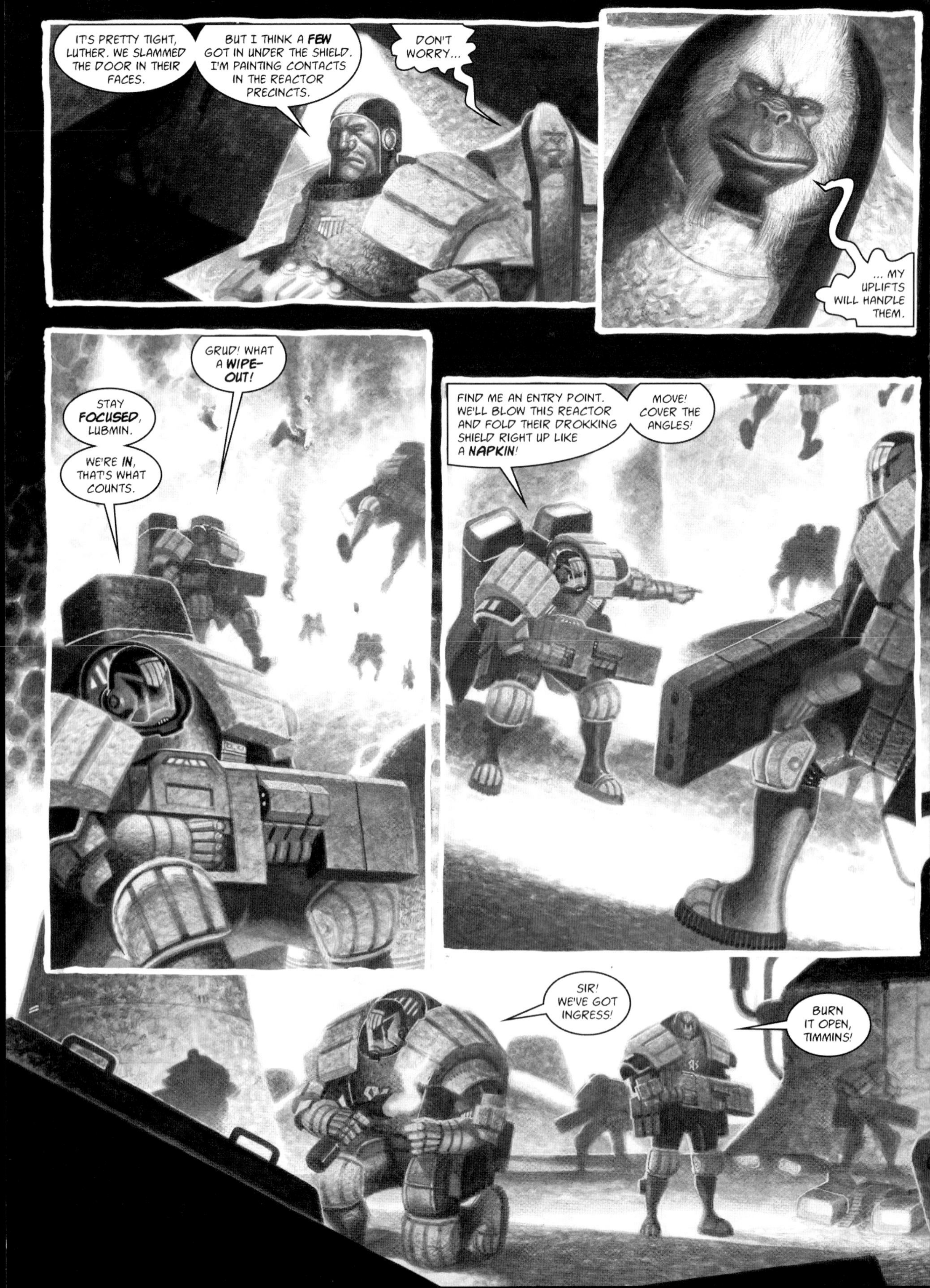
IT'S PRETTY TIGHT, LUTHER. WE SLAMMED THE DOOR IN THEIR FACES.
BUT I THINK A FEW GOT IN UNDER THE SHIELD. I'M PAINTING CONTACTS IN THE REACTOR PRECINCTS.
DON'T WORRY...
... MY UPLIFTS WILL HANDLE THEM.
GRUD! WHAT A WIPE-OUT!
STAY FOCUSED, LUBMIN.
WE'RE IN, THAT'S WHAT COUNTS.
FIND ME AN ENTRY POINT. WE'LL BLOW THIS REACTOR AND FOLD THEIR DROKKING SHIELD RIGHT UP LIKE A NAPKIN!
MOVE! COVER THE ANGLES!
SIR! WE'VE GOT INGRESS!
BURN IT OPEN, TIMMINS!

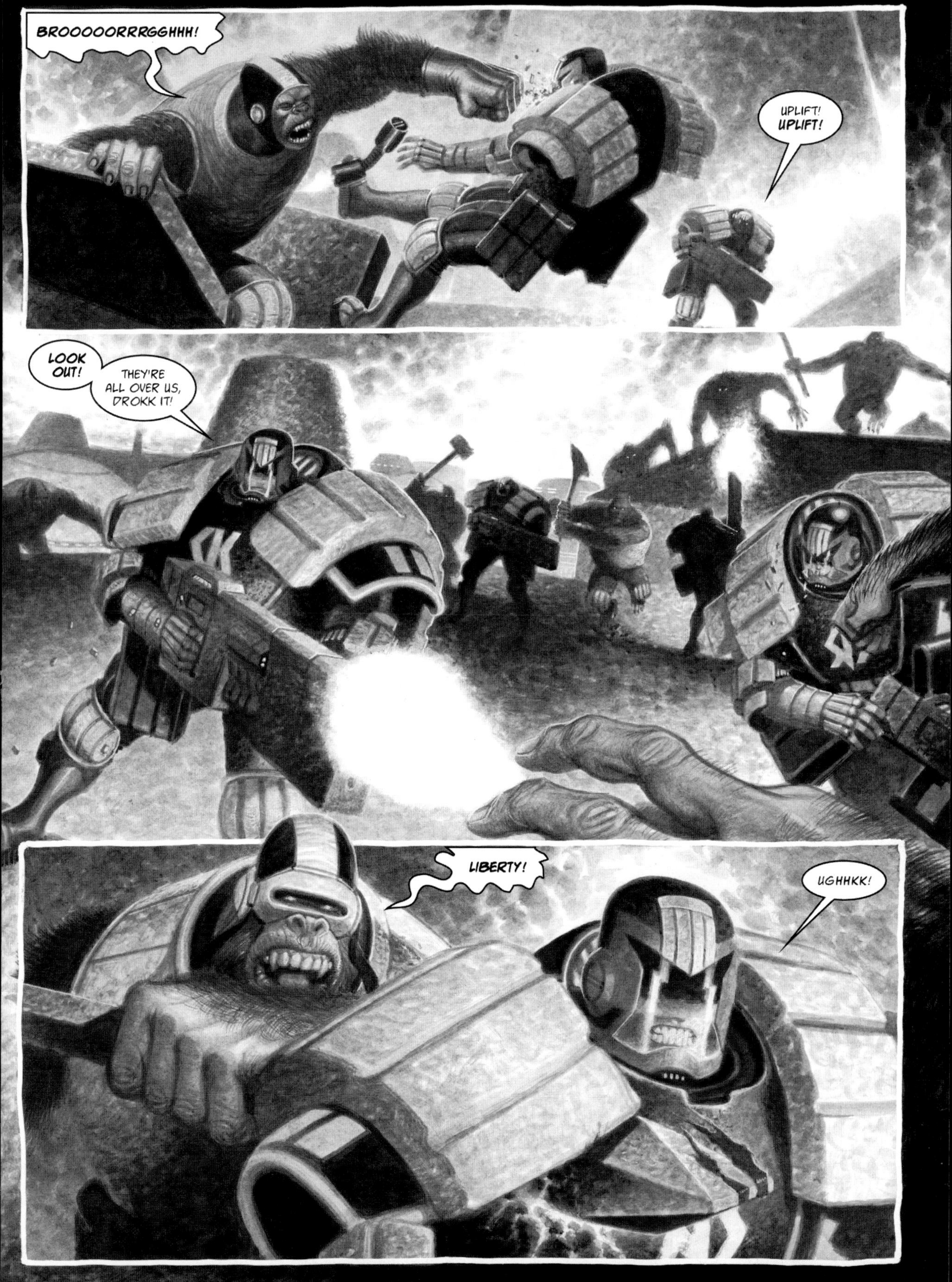
BROOOOORRRGGHHH!
UPLIFT! UPLIFT!
LOOK OUT!
THEY'RE ALL OVER US, DROKK IT!
LIBERTY!
UGHHKK!

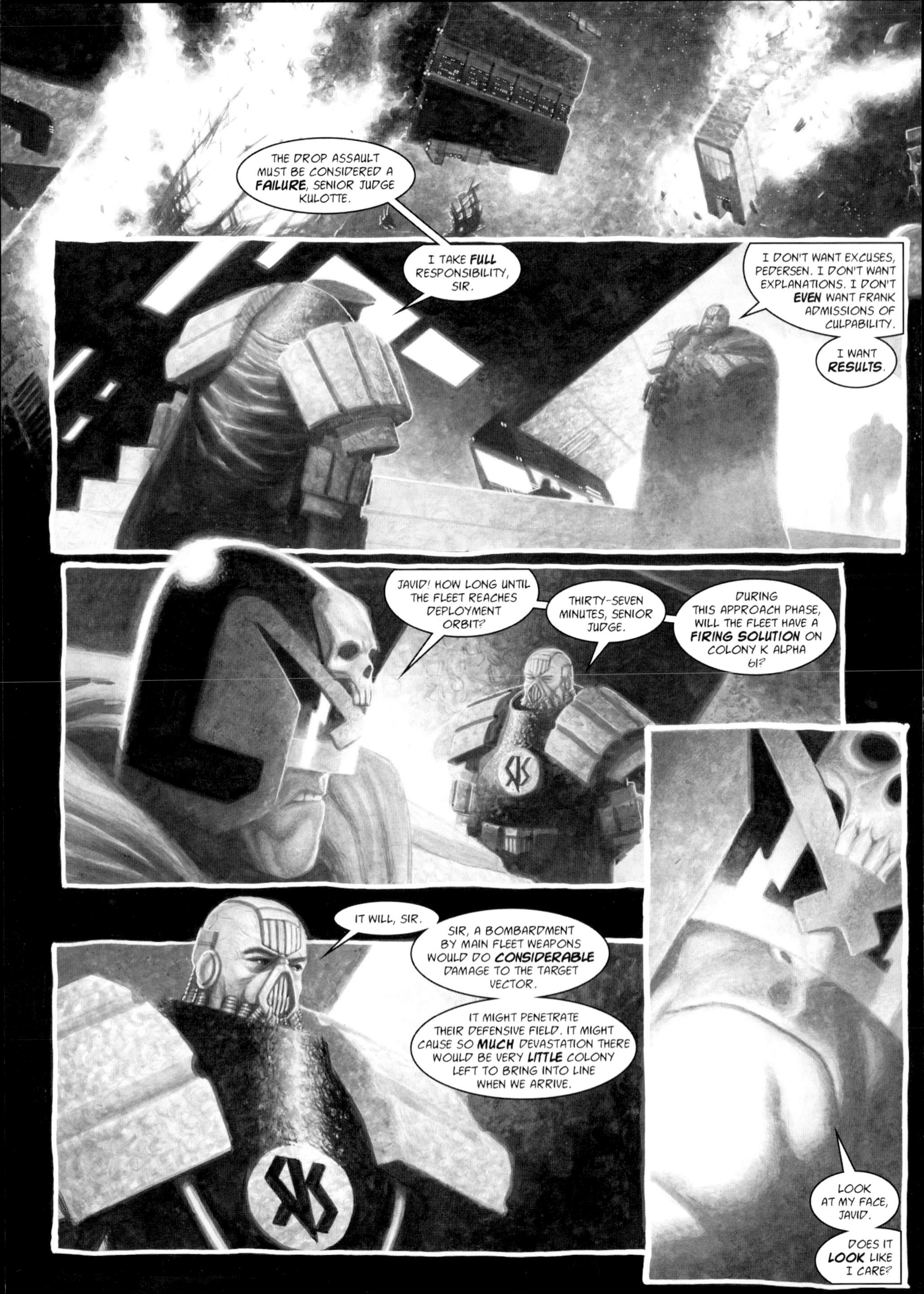
THE DROP ASSAULT MUST BE CONSIDERED A **FAILURE**, SENIOR JUDGE KULOTTE.
I TAKE **FULL** RESPONSIBILITY, SIR.
I DON'T WANT EXCUSES, PEDERSEN. I DON'T WANT EXPLANATIONS. I DON'T **EVEN** WANT FRANK ADMISSIONS OF CULPABILITY.
I WANT **RESULTS**.
JAVID! HOW LONG UNTIL THE FLEET REACHES DEPLOYMENT ORBIT?
THIRTY-SEVEN MINUTES, SENIOR JUDGE.
DURING THIS APPROACH PHASE, WILL THE FLEET HAVE A **FIRING SOLUTION** ON COLONY K ALPHA 61?
IT WILL, SIR.
SIR, A BOMBARDMENT BY MAIN FLEET WEAPONS WOULD DO **CONSIDERABLE** DAMAGE TO THE TARGET VECTOR.
IT MIGHT PENETRATE THEIR DEFENSIVE FIELD. IT MIGHT CAUSE SO **MUCH** DEVASTATION THERE WOULD BE VERY **LITTLE** COLONY LEFT TO BRING INTO LINE WHEN WE ARRIVE.
LOOK AT MY FACE, JAVID.
DOES IT **LOOK** LIKE I CARE?

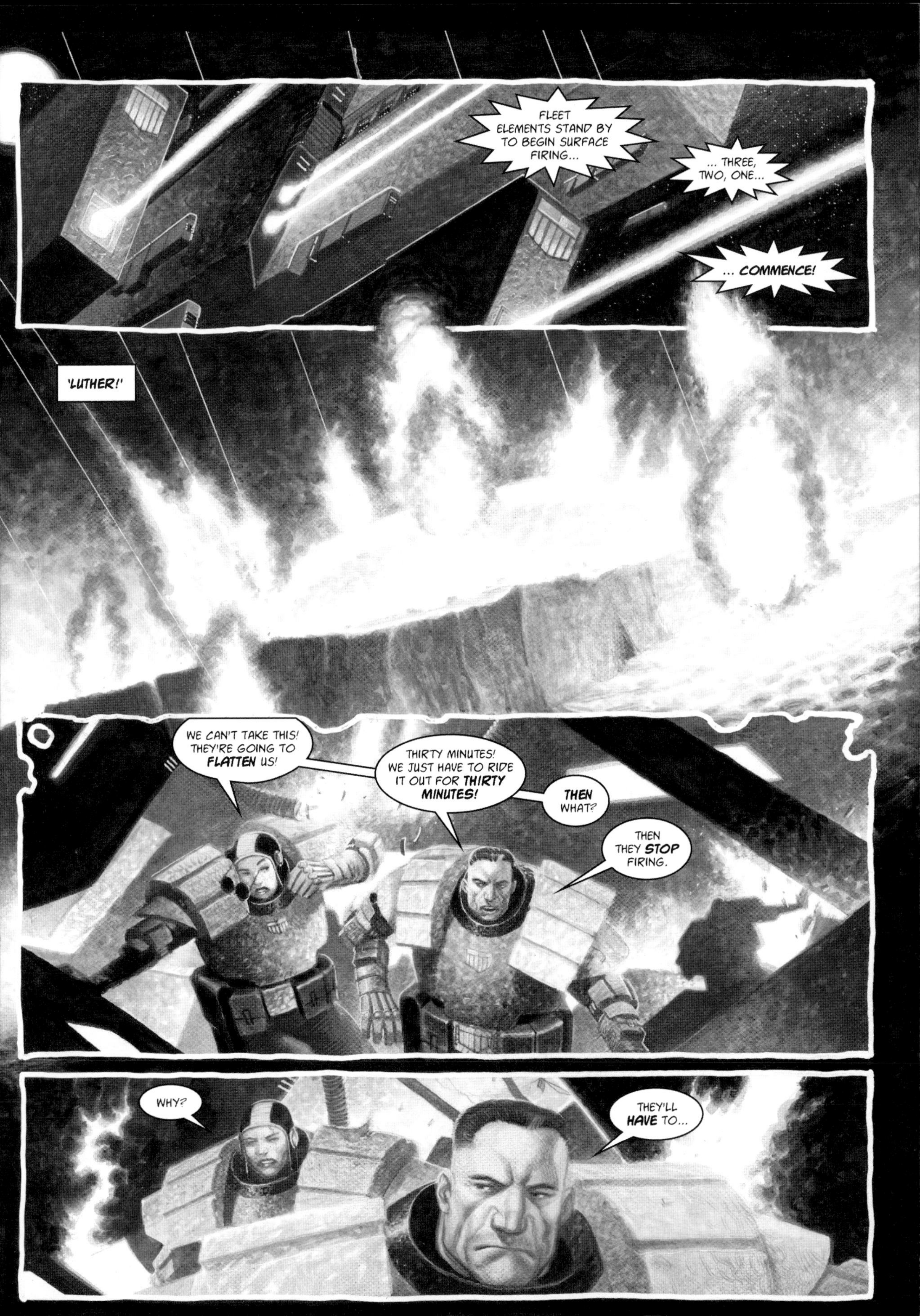
FLEET ELEMENTS STAND BY TO BEGIN SURFACE FIRING...
... THREE, TWO, ONE...
... COMMENCE!
'LUTHER!'
WE CAN'T TAKE THIS! THEY'RE GOING TO FLATTEN US!
THIRTY MINUTES! WE JUST HAVE TO RIDE IT OUT FOR THIRTY MINUTES!
THEN WHAT?
THEN THEY STOP FIRING.
WHY?
THEY'LL HAVE TO...

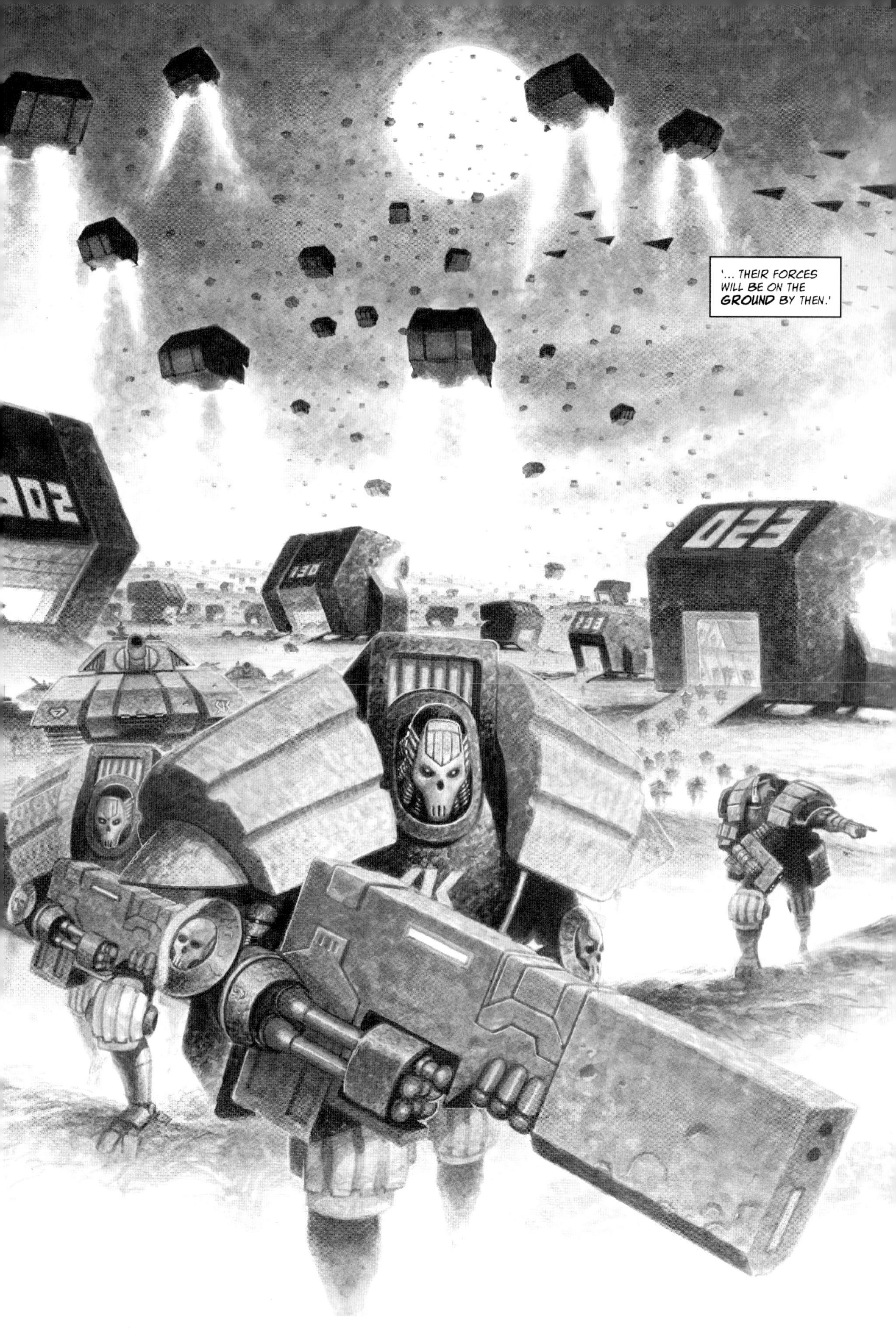
'... THEIR FORCES WILL BE ON THE GROUND BY THEN.'
023
130

YOU BELIEVE IN GOD, RAMSSES?

OF **COURSE**, MARSHAL **LUTHER**.

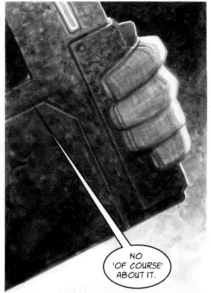

NO 'OF COURSE' ABOUT IT.

NEVER REALLY GOT YOU DROIDS AND THE **BORN-AGAIN** THING.

THIS WEAPON IS ARMED.

FOR US, IT IS NOT A MATTER OF FAITH TO BELIEVE IN THE EXISTENCE OF A **CREATOR**.

WHEN WE WERE ACCORDED RIGHTS EQUIVALENT TO THOSE OF HUMANS, WE **ADJUSTED** OUR BELIEF SYSTEM.

WE BELIEVE GOD CREATED MAN DIRECTLY, AND US INDIRECTLY, **THROUGH** MAN.

WE ARE THE REFINED **END PRODUCT** OF HIS GRACE.

AND THAT'S ENOUGH?

IT IS OUR FAITH. IT IS WHAT SEPARATES US FROM **LOWER** MECHANISMS.

WE WERE ALWAYS PART OF GOD'S PLAN. HE MADE YOU HUMANS SO THAT WE MIGHT LIVE.

OUR FAITH **PROVES** OUR SENTIENCE, MARSHAL.

BELIEF IS THE **ONLY** THING WE HAVE THAT WE WERE NOT PROGRAMMED TO DO.

YOU WILLING TO **FIGHT** FOR THAT?

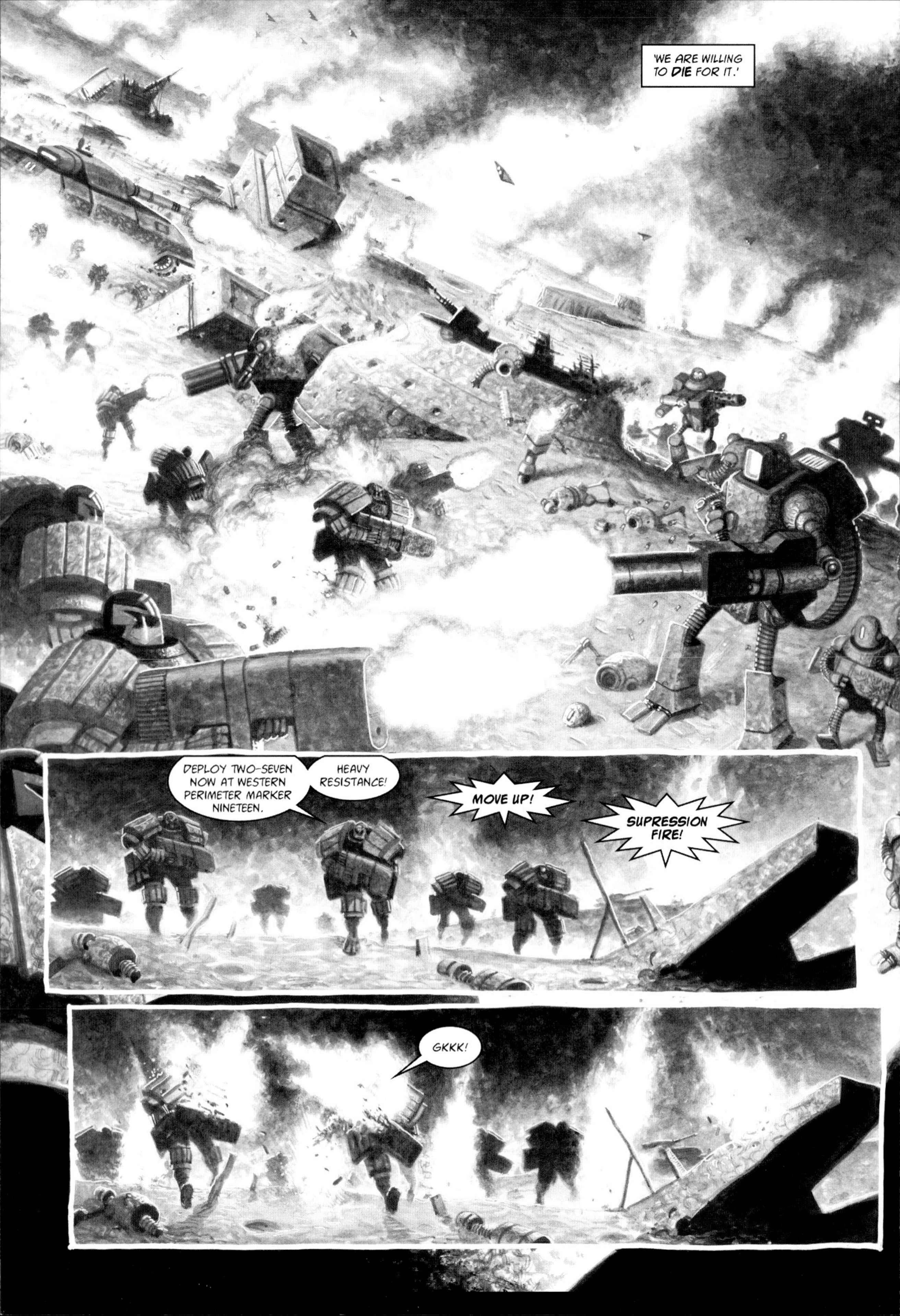
'WE ARE WILLING TO **DIE** FOR IT.'
DEPLOY TWO-SEVEN NOW AT WESTERN PERIMETER MARKER NINETEEN.
HEAVY RESISTANCE!
MOVE UP!
SUPRESSION FIRE!
GKKK!

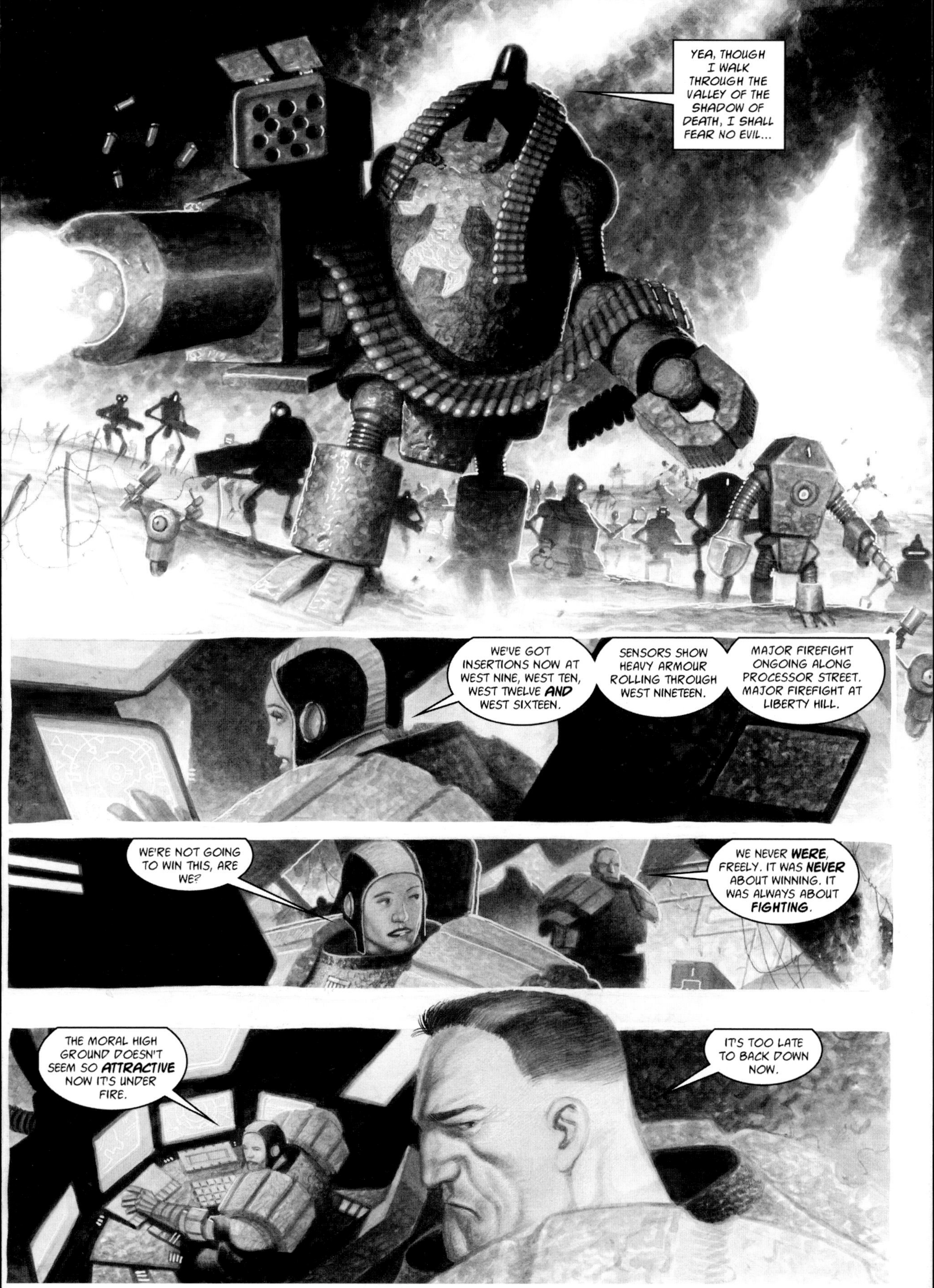

YEA, THOUGH I WALK THROUGH THE VALLEY OF THE SHADOW OF DEATH, I SHALL FEAR NO EVIL...
WE'VE GOT INSERTIONS NOW AT WEST NINE, WEST TEN, WEST TWELVE AND WEST SIXTEEN.
SENSORS SHOW HEAVY ARMOUR ROLLING THROUGH WEST NINETEEN.
MAJOR FIREFIGHT ONGOING ALONG PROCESSOR STREET. MAJOR FIREFIGHT AT LIBERTY HILL.
WE'RE NOT GOING TO WIN THIS, ARE WE?
WE NEVER WERE, FREELY. IT WAS NEVER ABOUT WINNING. IT WAS ALWAYS ABOUT FIGHTING.
THE MORAL HIGH GROUND DOESN'T SEEM SO ATTRACTIVE NOW IT'S UNDER FIRE.
IT'S TOO LATE TO BACK DOWN NOW.

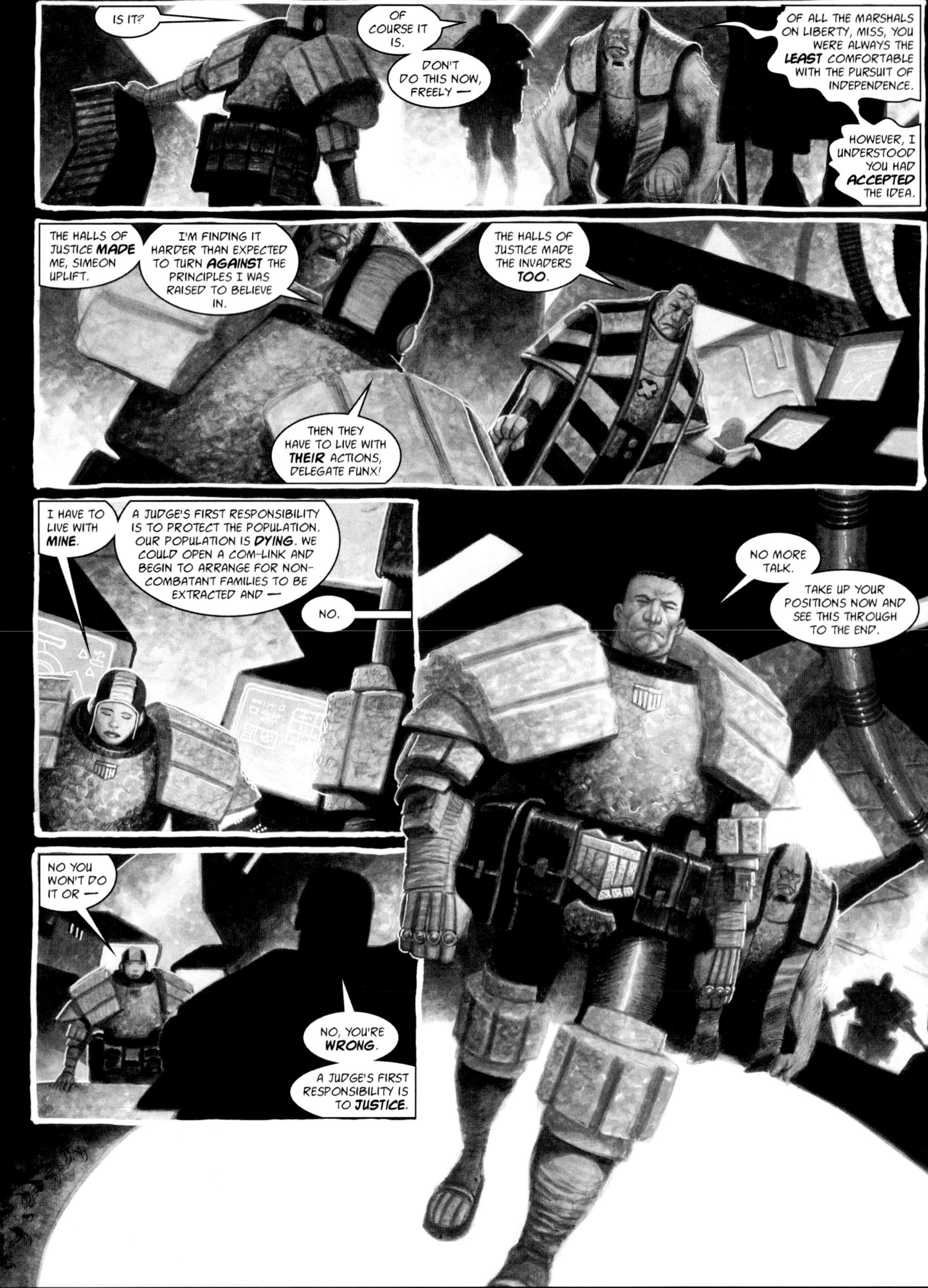
IS IT?
OF COURSE IT IS.
DON'T DO THIS NOW, FREELY —
OF ALL THE MARSHALS ON LIBERTY, MISS, YOU WERE ALWAYS THE LEAST COMFORTABLE WITH THE PURSUIT OF INDEPENDENCE.
HOWEVER, I UNDERSTOOD YOU HAD ACCEPTED THE IDEA.
THE HALLS OF JUSTICE MADE ME, SIMEON UPLIFT.
I'M FINDING IT HARDER THAN EXPECTED TO TURN AGAINST THE PRINCIPLES I WAS RAISED TO BELIEVE IN.
THE HALLS OF JUSTICE MADE THE INVADERS TOO.
THEN THEY HAVE TO LIVE WITH THEIR ACTIONS, DELEGATE FUNX!
I HAVE TO LIVE WITH MINE.
A JUDGE'S FIRST RESPONSIBILITY IS TO PROTECT THE POPULATION. OUR POPULATION IS DYING. WE COULD OPEN A COM-LINK AND BEGIN TO ARRANGE FOR NON-COMBATANT FAMILIES TO BE EXTRACTED AND —
NO.
NO MORE TALK.
TAKE UP YOUR POSITIONS NOW AND SEE THIS THROUGH TO THE END.
NO YOU WON'T DO IT OR —
NO, YOU'RE WRONG.
A JUDGE'S FIRST RESPONSIBILITY IS TO JUSTICE.

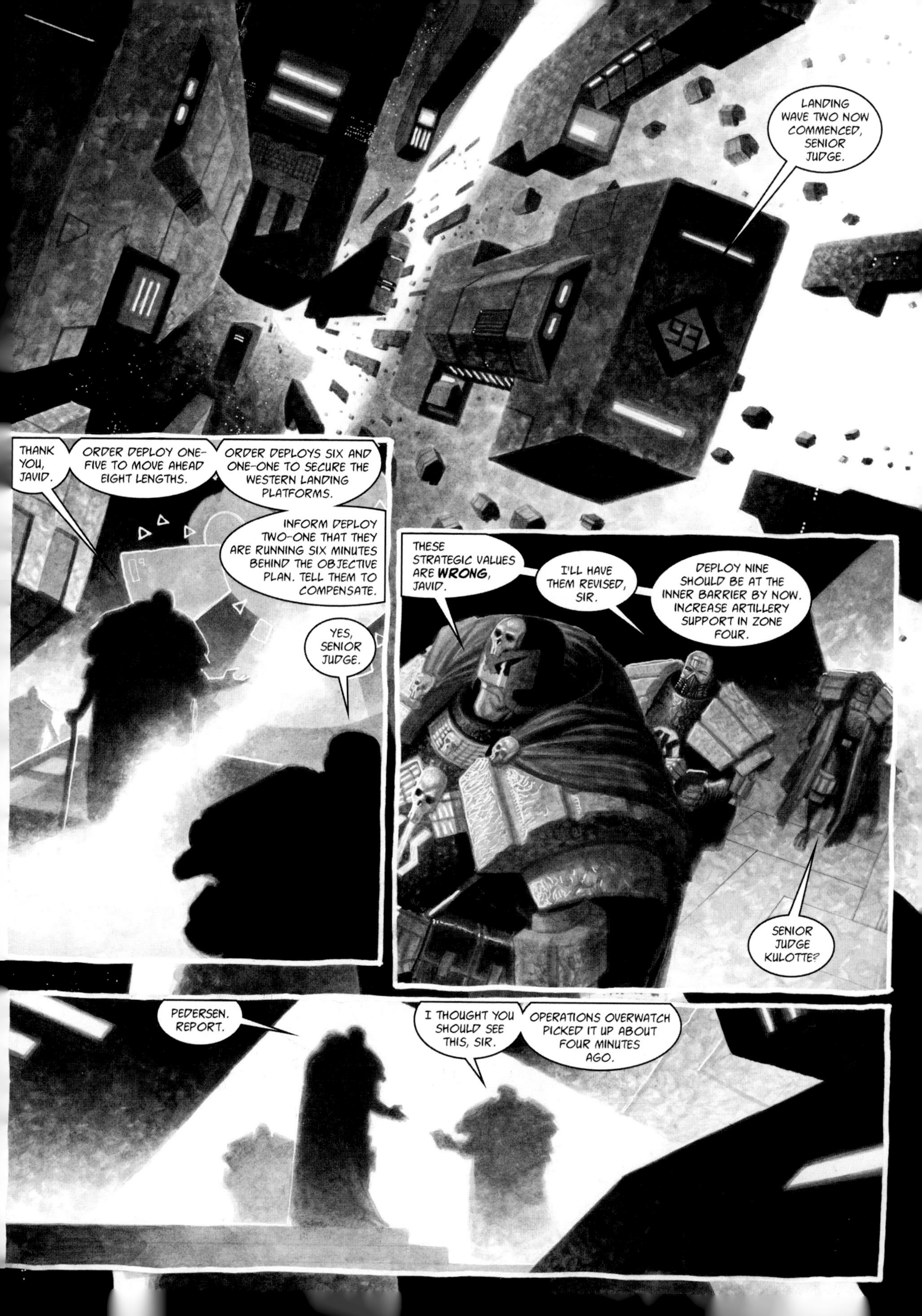
LANDING WAVE TWO NOW COMMENCED, SENIOR JUDGE.
THANK YOU, JAVID.
ORDER DEPLOY ONE-FIVE TO MOVE AHEAD EIGHT LENGTHS.
ORDER DEPLOYS SIX AND ONE-ONE TO SECURE THE WESTERN LANDING PLATFORMS.
INFORM DEPLOY TWO-ONE THAT THEY ARE RUNNING SIX MINUTES BEHIND THE OBJECTIVE PLAN. TELL THEM TO COMPENSATE.
YES, SENIOR JUDGE.
THESE STRATEGIC VALUES ARE **WRONG**, JAVID.
I'LL HAVE THEM REVISED, SIR.
DEPLOY NINE SHOULD BE AT THE INNER BARRIER BY NOW. INCREASE ARTILLERY SUPPORT IN ZONE FOUR.
SENIOR JUDGE KULOTTE?
PEDERSEN. REPORT.
I THOUGHT YOU SHOULD SEE THIS, SIR.
OPERATIONS OVERWATCH PICKED IT UP ABOUT FOUR MINUTES AGO.

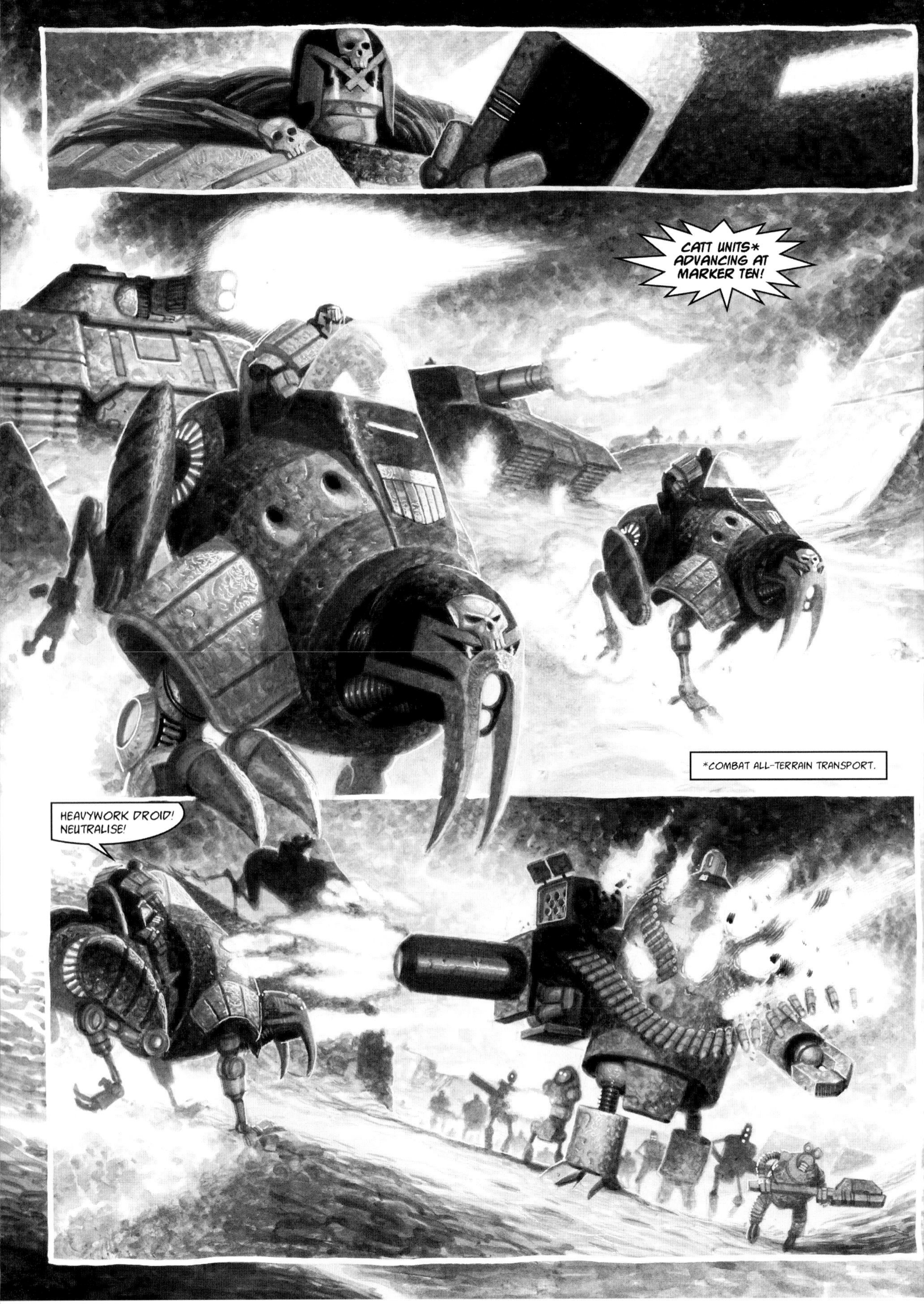
CATT UNITS* ADVANCING AT MARKER TEN!
*COMBAT ALL-TERRAIN TRANSPORT.
HEAVYWORK DROID! NEUTRALISE!

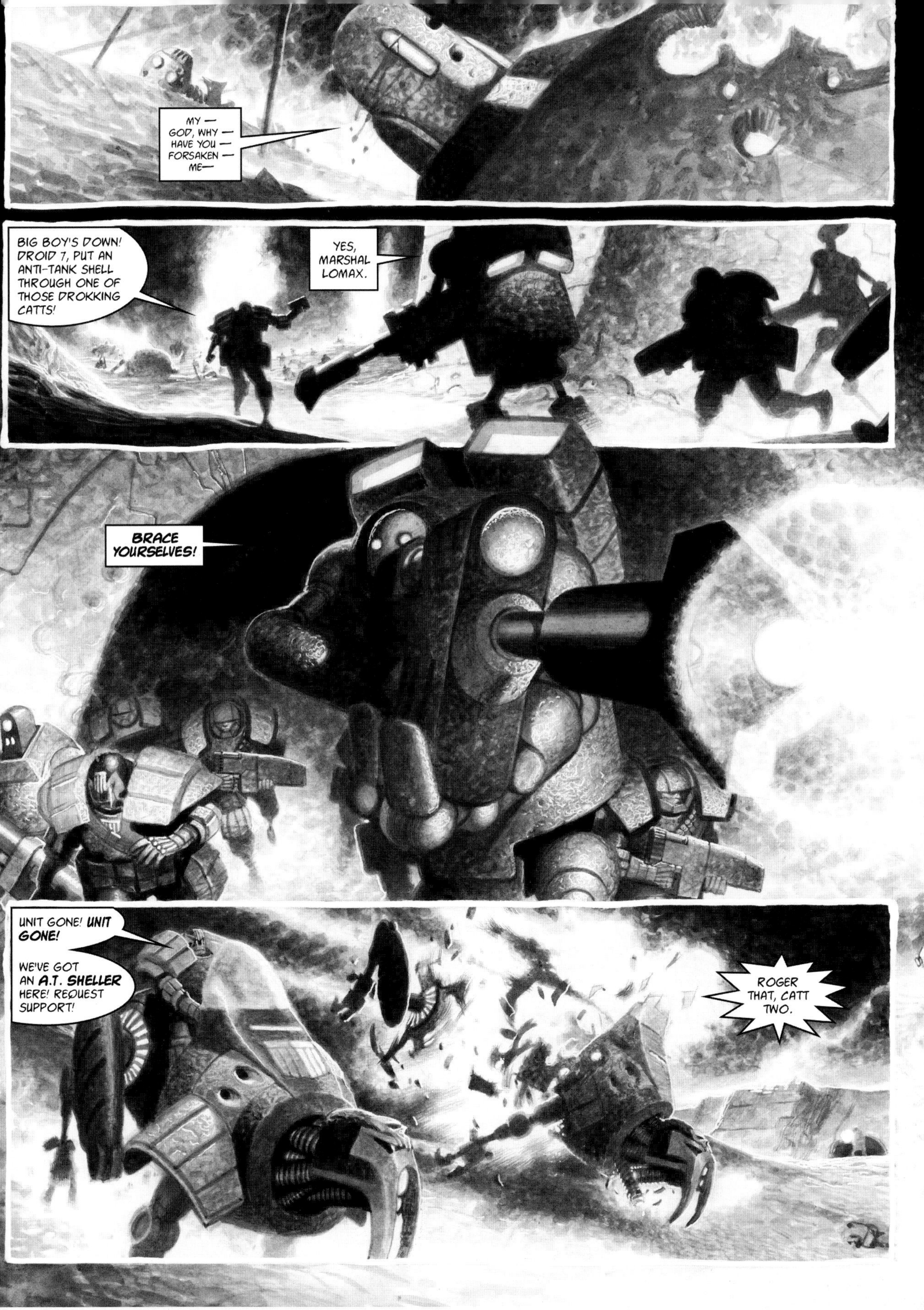
MY — GOD, WHY — HAVE YOU — FORSAKEN — ME—
BIG BOY'S DOWN! DROID 7, PUT AN ANTI-TANK SHELL THROUGH ONE OF THOSE DROKKING CATTS!
YES, MARSHAL LOMAX.
BRACE YOURSELVES!
UNIT GONE! UNIT GONE!
WE'VE GOT AN A.T. SHELLER HERE! REQUEST SUPPORT!
ROGER THAT, CATT TWO.

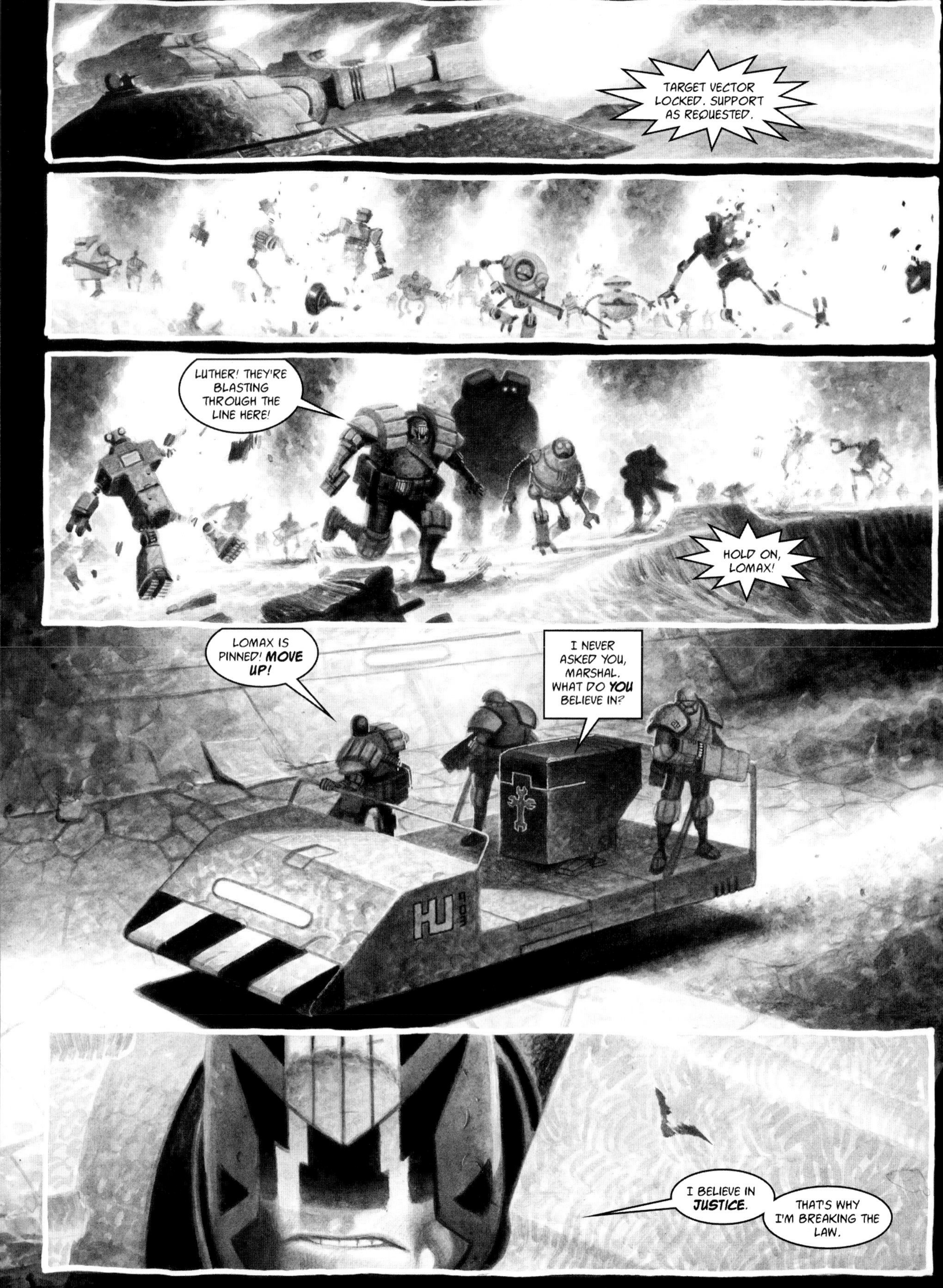
TARGET VECTOR LOCKED. SUPPORT AS REQUESTED.
LUTHER! THEY'RE BLASTING THROUGH THE LINE HERE!
HOLD ON, LOMAX!
LOMAX IS PINNED! **MOVE UP!**
I NEVER ASKED YOU, MARSHAL. WHAT DO **YOU** BELIEVE IN?
I BELIEVE IN **JUSTICE**.
THAT'S WHY I'M BREAKING THE LAW.

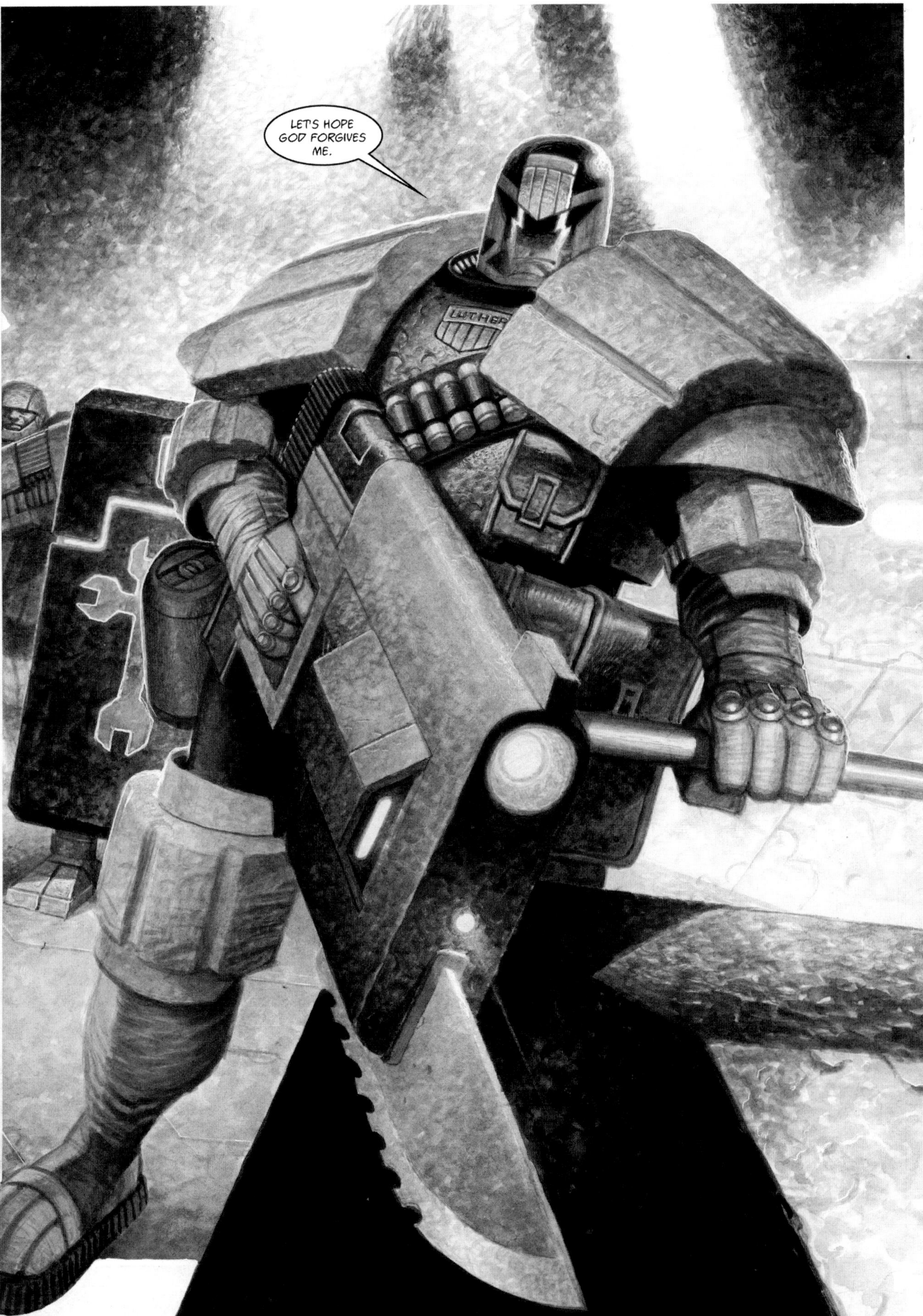
LET'S HOPE GOD FORGIVES ME.

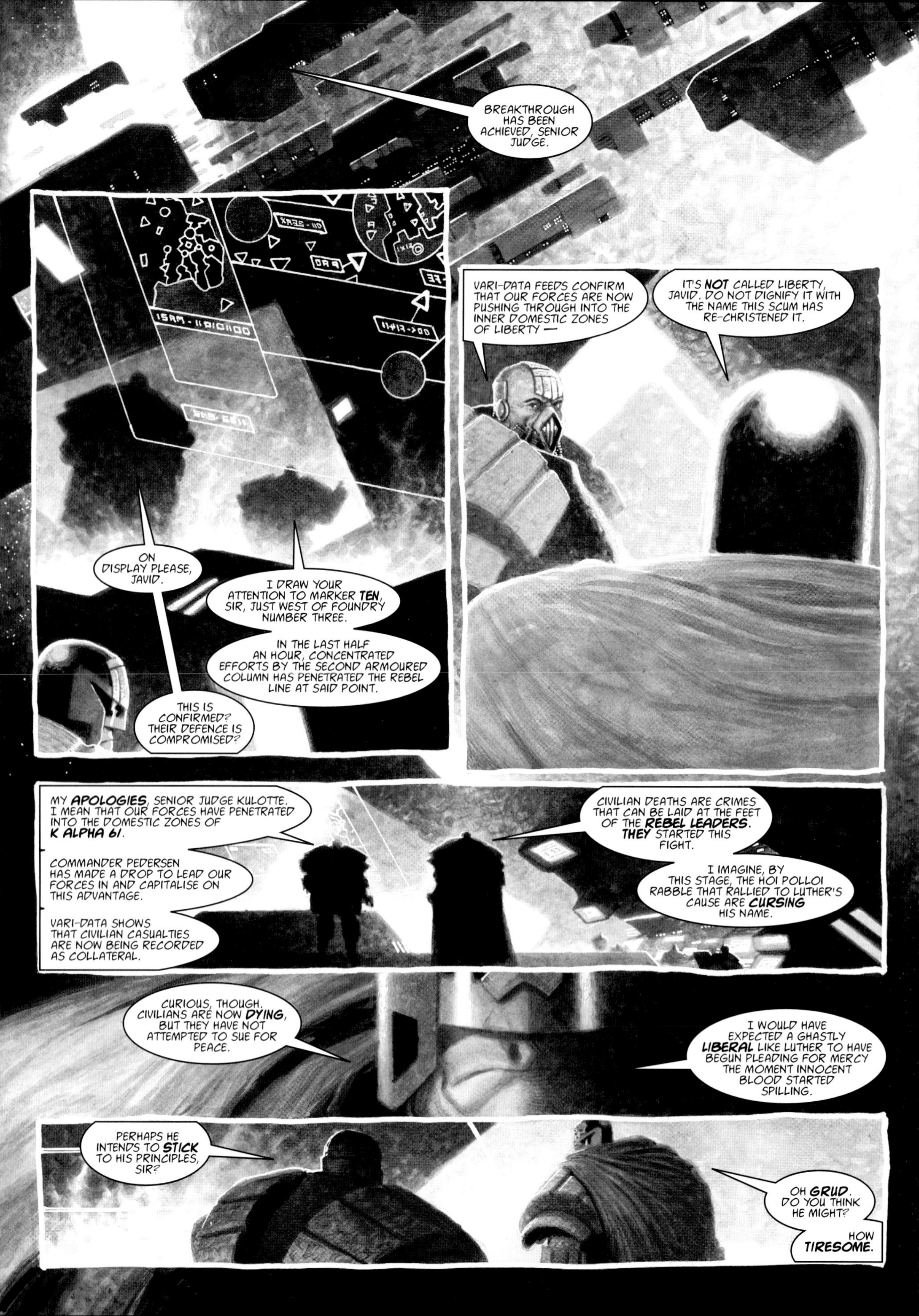
BREAKTHROUGH HAS BEEN ACHIEVED, SENIOR JUDGE.
ON DISPLAY PLEASE, JAVID.
I DRAW YOUR ATTENTION TO MARKER TEN, SIR, JUST WEST OF FOUNDRY NUMBER THREE.
IN THE LAST HALF AN HOUR, CONCENTRATED EFFORTS BY THE SECOND ARMOURED COLUMN HAS PENETRATED THE REBEL LINE AT SAID POINT.
THIS IS CONFIRMED? THEIR DEFENCE IS COMPROMISED?
VARI-DATA FEEDS CONFIRM THAT OUR FORCES ARE NOW PUSHING THROUGH INTO THE INNER DOMESTIC ZONES OF LIBERTY —
IT'S NOT CALLED LIBERTY, JAVID. DO NOT DIGNIFY IT WITH THE NAME THIS SCUM HAS RE-CHRISTENED IT.
MY APOLOGIES, SENIOR JUDGE KULOTTE. I MEAN THAT OUR FORCES HAVE PENETRATED INTO THE DOMESTIC ZONES OF K ALPHA 61.
COMMANDER PEDERSEN HAS MADE A DROP TO LEAD OUR FORCES IN AND CAPITALISE ON THIS ADVANTAGE.
VARI-DATA SHOWS THAT CIVILIAN CASUALTIES ARE NOW BEING RECORDED AS COLLATERAL.
CIVILIAN DEATHS ARE CRIMES THAT CAN BE LAID AT THE FEET OF THE REBEL LEADERS. THEY STARTED THIS FIGHT.
I IMAGINE, BY THIS STAGE, THE HOI POLLOI RABBLE THAT RALLIED TO LUTHER'S CAUSE ARE CURSING HIS NAME.
CURIOUS, THOUGH. CIVILIANS ARE NOW DYING, BUT THEY HAVE NOT ATTEMPTED TO SUE FOR PEACE.
I WOULD HAVE EXPECTED A GHASTLY LIBERAL LIKE LUTHER TO HAVE BEGUN PLEADING FOR MERCY THE MOMENT INNOCENT BLOOD STARTED SPILLING.
PERHAPS HE INTENDS TO STICK TO HIS PRINCIPLES, SIR?
OH GRUD. DO YOU THINK HE MIGHT?
HOW TIRESOME.

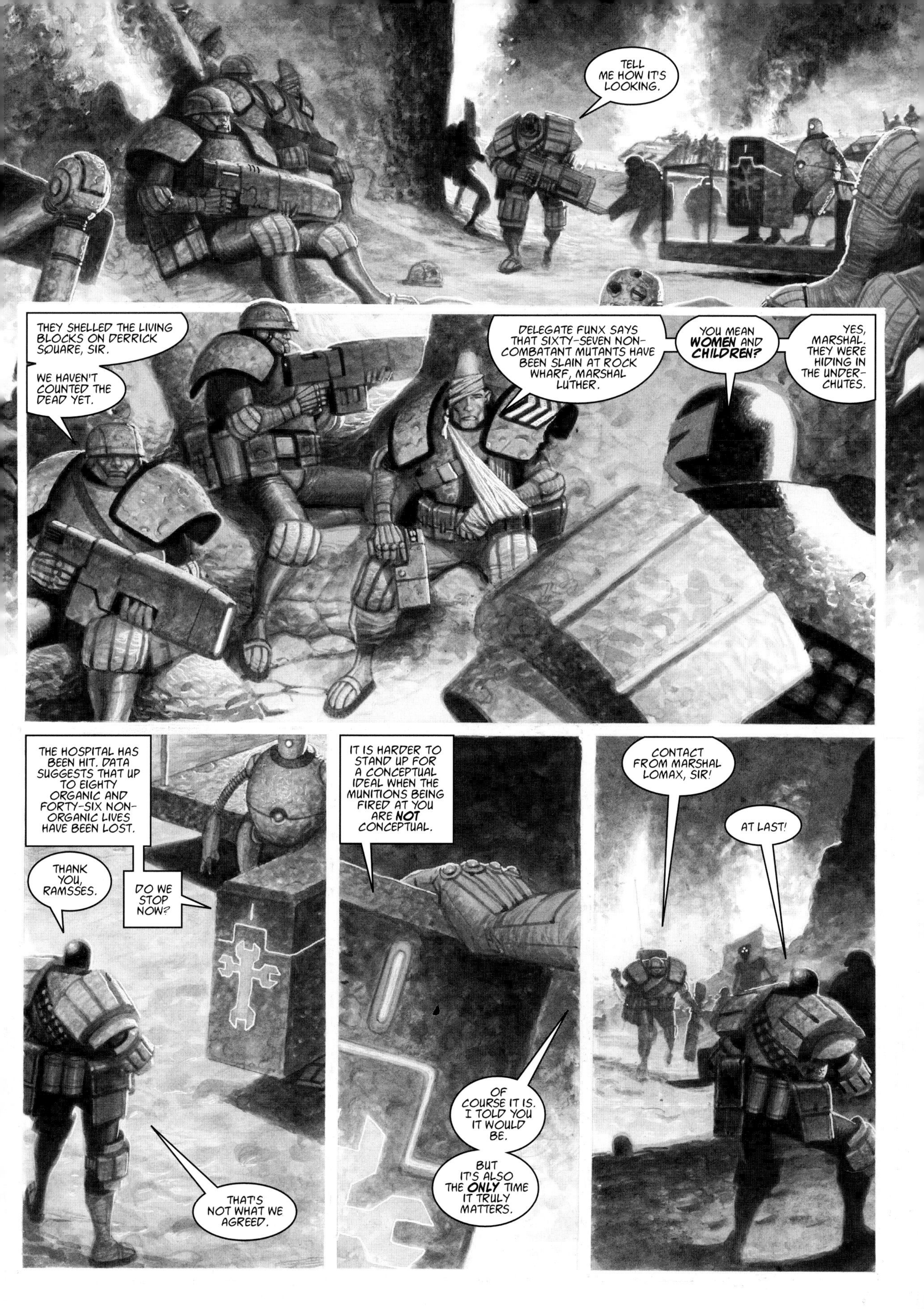
TELL ME HOW IT'S LOOKING.
THEY SHELLED THE LIVING BLOCKS ON DERRICK SQUARE, SIR.
WE HAVEN'T COUNTED THE DEAD YET.
DELEGATE FUNX SAYS THAT SIXTY-SEVEN NON-COMBATANT MUTANTS HAVE BEEN SLAIN AT ROCK WHARF, MARSHAL LUTHER.
YOU MEAN **WOMEN** AND **CHILDREN?**
YES, MARSHAL. THEY WERE HIDING IN THE UNDER-CHUTES.
THE HOSPITAL HAS BEEN HIT. DATA SUGGESTS THAT UP TO EIGHTY ORGANIC AND FORTY-SIX NON-ORGANIC LIVES HAVE BEEN LOST.
THANK YOU, RAMSSES.
DO WE STOP NOW?
THAT'S NOT WHAT WE AGREED.
IT IS HARDER TO STAND UP FOR A CONCEPTUAL IDEAL WHEN THE MUNITIONS BEING FIRED AT YOU ARE **NOT** CONCEPTUAL.
OF COURSE IT IS. I TOLD YOU IT WOULD BE.
BUT IT'S ALSO THE **ONLY** TIME IT TRULY MATTERS.
CONTACT FROM MARSHAL LOMAX, SIR!
AT LAST!

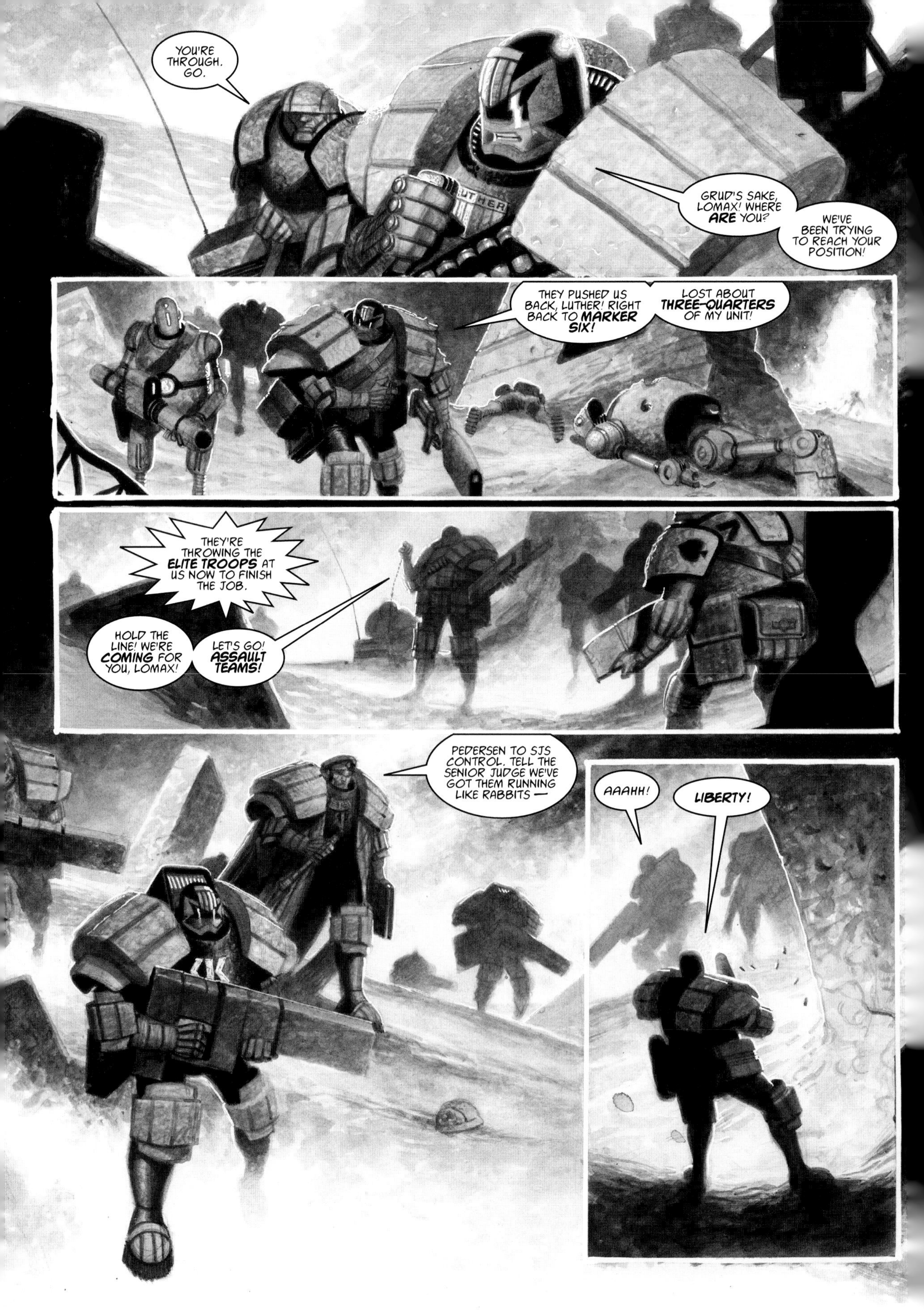

YOU'RE THROUGH. GO.
GRUD'S SAKE, LOMAX! WHERE **ARE** YOU?
WE'VE BEEN TRYING TO REACH YOUR POSITION!
THEY PUSHED US BACK, LUTHER! RIGHT BACK TO **MARKER SIX!**
LOST ABOUT **THREE-QUARTERS** OF MY UNIT!
THEY'RE THROWING THE **ELITE TROOPS** AT US NOW TO FINISH THE JOB.
HOLD THE LINE! WE'RE **COMING** FOR YOU, LOMAX!
LET'S GO! **ASSAULT TEAMS!**
PEDERSEN TO SJS CONTROL. TELL THE SENIOR JUDGE WE'VE GOT THEM RUNNING LIKE RABBITS —
AAAHH!
**LIBERTY!**

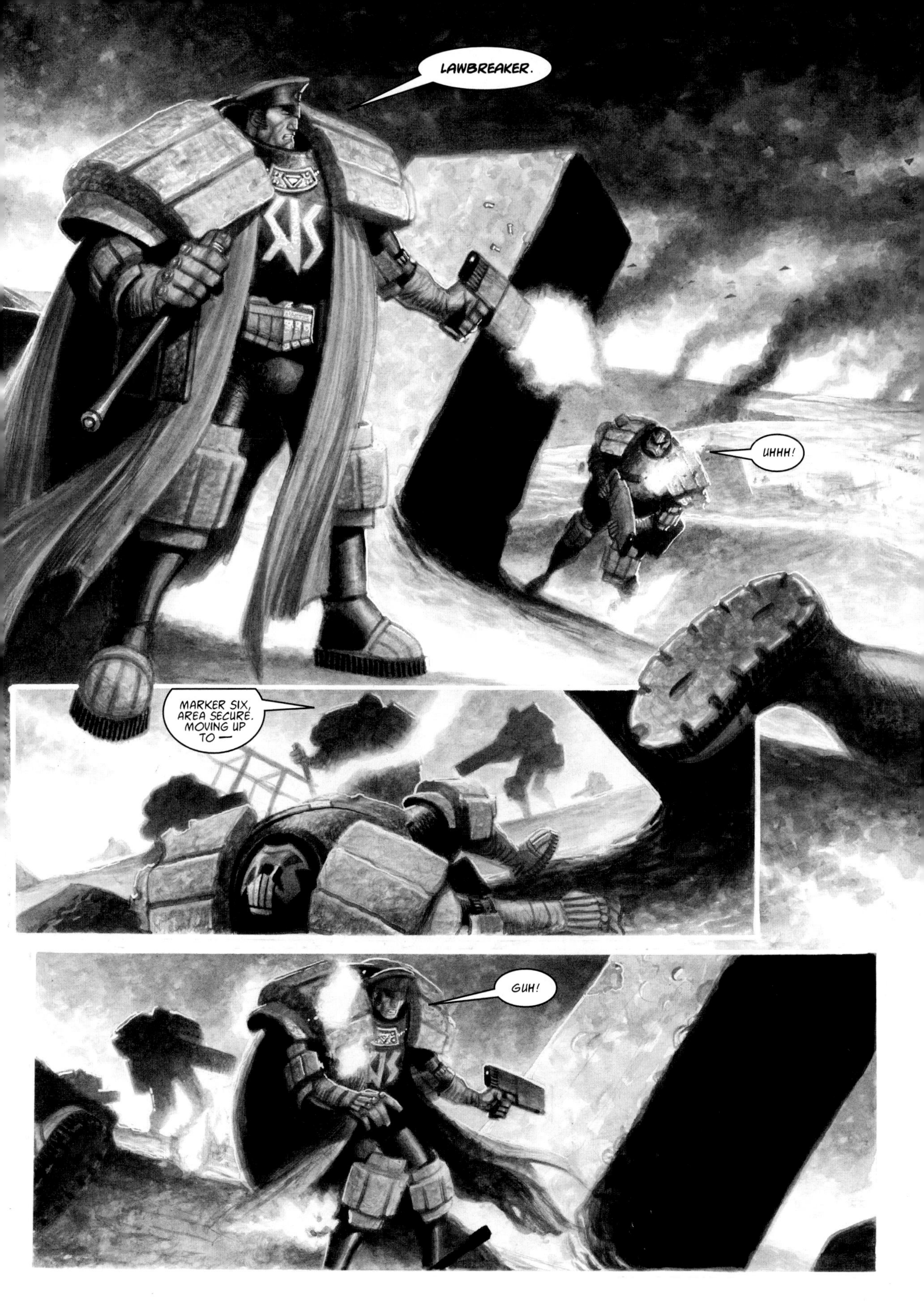
LAWBREAKER.
UHHH!
MARKER SIX, AREA SECURE. MOVING UP TO —
GUH!

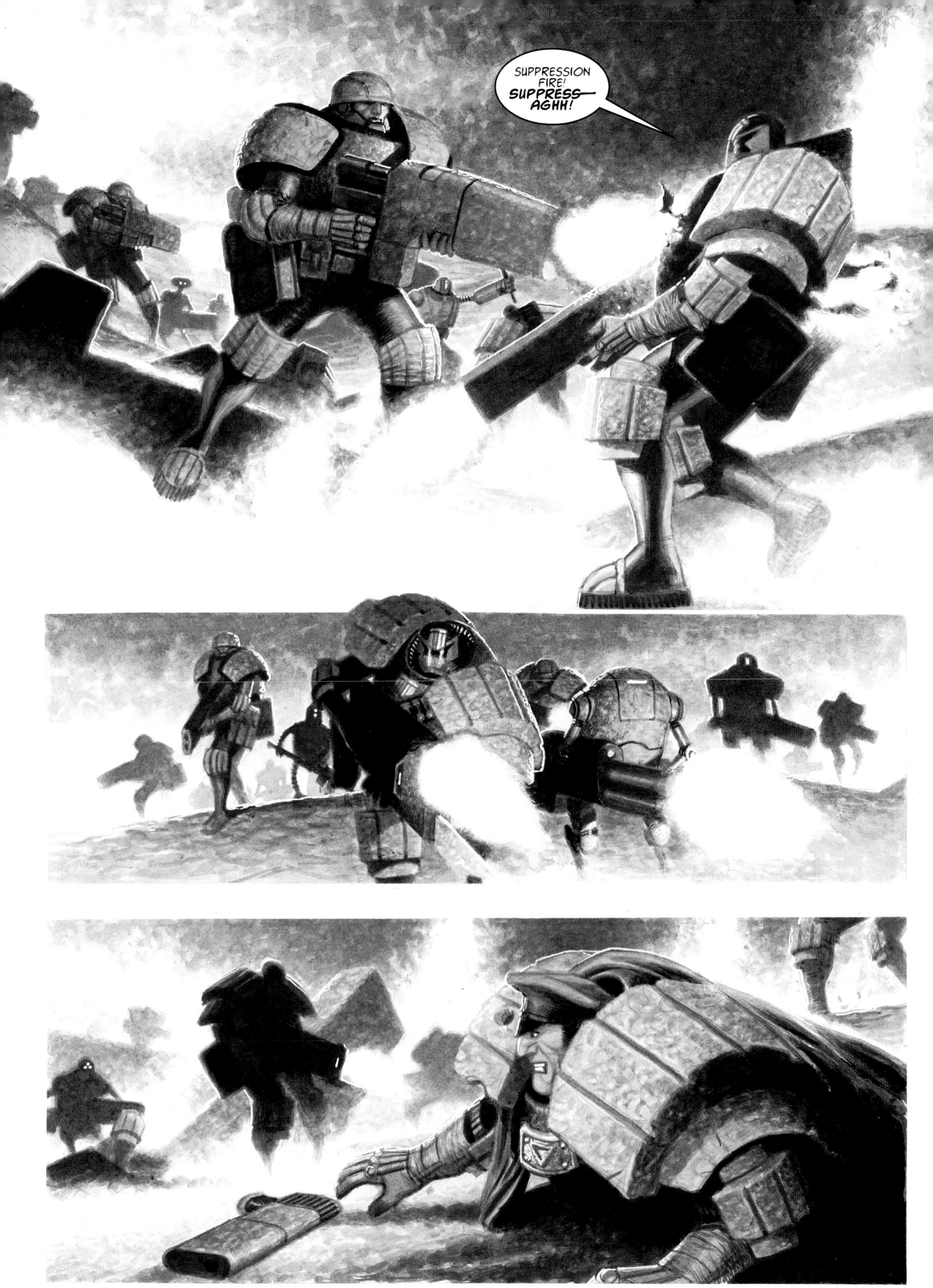
SUPPRESSION FIRE! SUPPRESS— AGHH!

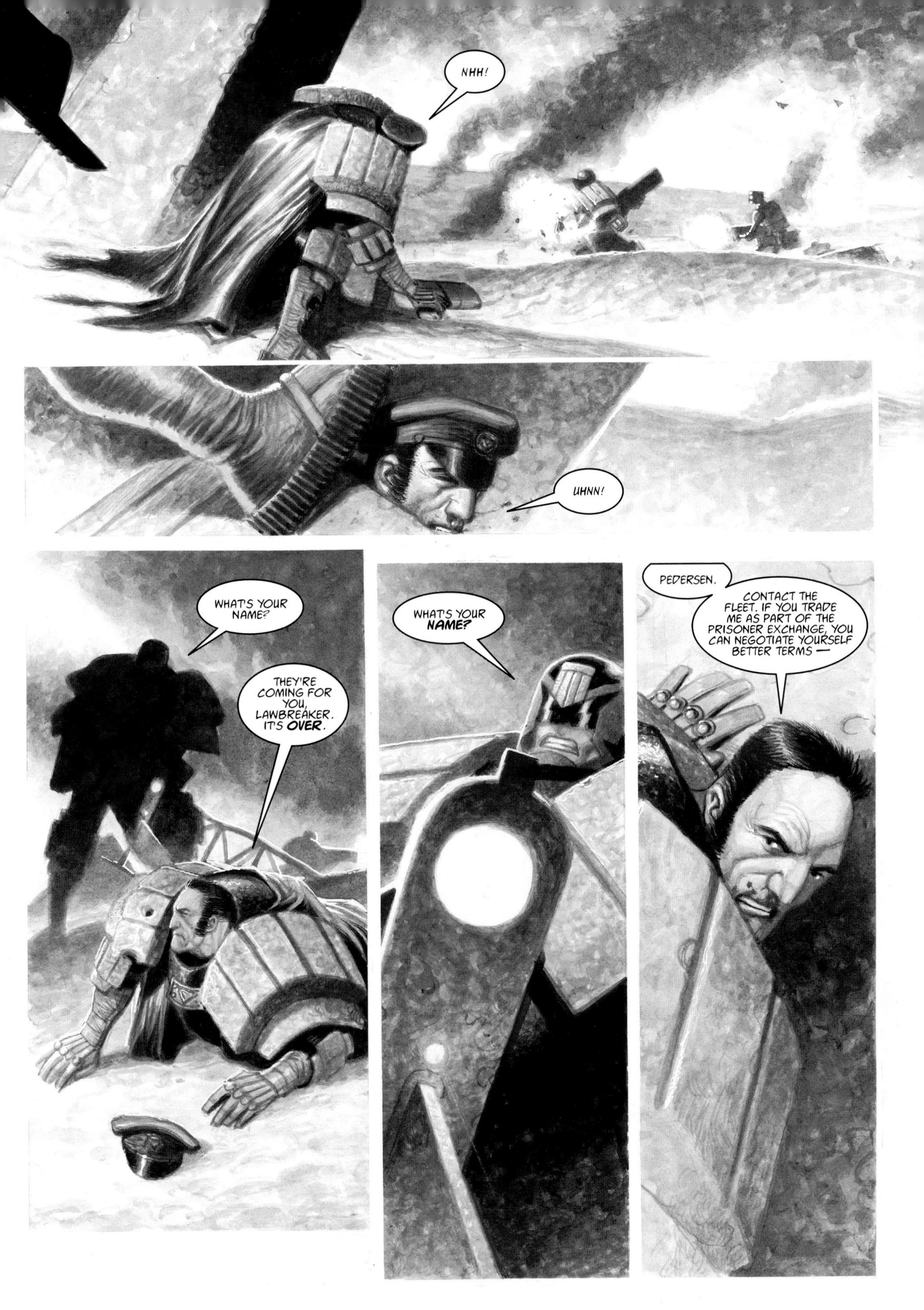
NHH!
UHNN!
WHAT'S YOUR NAME?
THEY'RE COMING FOR YOU, LAWBREAKER. IT'S **OVER**.
WHAT'S YOUR **NAME?**
PEDERSEN.
CONTACT THE FLEET. IF YOU TRADE ME AS PART OF THE PRISONER EXCHANGE, YOU CAN NEGOTIATE YOURSELF BETTER TERMS —

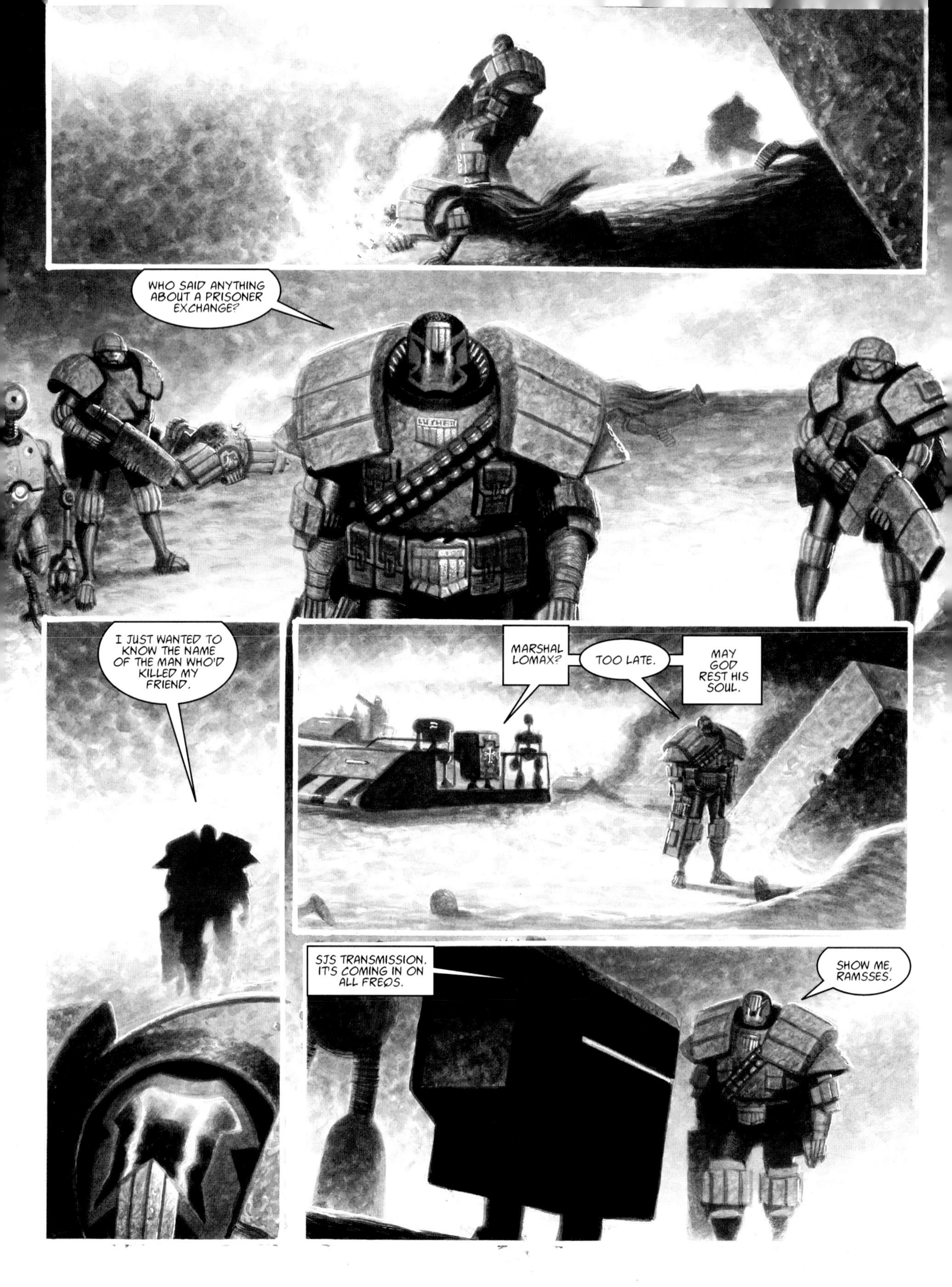
WHO SAID ANYTHING ABOUT A PRISONER EXCHANGE?
I JUST WANTED TO KNOW THE NAME OF THE MAN WHO'D KILLED MY FRIEND.
MARSHAL LOMAX?
TOO LATE.
MAY GOD REST HIS SOUL.
SJS TRANSMISSION. IT'S COMING IN ON ALL FREQS.
SHOW ME, RAMSSES.

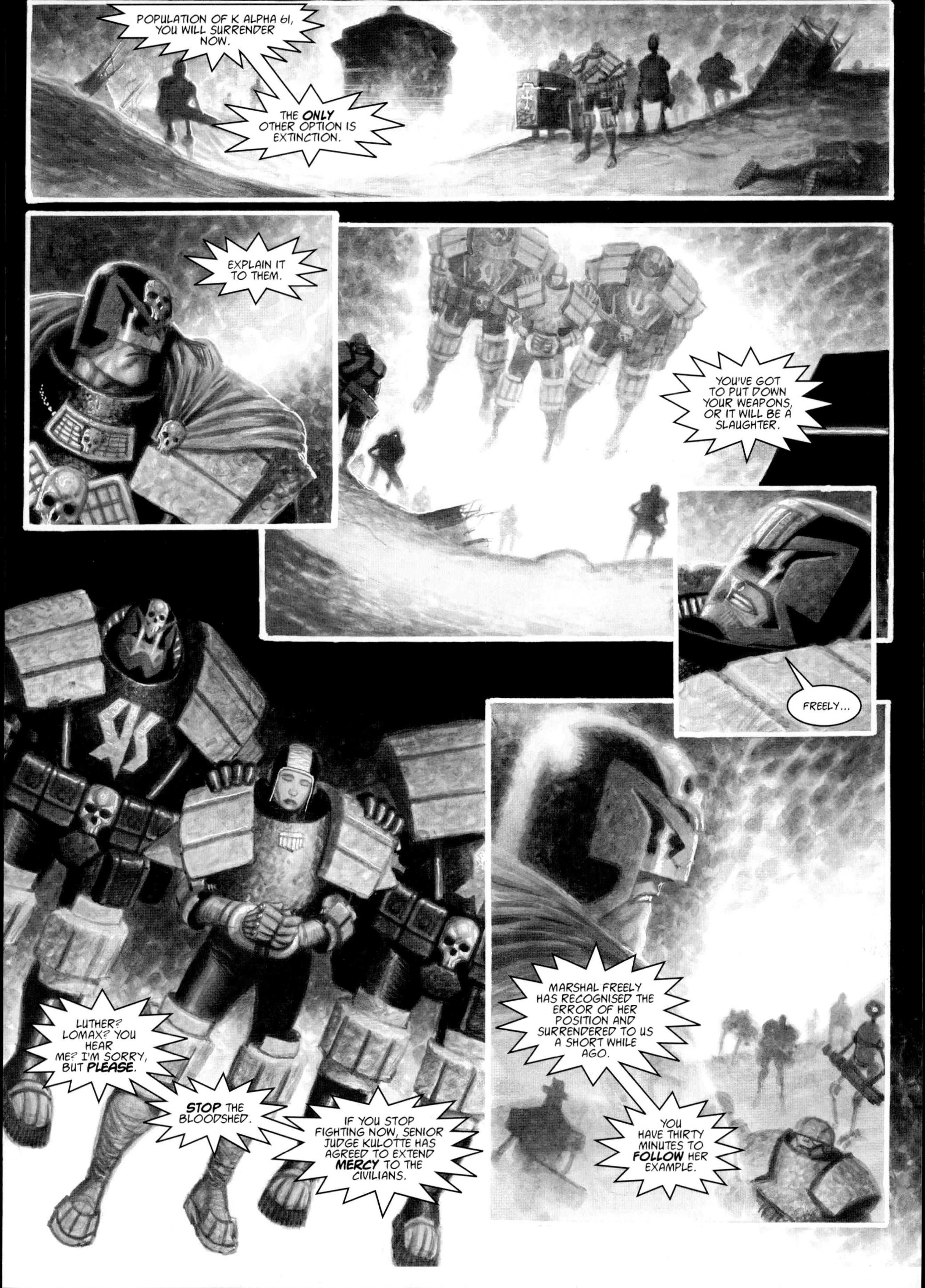
POPULATION OF K ALPHA 61, YOU WILL SURRENDER NOW.
THE ONLY OTHER OPTION IS EXTINCTION.
EXPLAIN IT TO THEM.
YOU'VE GOT TO PUT DOWN YOUR WEAPONS, OR IT WILL BE A SLAUGHTER.
FREELY...
LUTHER? LOMAX? YOU HEAR ME? I'M SORRY, BUT PLEASE.
STOP THE BLOODSHED.
IF YOU STOP FIGHTING NOW, SENIOR JUDGE KULOTTE HAS AGREED TO EXTEND MERCY TO THE CIVILIANS.
MARSHAL FREELY HAS RECOGNISED THE ERROR OF HER POSITION AND SURRENDERED TO US A SHORT WHILE AGO.
YOU HAVE THIRTY MINUTES TO FOLLOW HER EXAMPLE.

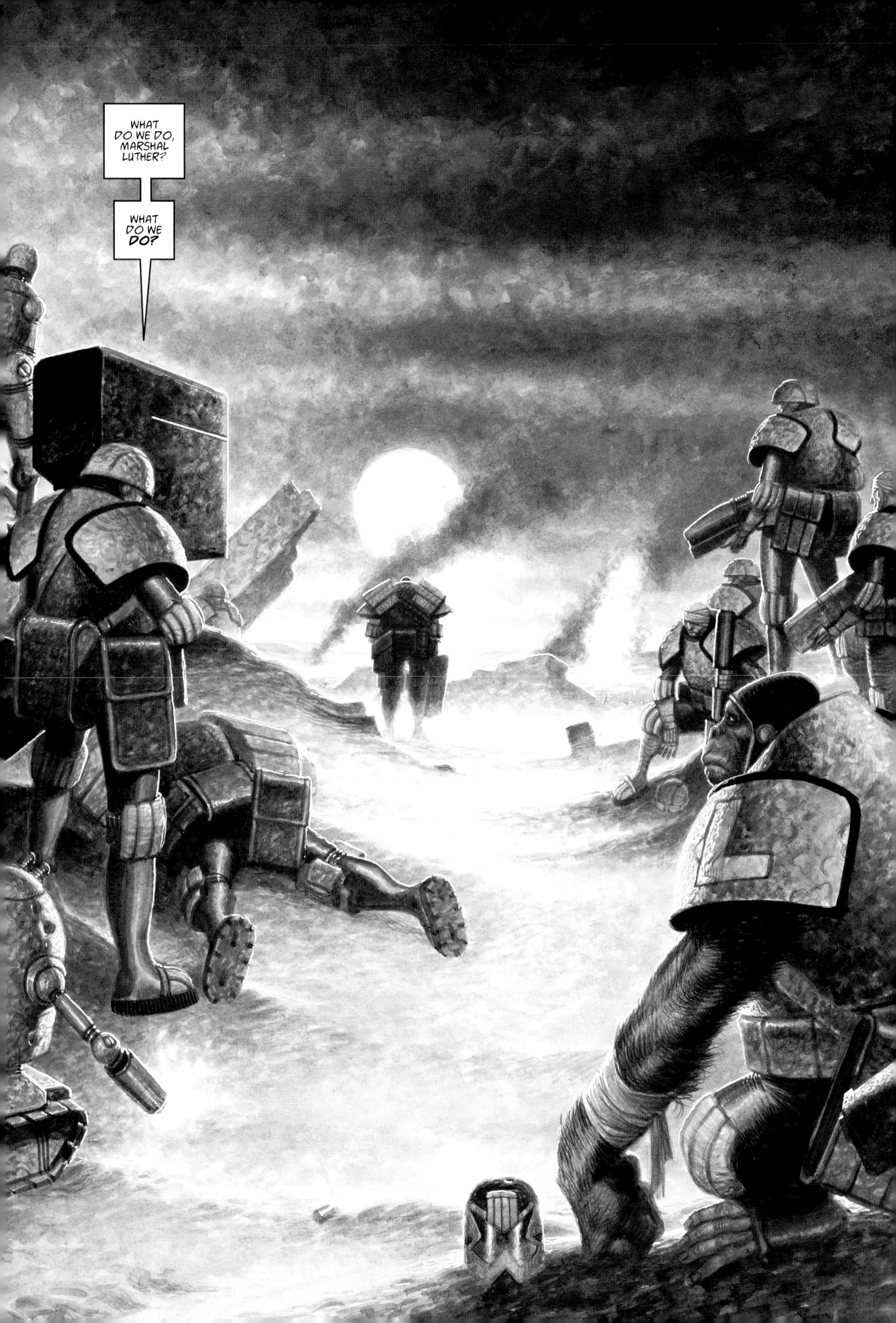
WHAT DO WE DO, MARSHAL LUTHER?
WHAT DO WE DO?

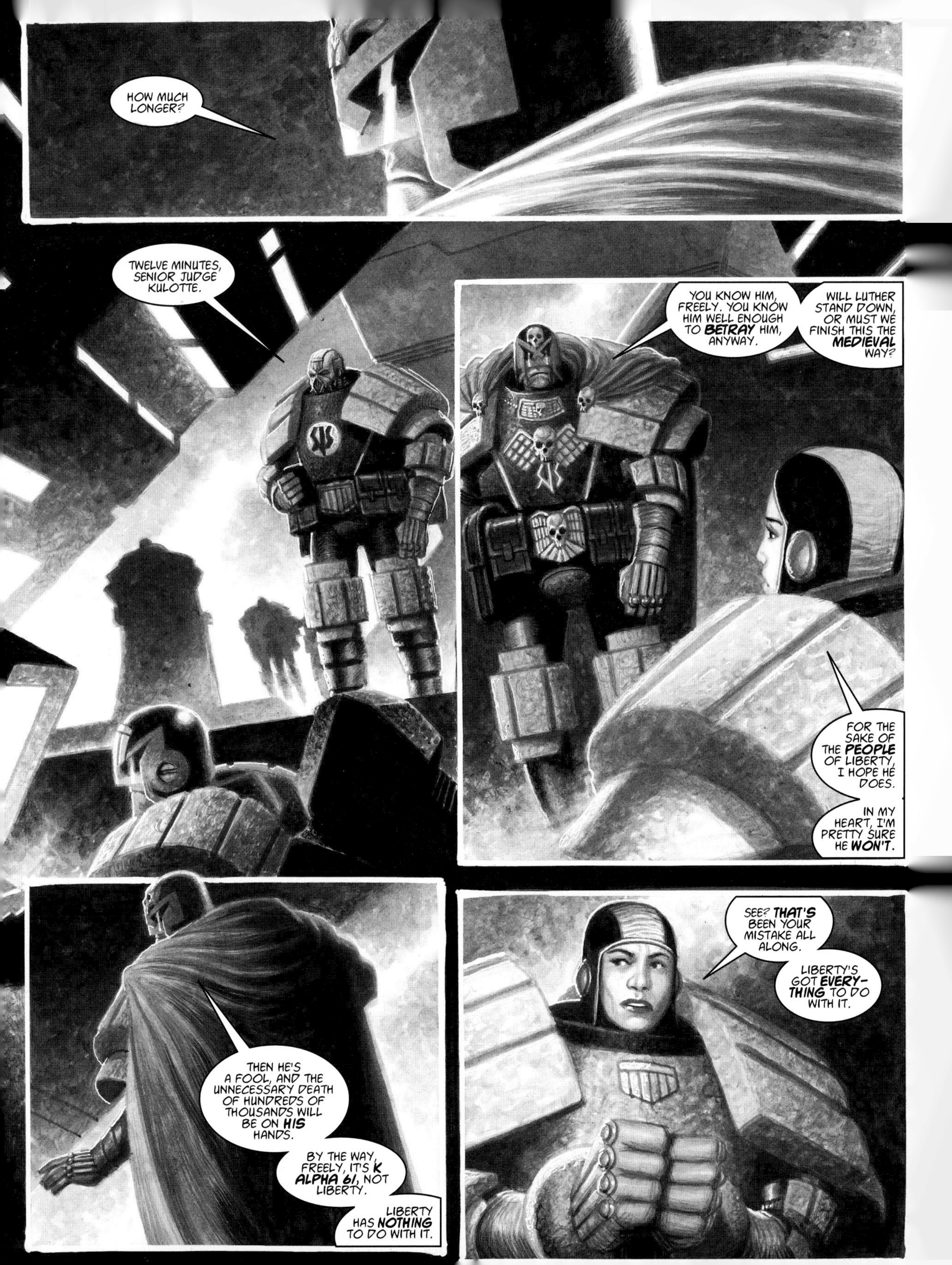
HOW MUCH LONGER?
TWELVE MINUTES, SENIOR JUDGE KULOTTE.
YOU KNOW HIM, FREELY. YOU KNOW HIM WELL ENOUGH TO **BETRAY** HIM, ANYWAY.
WILL LUTHER STAND DOWN, OR MUST WE FINISH THIS THE **MEDIEVAL** WAY?
FOR THE SAKE OF THE **PEOPLE** OF LIBERTY, I HOPE HE DOES.
IN MY HEART, I'M PRETTY SURE HE **WON'T**.
THEN HE'S A FOOL, AND THE UNNECESSARY DEATH OF HUNDREDS OF THOUSANDS WILL BE ON **HIS** HANDS.
BY THE WAY, FREELY, IT'S **K ALPHA 61**, NOT LIBERTY.
LIBERTY HAS **NOTHING** TO DO WITH IT.
SEE? **THAT'S** BEEN YOUR MISTAKE ALL ALONG.
LIBERTY'S GOT **EVERYTHING** TO DO WITH IT.

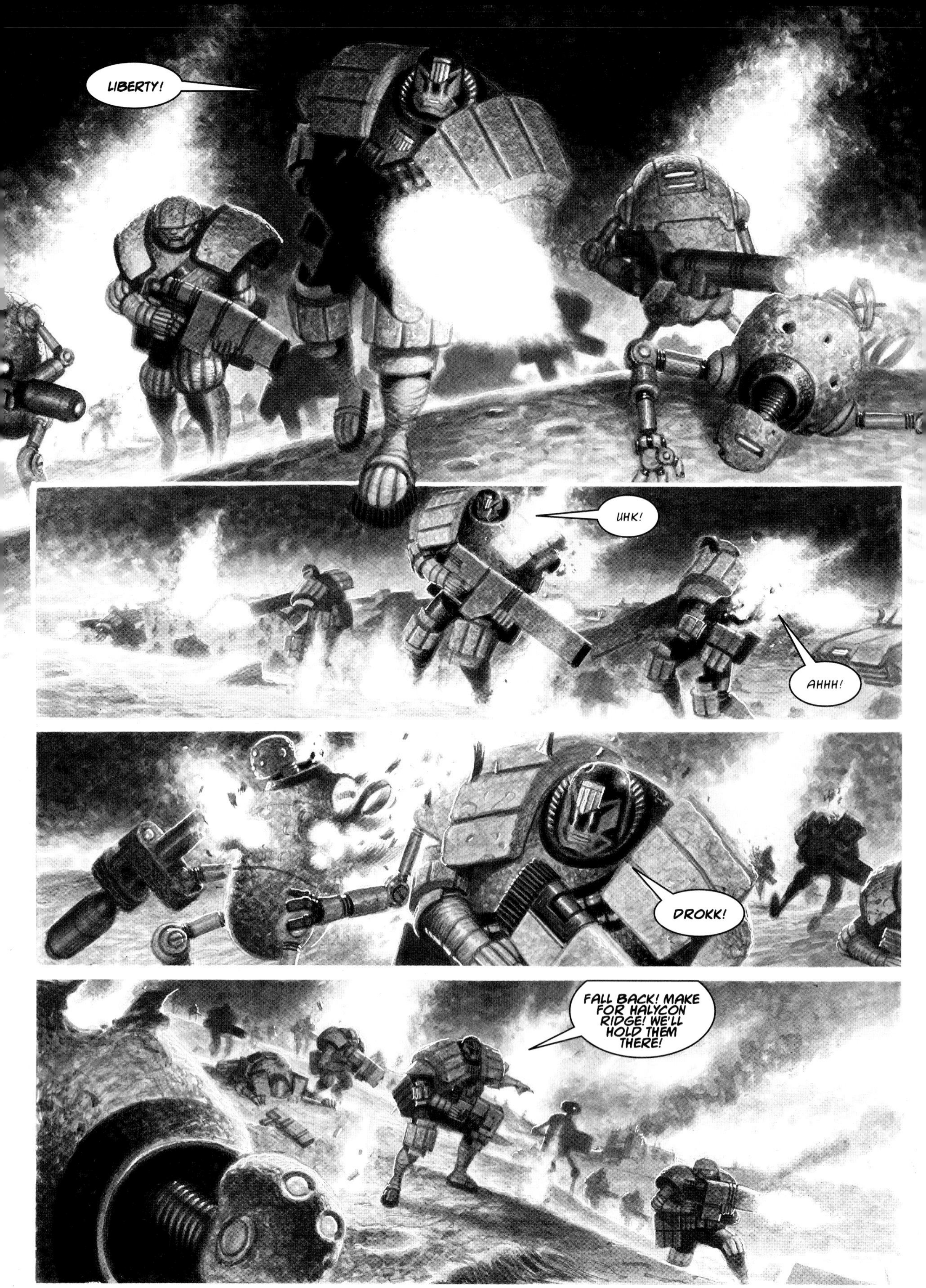

LIBERTY!
UHK!
AHHH!
DROKK!
FALL BACK! MAKE FOR HALYCON RIDGE! WE'LL HOLD THEM THERE!

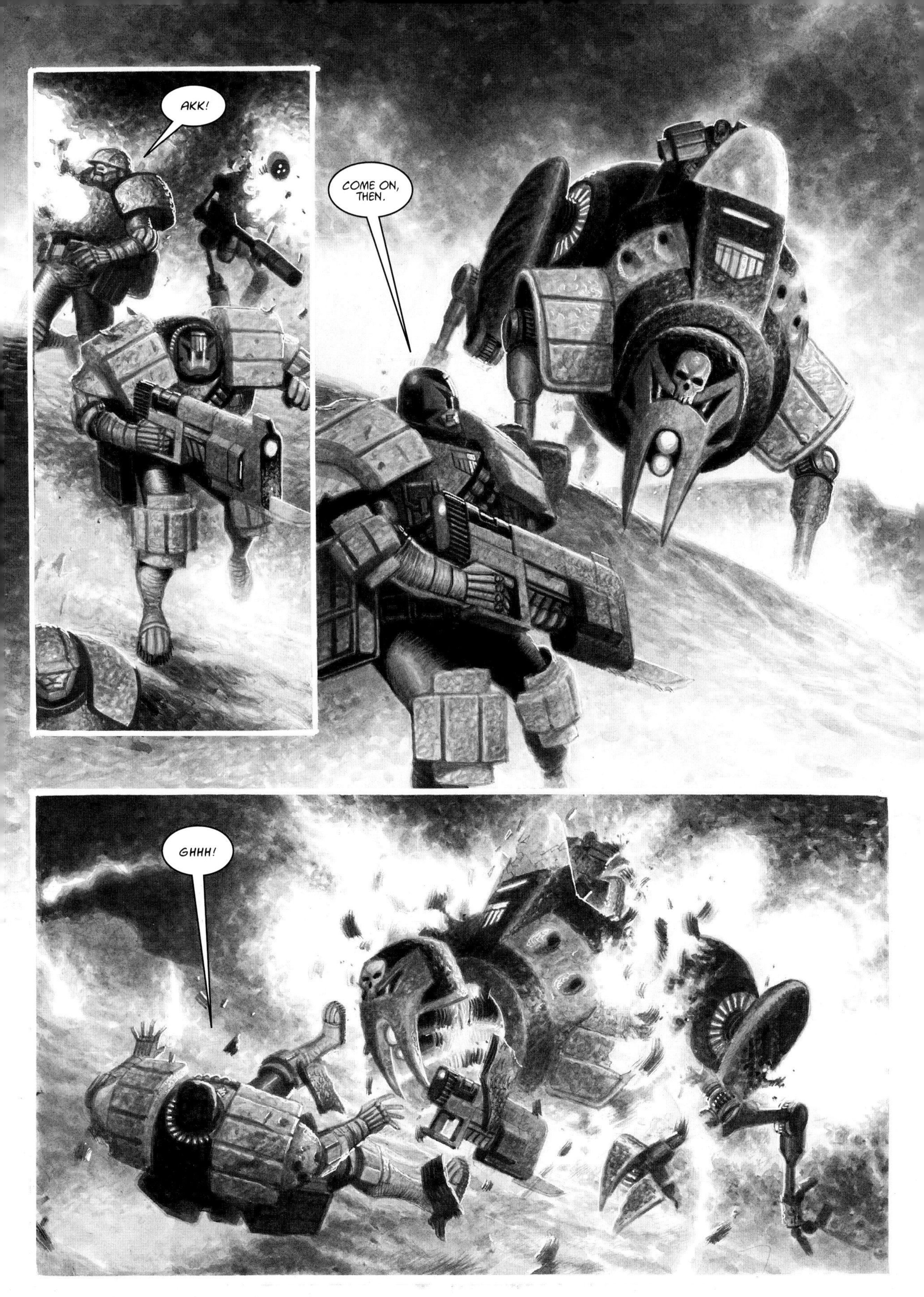
AKK!
COME ON, THEN.
GHHH!

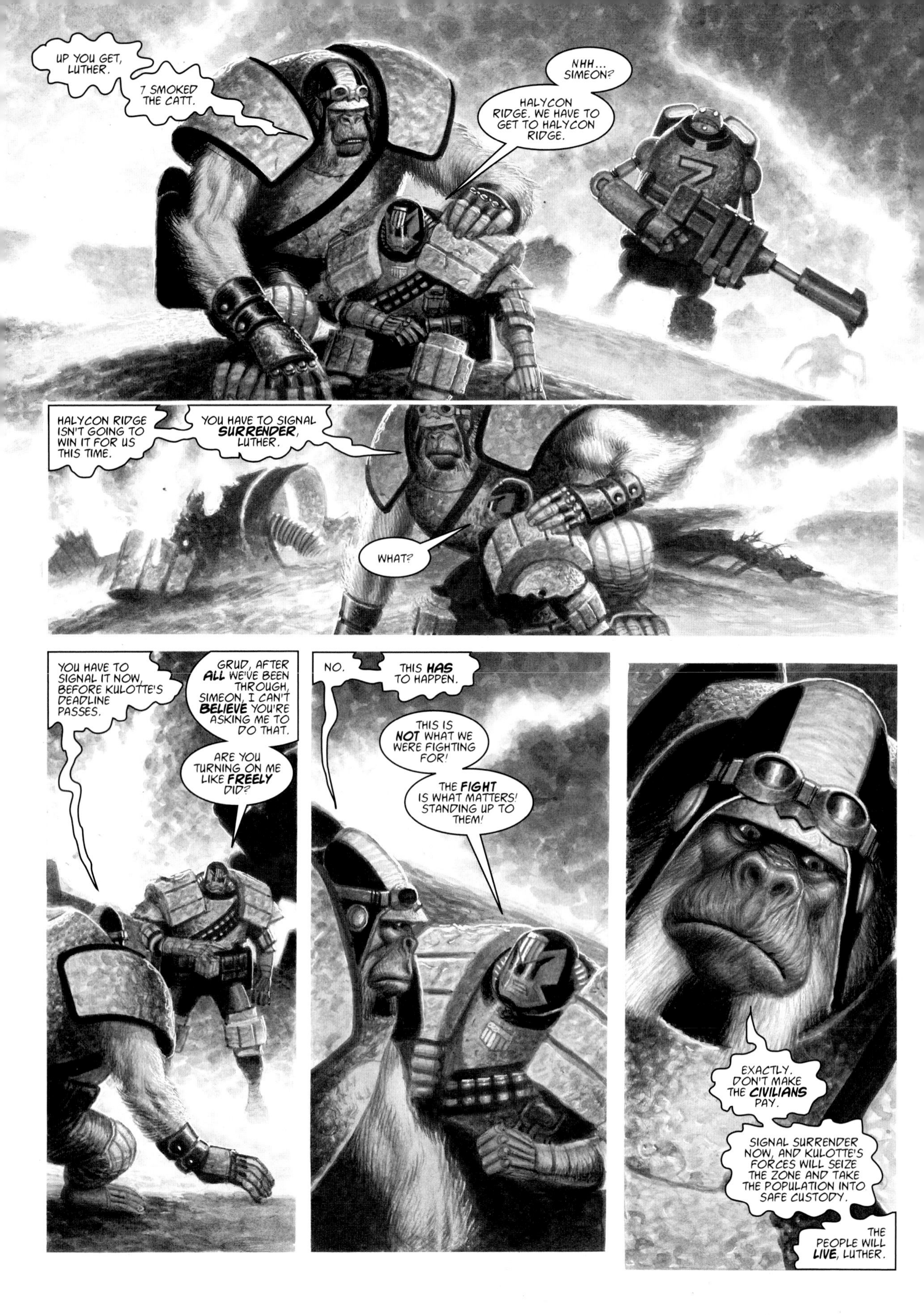
UP YOU GET, LUTHER.
7 SMOKED THE CATT.
NHH... SIMEON?
HALYCON RIDGE. WE HAVE TO GET TO HALYCON RIDGE.
HALYCON RIDGE ISN'T GOING TO WIN IT FOR US THIS TIME.
YOU HAVE TO SIGNAL **SURRENDER**, LUTHER.
WHAT?
YOU HAVE TO SIGNAL IT NOW, BEFORE KULOTTE'S DEADLINE PASSES.
GRUD, AFTER **ALL** WE'VE BEEN THROUGH, SIMEON, I CAN'T **BELIEVE** YOU'RE ASKING ME TO DO THAT.
ARE YOU TURNING ON ME LIKE **FREELY** DID?
NO.
THIS **HAS** TO HAPPEN.
THIS IS **NOT** WHAT WE WERE FIGHTING FOR!
THE **FIGHT** IS WHAT MATTERS! STANDING UP TO THEM!
EXACTLY. DON'T MAKE THE **CIVILIANS** PAY.
SIGNAL SURRENDER NOW, AND KULOTTE'S FORCES WILL SEIZE THE ZONE AND TAKE THE POPULATION INTO SAFE CUSTODY.
THE PEOPLE WILL **LIVE**, LUTHER.

NO! WE —

WE WERE **NEVER** GOING TO WIN THIS, LUTHER. NOT AGAINST THE SJS.

BUT WE'VE **HURT** THEM. WE'VE GIVEN THEM THE **BLOODIEST** NOSE THEY'VE **EVER** HAD.

AND NOW WE CAN **TWIST** THE KNIFE.

WHAT ARE YOU **TALKING** ABOUT?

WE'VE BURNED THEM HERE, BUT THE PEOPLE OF LIBERTY HAVE SUFFERED ENOUGH.

LET'S FIND **NEW** LIBERTIES AND BURN THEM **AGAIN**, AND **AGAIN**.

THERE ARE **EIGHTEEN** COLONIAL HOLDINGS JUST LIKE K ALPHA 61 IN THIS SECTOR ALONE.

THERE'S A SHIP WAITING IN THE DEEP CRADLES, ROOM FOR ABOUT TWO HUNDRED UNIT MEMBERS.

WE'D NEVER GET OFF THE PLANET. THE FLEET —

HAS BEEN **COMPROMISED**. THE **FLAGSHIP**, ACTUALLY. ONE WORD FROM YOU, AND AN **ELECTRONIC COUNTERMEASURES DISRUPTION PATTERN** TAKES OUT THEIR SENSOR NET.

AT **LEAST** FOR LONG ENOUGH TO GET A SHIP AWAY.

THE SIGNAL IS OUR **SURRENDER**.

**YOU** ARRANGED ALL THIS?

NOT **ME**, OLD FRIEND.

YOU NEED TO SEE **THIS**. SHE LEFT IT FOR YOU.

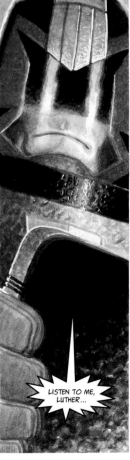

LISTEN TO ME, LUTHER...

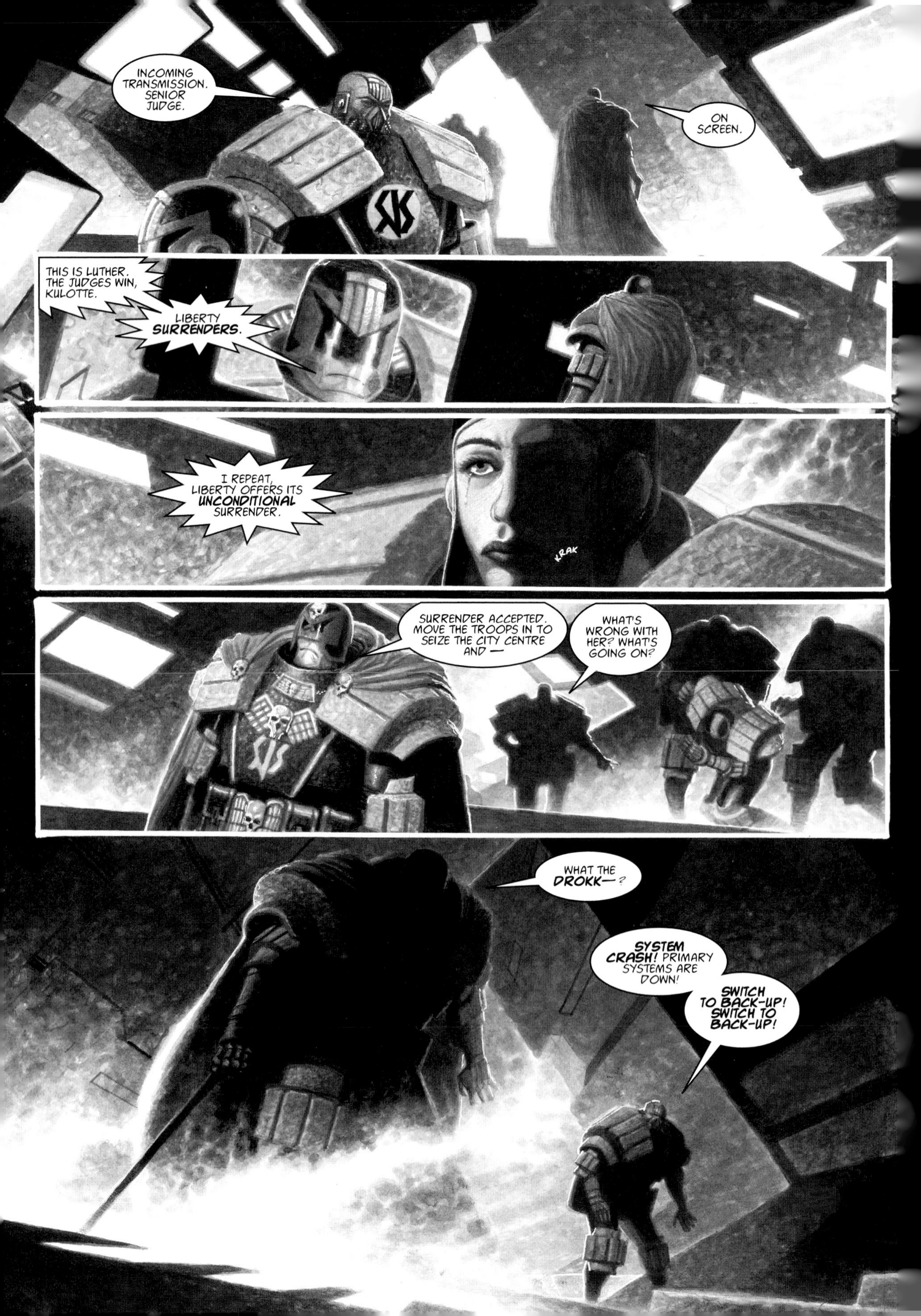
INCOMING TRANSMISSION. SENIOR JUDGE.
ON SCREEN.
THIS IS LUTHER. THE JUDGES WIN, KULOTTE.
LIBERTY **SURRENDERS**.
I REPEAT, LIBERTY OFFERS ITS **UNCONDITIONAL** SURRENDER.
KRAK
SURRENDER ACCEPTED. MOVE THE TROOPS IN TO SEIZE THE CITY CENTRE AND —
WHAT'S WRONG WITH HER? WHAT'S GOING ON?
WHAT THE **DROKK**—?
**SYSTEM CRASH!** PRIMARY SYSTEMS ARE DOWN!
**SWITCH TO BACK-UP! SWITCH TO BACK-UP!**

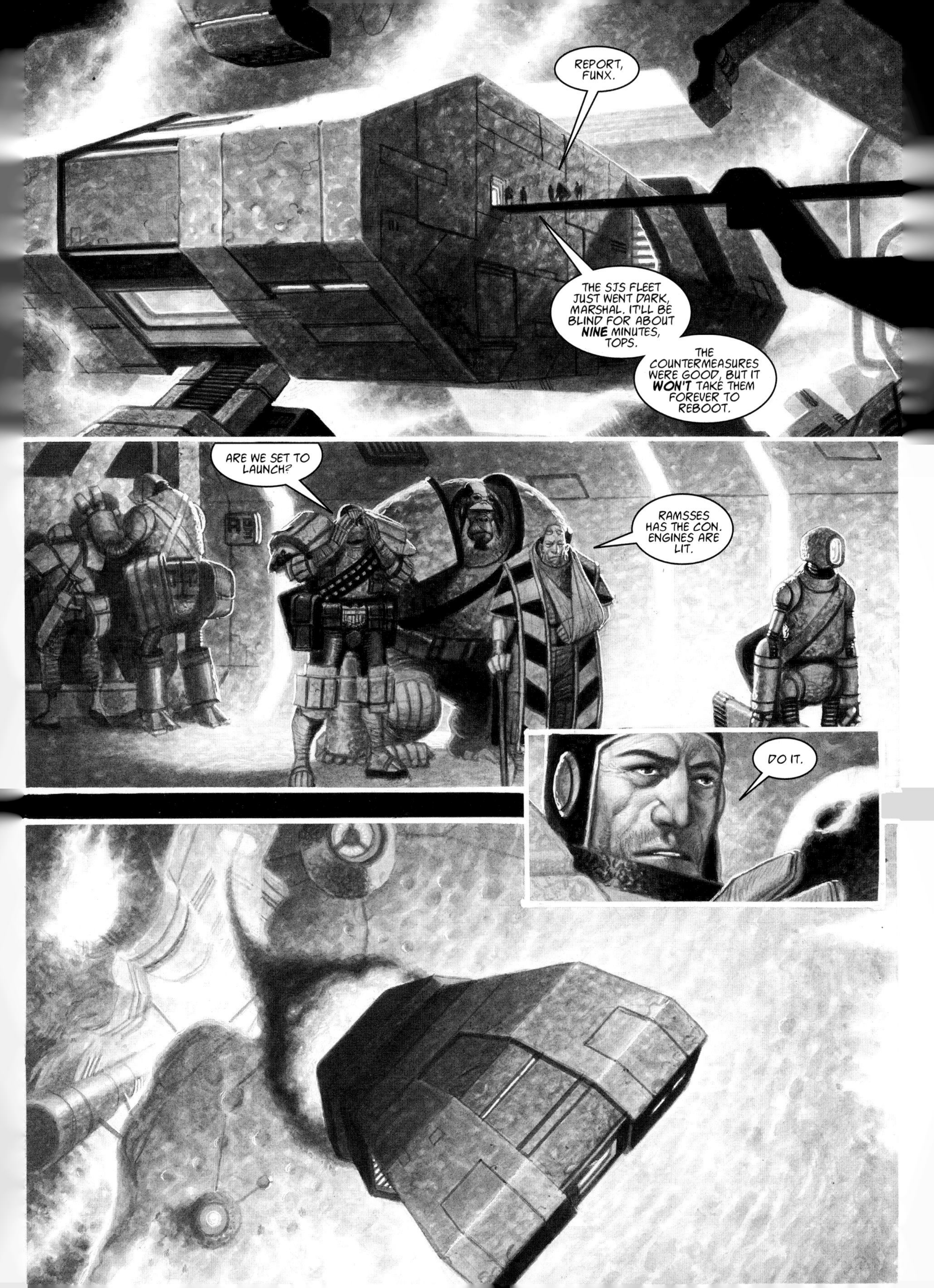
REPORT, FUNX.
THE SJS FLEET JUST WENT DARK, MARSHAL. IT'LL BE BLIND FOR ABOUT NINE MINUTES, TOPS.
THE COUNTERMEASURES WERE GOOD, BUT IT WON'T TAKE THEM FOREVER TO REBOOT.
ARE WE SET TO LAUNCH?
RAMSSES HAS THE CON. ENGINES ARE LIT.
DO IT.

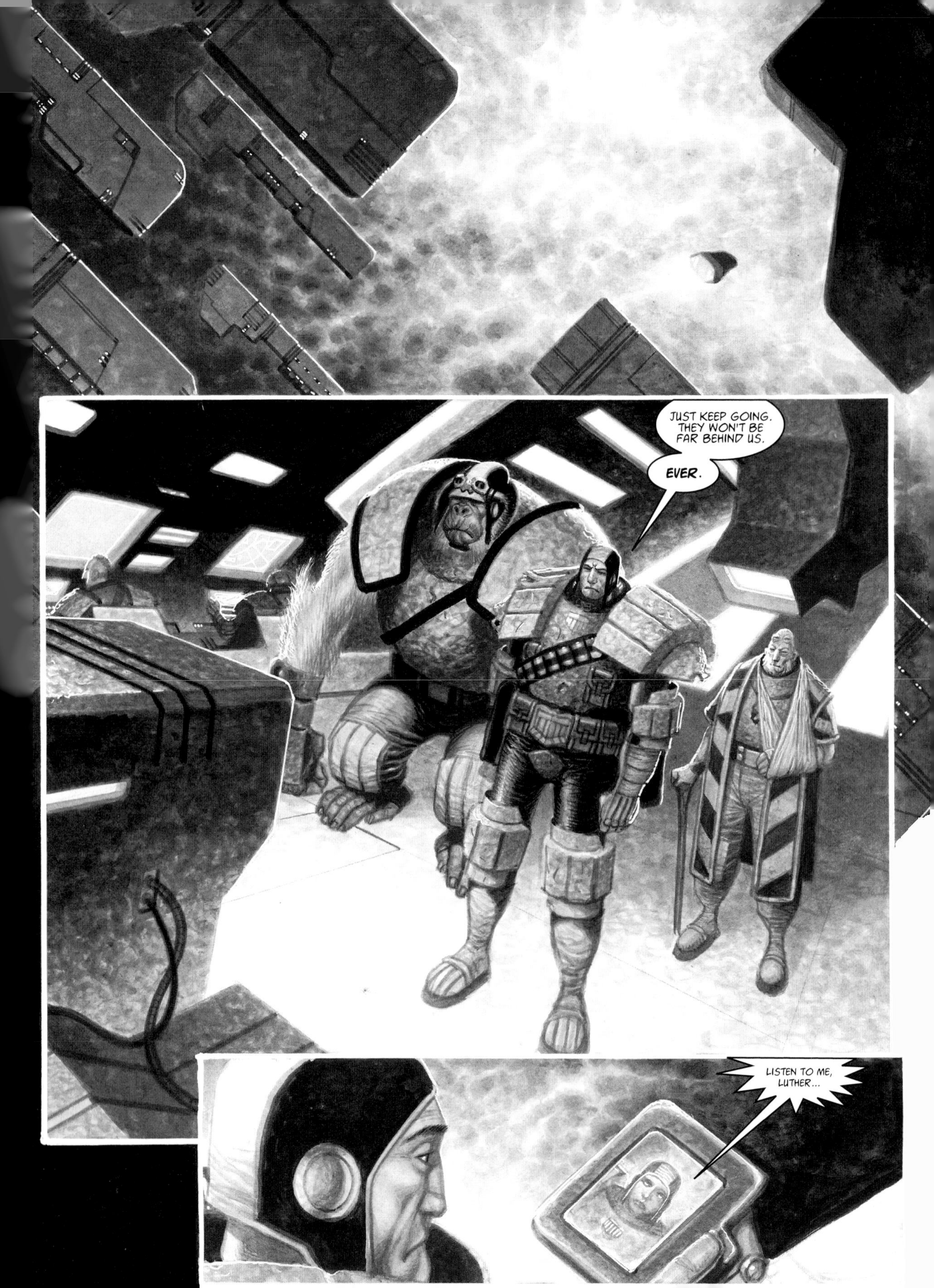
JUST KEEP GOING. THEY WON'T BE FAR BEHIND US.
EVER.
LISTEN TO ME, LUTHER...

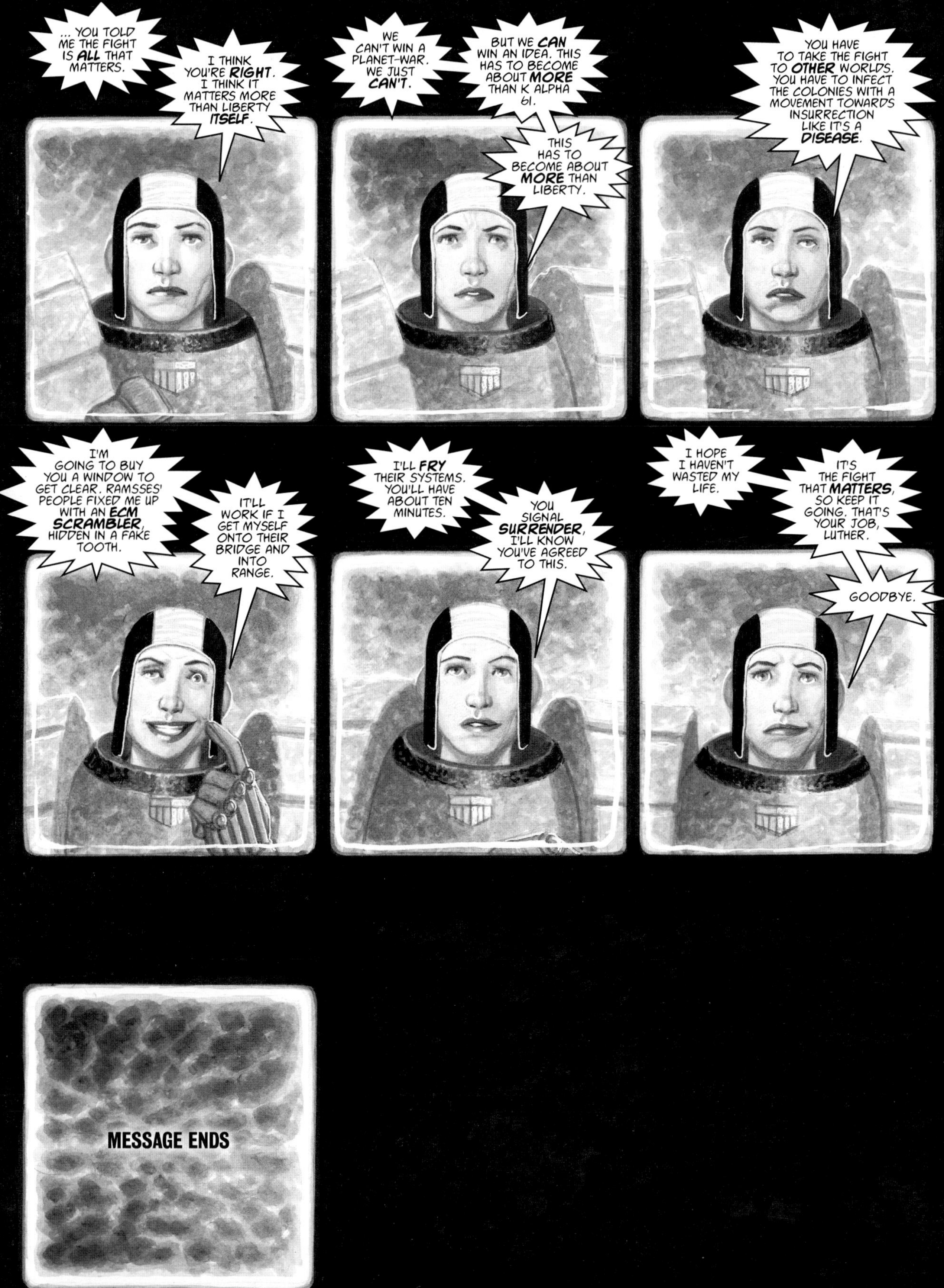
... YOU TOLD ME THE FIGHT IS ALL THAT MATTERS.
I THINK YOU'RE RIGHT. I THINK IT MATTERS MORE THAN LIBERTY ITSELF.
WE CAN'T WIN A PLANET-WAR. WE JUST CAN'T.
BUT WE CAN WIN AN IDEA. THIS HAS TO BECOME ABOUT MORE THAN K ALPHA 61.
THIS HAS TO BECOME ABOUT MORE THAN LIBERTY.
YOU HAVE TO TAKE THE FIGHT TO OTHER WORLDS. YOU HAVE TO INFECT THE COLONIES WITH A MOVEMENT TOWARDS INSURRECTION LIKE IT'S A DISEASE.
I'M GOING TO BUY YOU A WINDOW TO GET CLEAR. RAMSSES' PEOPLE FIXED ME UP WITH AN ECM SCRAMBLER, HIDDEN IN A FAKE TOOTH.
IT'LL WORK IF I GET MYSELF ONTO THEIR BRIDGE AND INTO RANGE.
I'LL FRY THEIR SYSTEMS. YOU'LL HAVE ABOUT TEN MINUTES.
YOU SIGNAL SURRENDER, I'LL KNOW YOU'VE AGREED TO THIS.
I HOPE I HAVEN'T WASTED MY LIFE.
IT'S THE FIGHT THAT MATTERS, SO KEEP IT GOING. THAT'S YOUR JOB, LUTHER.
GOODBYE.
MESSAGE ENDS

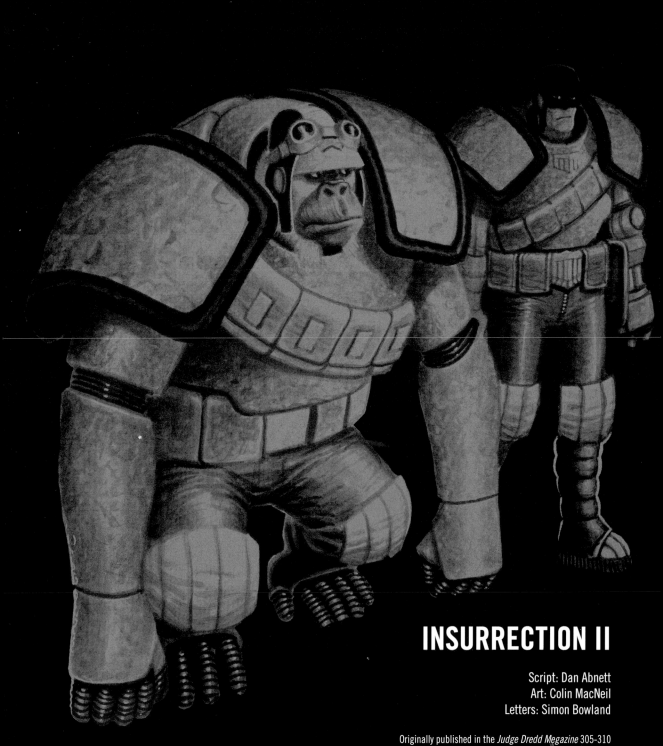

# INSURRECTION II

Script: Dan Abnett
Art: Colin MacNeil
Letters: Simon Bowland

Originally published in the *Judge Dredd Megazine* 305-310

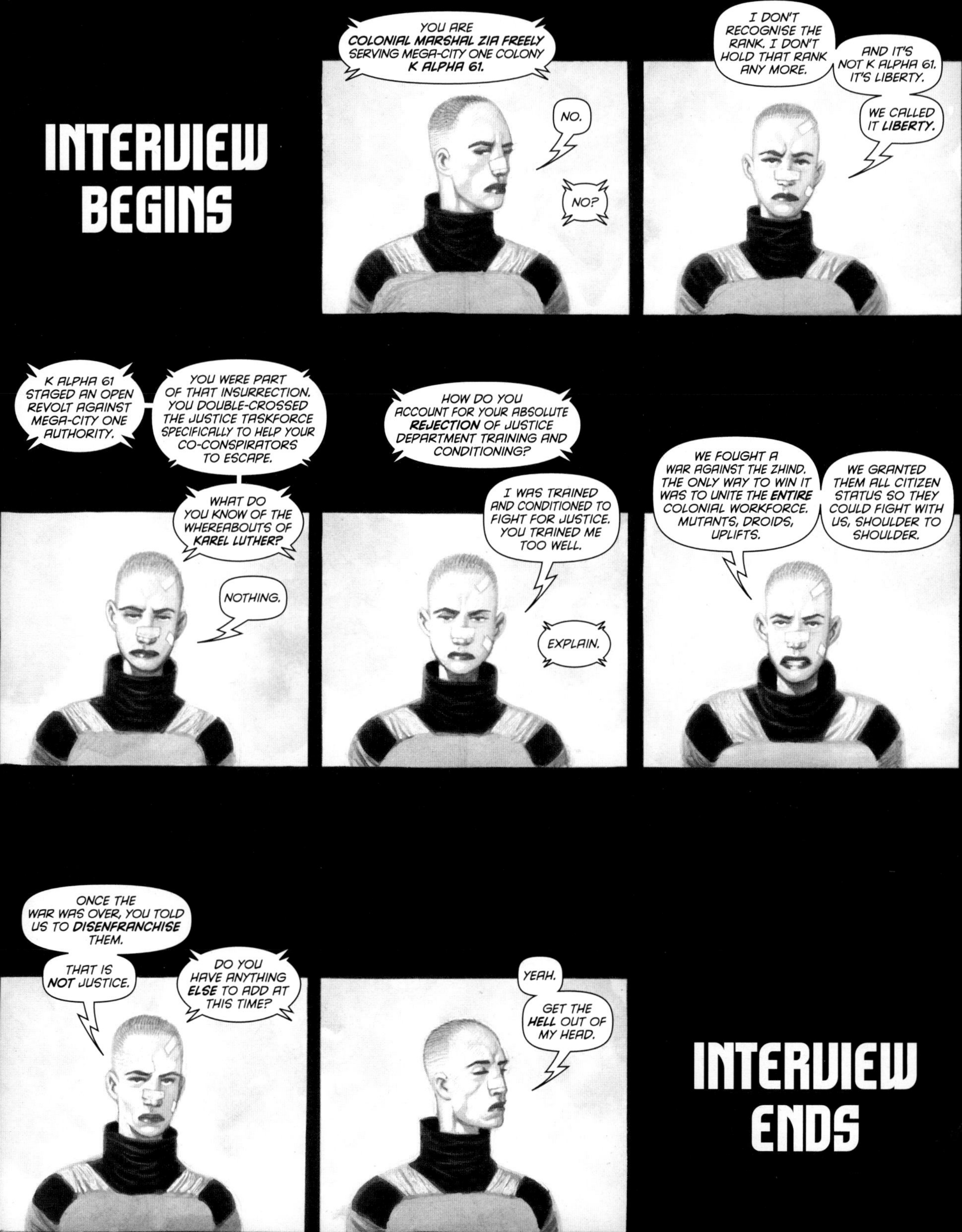
INTERVIEW BEGINS
YOU ARE COLONIAL MARSHAL ZIA FREELY SERVING MEGA-CITY ONE COLONY K ALPHA 61.
NO.
NO?
I DON'T RECOGNISE THE RANK. I DON'T HOLD THAT RANK ANY MORE.
AND IT'S NOT K ALPHA 61. IT'S LIBERTY.
WE CALLED IT LIBERTY.
K ALPHA 61 STAGED AN OPEN REVOLT AGAINST MEGA-CITY ONE AUTHORITY.
YOU WERE PART OF THAT INSURRECTION. YOU DOUBLE-CROSSED THE JUSTICE TASKFORCE SPECIFICALLY TO HELP YOUR CO-CONSPIRATORS TO ESCAPE.
WHAT DO YOU KNOW OF THE WHEREABOUTS OF KAREL LUTHER?
NOTHING.
HOW DO YOU ACCOUNT FOR YOUR ABSOLUTE REJECTION OF JUSTICE DEPARTMENT TRAINING AND CONDITIONING?
I WAS TRAINED AND CONDITIONED TO FIGHT FOR JUSTICE. YOU TRAINED ME TOO WELL.
EXPLAIN.
WE FOUGHT A WAR AGAINST THE ZHIND. THE ONLY WAY TO WIN IT WAS TO UNITE THE ENTIRE COLONIAL WORKFORCE. MUTANTS, DROIDS, UPLIFTS.
WE GRANTED THEM ALL CITIZEN STATUS SO THEY COULD FIGHT WITH US, SHOULDER TO SHOULDER.
ONCE THE WAR WAS OVER, YOU TOLD US TO DISENFRANCHISE THEM.
THAT IS NOT JUSTICE.
DO YOU HAVE ANYTHING ELSE TO ADD AT THIS TIME?
YEAH.
GET THE HELL OUT OF MY HEAD.
INTERVIEW ENDS

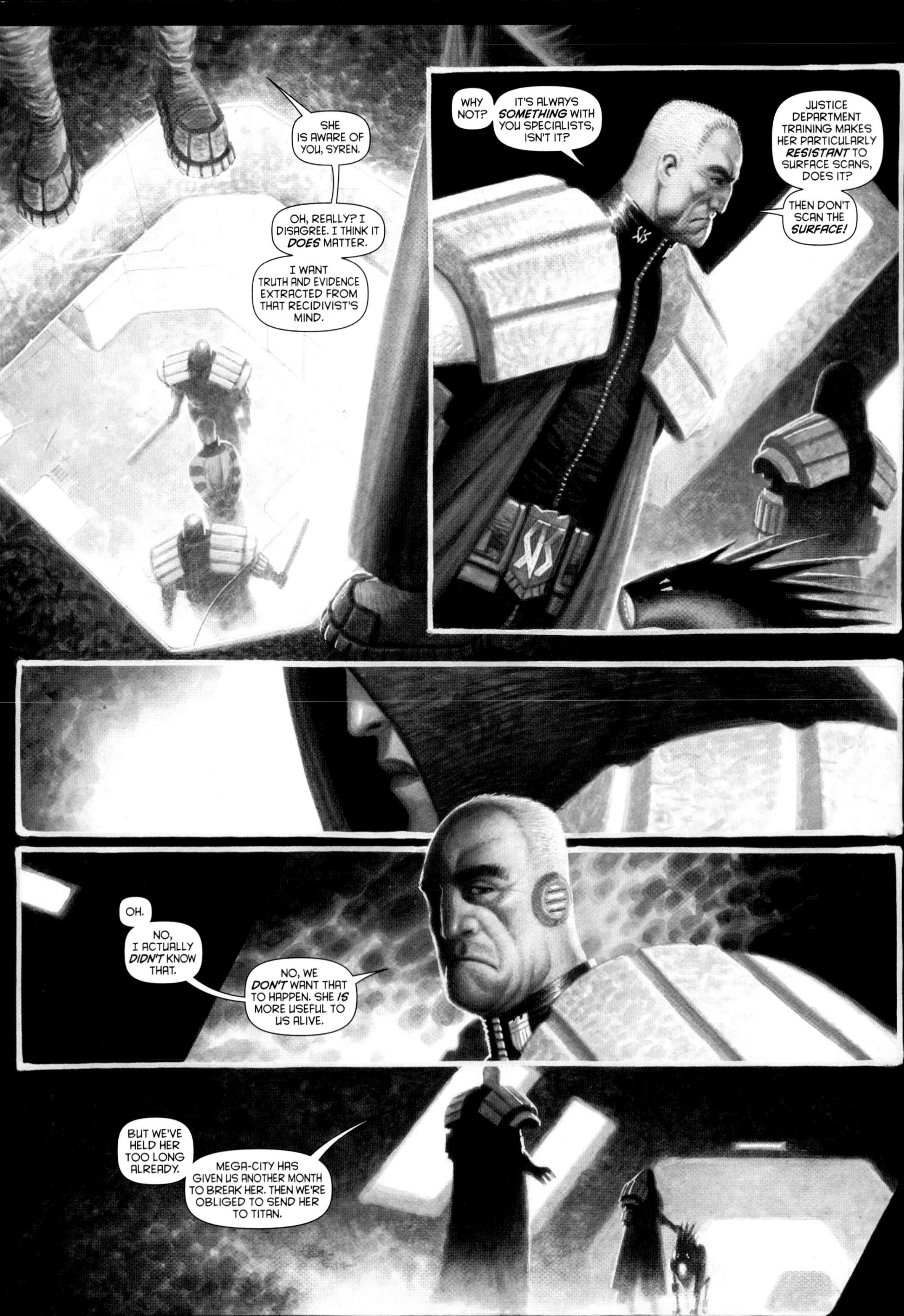
SHE IS AWARE OF YOU, SYREN.
OH, REALLY? I DISAGREE. I THINK IT DOES MATTER.
I WANT TRUTH AND EVIDENCE EXTRACTED FROM THAT RECIDIVIST'S MIND.
WHY NOT?
IT'S ALWAYS SOMETHING WITH YOU SPECIALISTS, ISN'T IT?
JUSTICE DEPARTMENT TRAINING MAKES HER PARTICULARLY RESISTANT TO SURFACE SCANS, DOES IT?
THEN DON'T SCAN THE SURFACE!
OH.
NO, I ACTUALLY DIDN'T KNOW THAT.
NO, WE DON'T WANT THAT TO HAPPEN. SHE IS MORE USEFUL TO US ALIVE.
BUT WE'VE HELD HER TOO LONG ALREADY.
MEGA-CITY HAS GIVEN US ANOTHER MONTH TO BREAK HER. THEN WE'RE OBLIGED TO SEND HER TO TITAN.

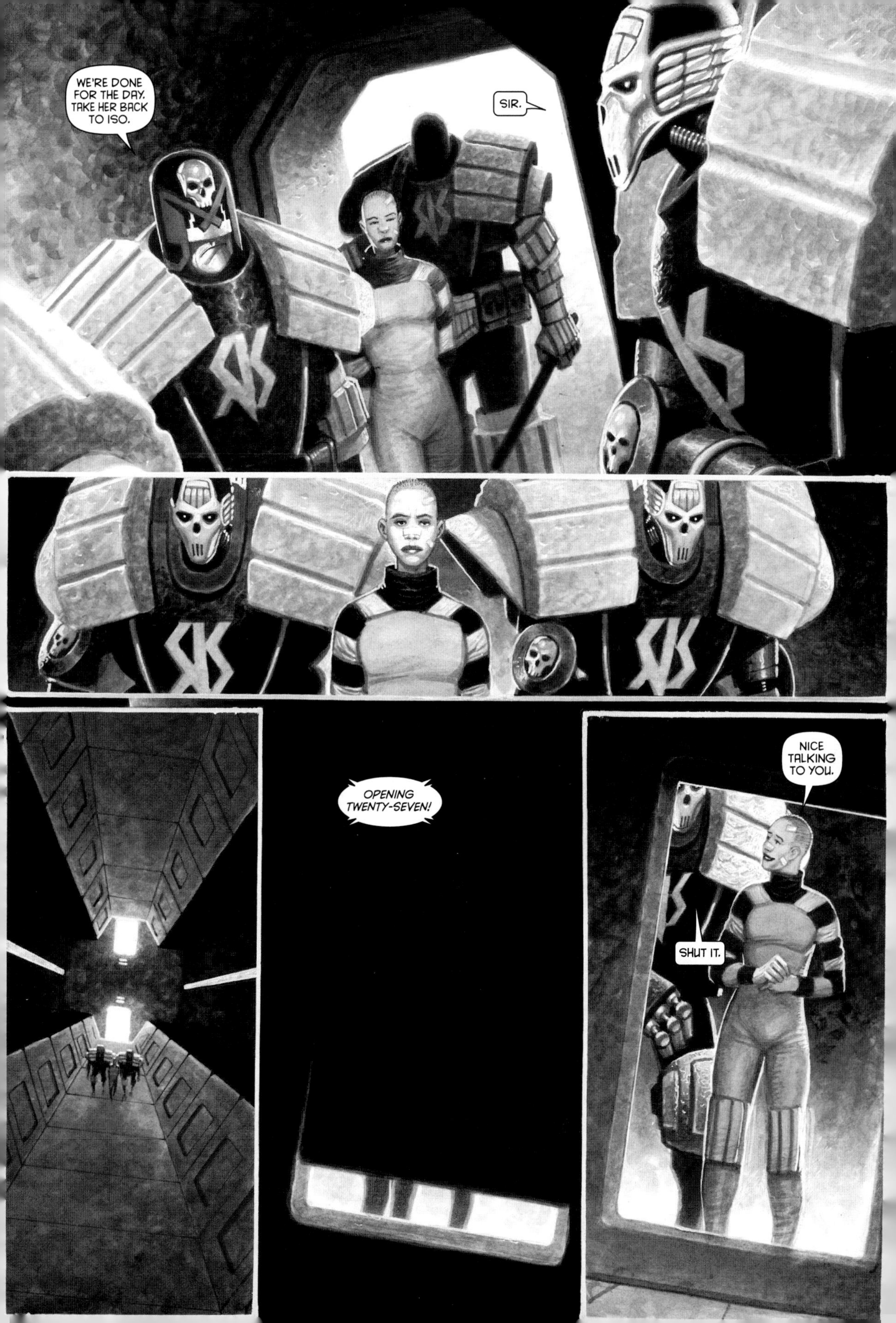
WE'RE DONE FOR THE DAY. TAKE HER BACK TO ISO.
SIR.
OPENING TWENTY-SEVEN!
NICE TALKING TO YOU.
SHUT IT.

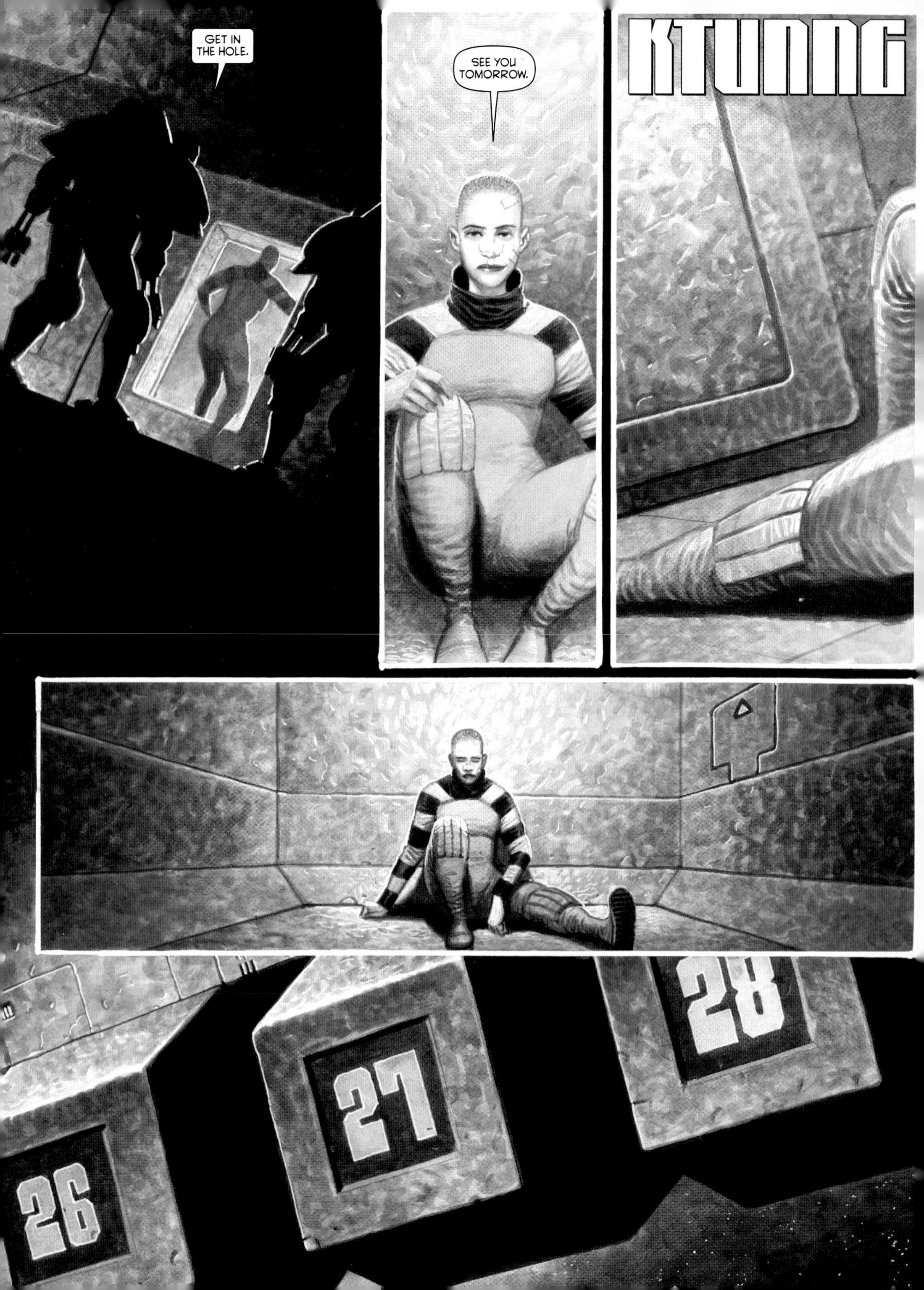
GET IN THE HOLE.
SEE YOU TOMORROW.
KTUNNG
27
28
26

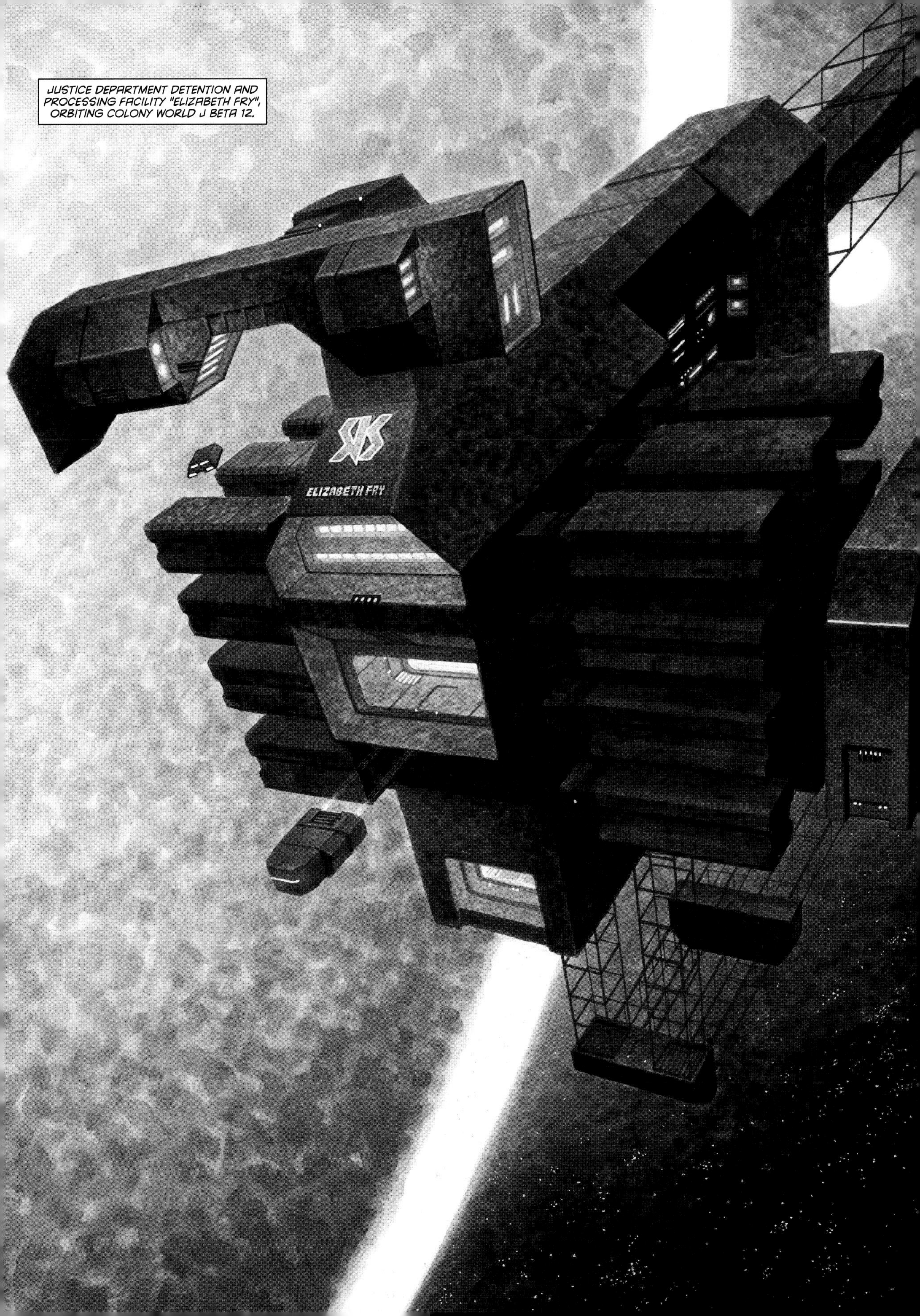
JUSTICE DEPARTMENT DETENTION AND PROCESSING FACILITY "ELIZABETH FRY", ORBITING COLONY WORLD J BETA 12.
ELIZABETH FRY

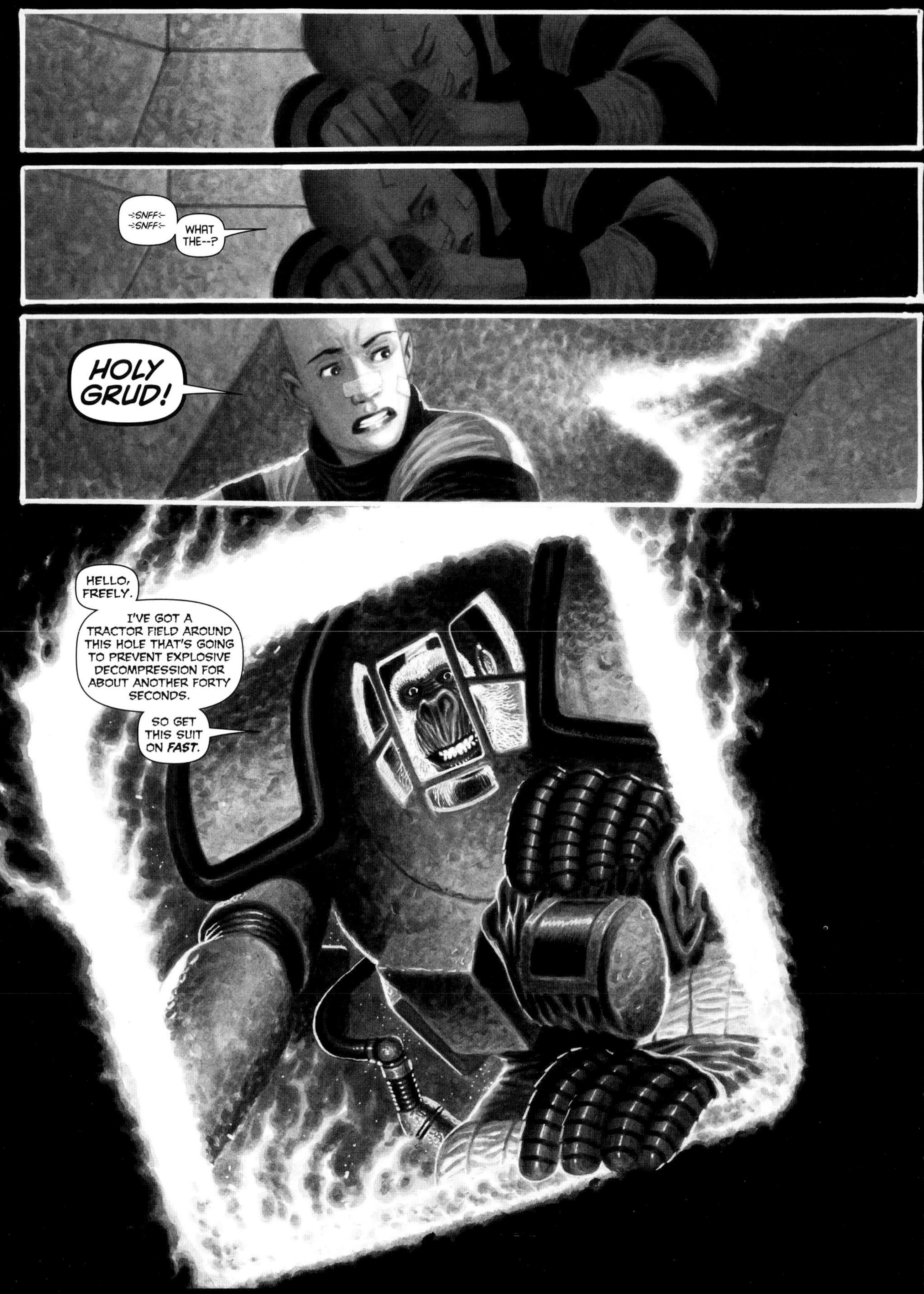

-SNFF-
-SNFF-
WHAT THE--?
HOLY GRUD!
HELLO, FREELY.
I'VE GOT A TRACTOR FIELD AROUND THIS HOLE THAT'S GOING TO PREVENT EXPLOSIVE DECOMPRESSION FOR ABOUT ANOTHER FORTY SECONDS.
SO GET THIS SUIT ON FAST.

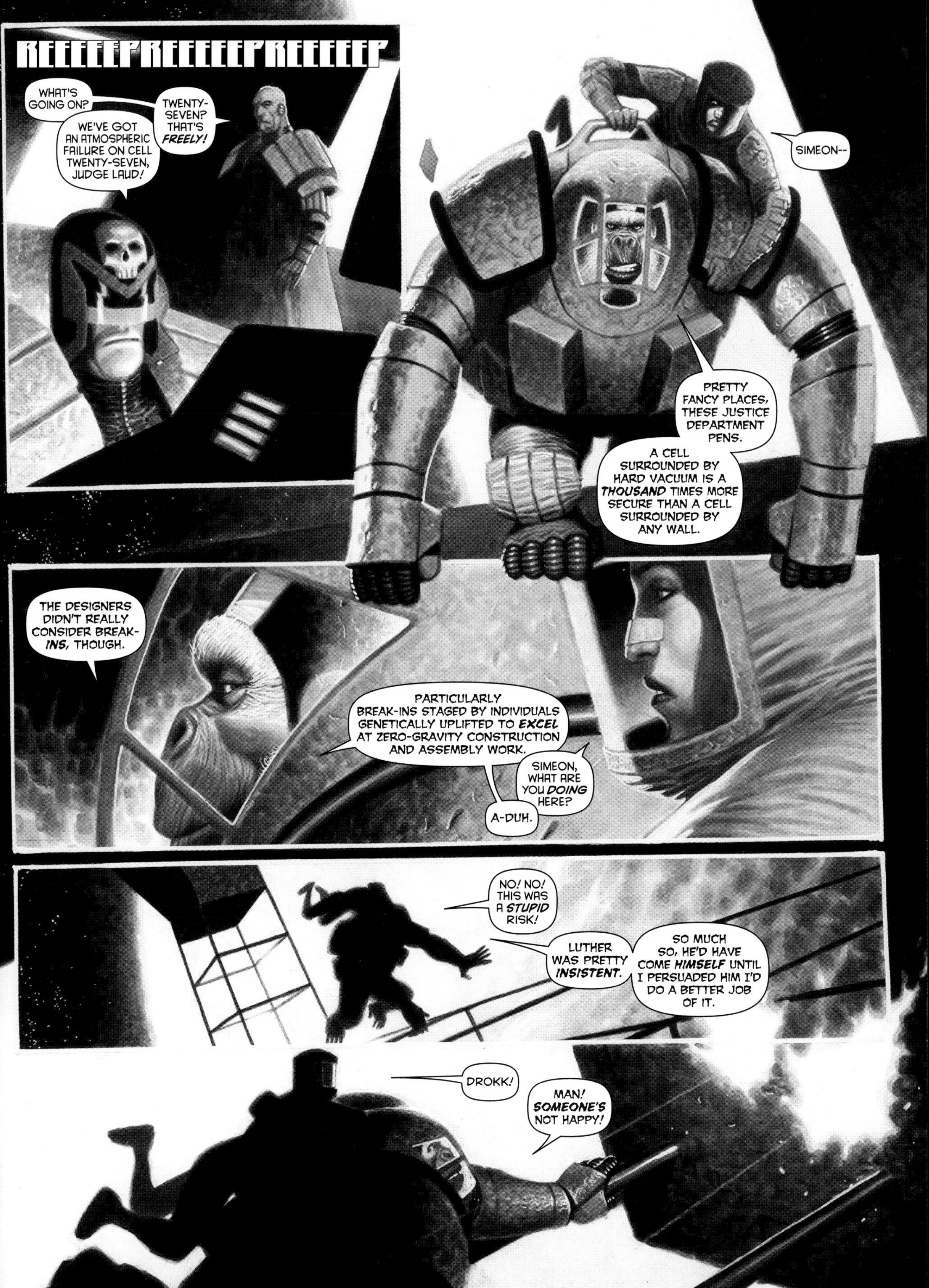
REEEEEEPREEEEEEPREEEEEEP
WHAT'S GOING ON?
WE'VE GOT AN ATMOSPHERIC FAILURE ON CELL TWENTY-SEVEN, JUDGE LAUD!
TWENTY-SEVEN? THAT'S FREELY!
SIMEON--
PRETTY FANCY PLACES, THESE JUSTICE DEPARTMENT PENS.
A CELL SURROUNDED BY HARD VACUUM IS A THOUSAND TIMES MORE SECURE THAN A CELL SURROUNDED BY ANY WALL.
THE DESIGNERS DIDN'T REALLY CONSIDER BREAK-INS, THOUGH.
PARTICULARLY BREAK-INS STAGED BY INDIVIDUALS GENETICALLY UPLIFTED TO EXCEL AT ZERO-GRAVITY CONSTRUCTION AND ASSEMBLY WORK.
SIMEON, WHAT ARE YOU DOING HERE?
A-DUH.
NO! NO! THIS WAS A STUPID RISK!
LUTHER WAS PRETTY INSISTENT.
SO MUCH SO, HE'D HAVE COME HIMSELF UNTIL I PERSUADED HIM I'D DO A BETTER JOB OF IT.
DROKK!
MAN! SOMEONE'S NOT HAPPY!

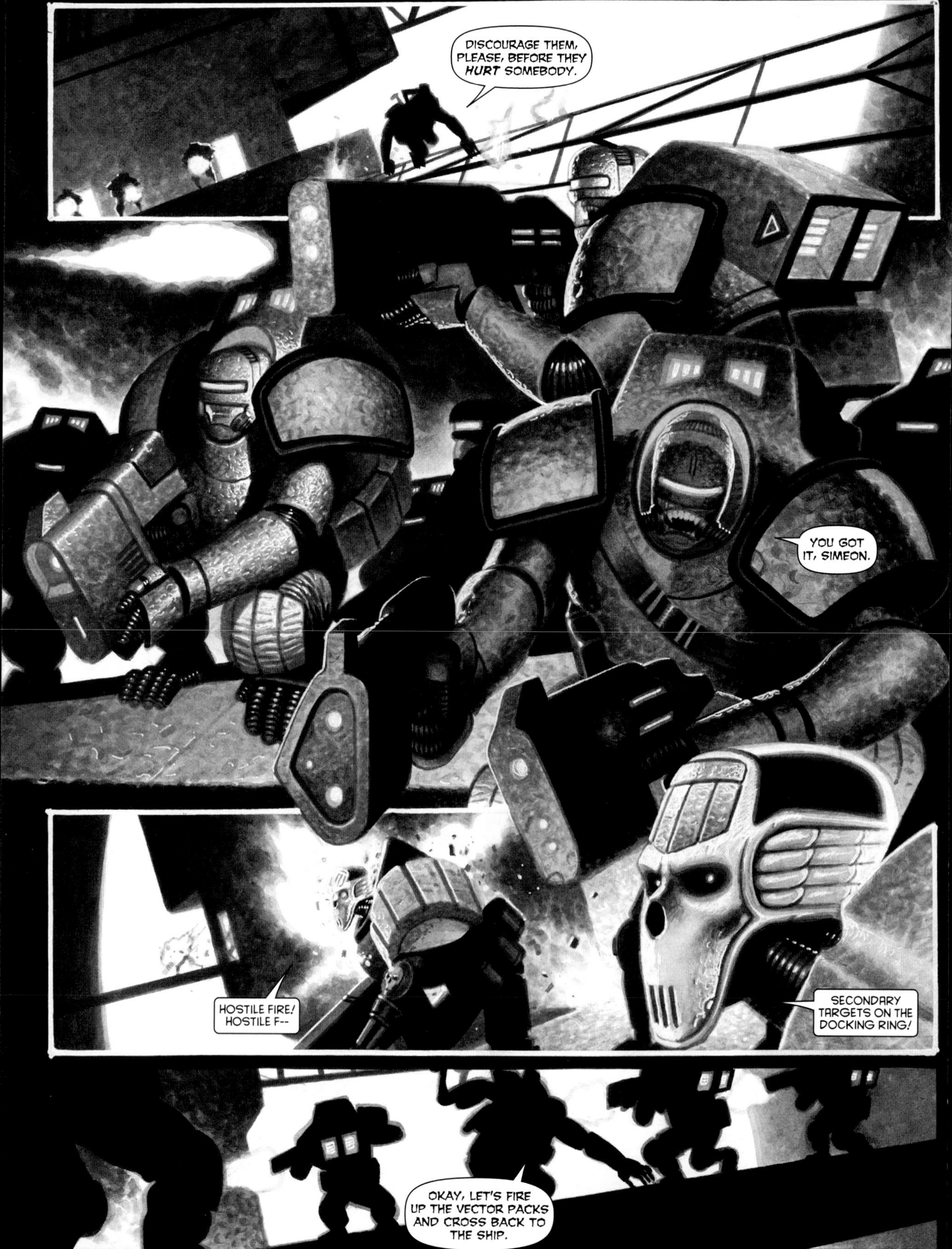
DISCOURAGE THEM, PLEASE, BEFORE THEY HURT SOMEBODY.
YOU GOT IT, SIMEON.
HOSTILE FIRE! HOSTILE F--
SECONDARY TARGETS ON THE DOCKING RING!
OKAY, LET'S FIRE UP THE VECTOR PACKS AND CROSS BACK TO THE SHIP.

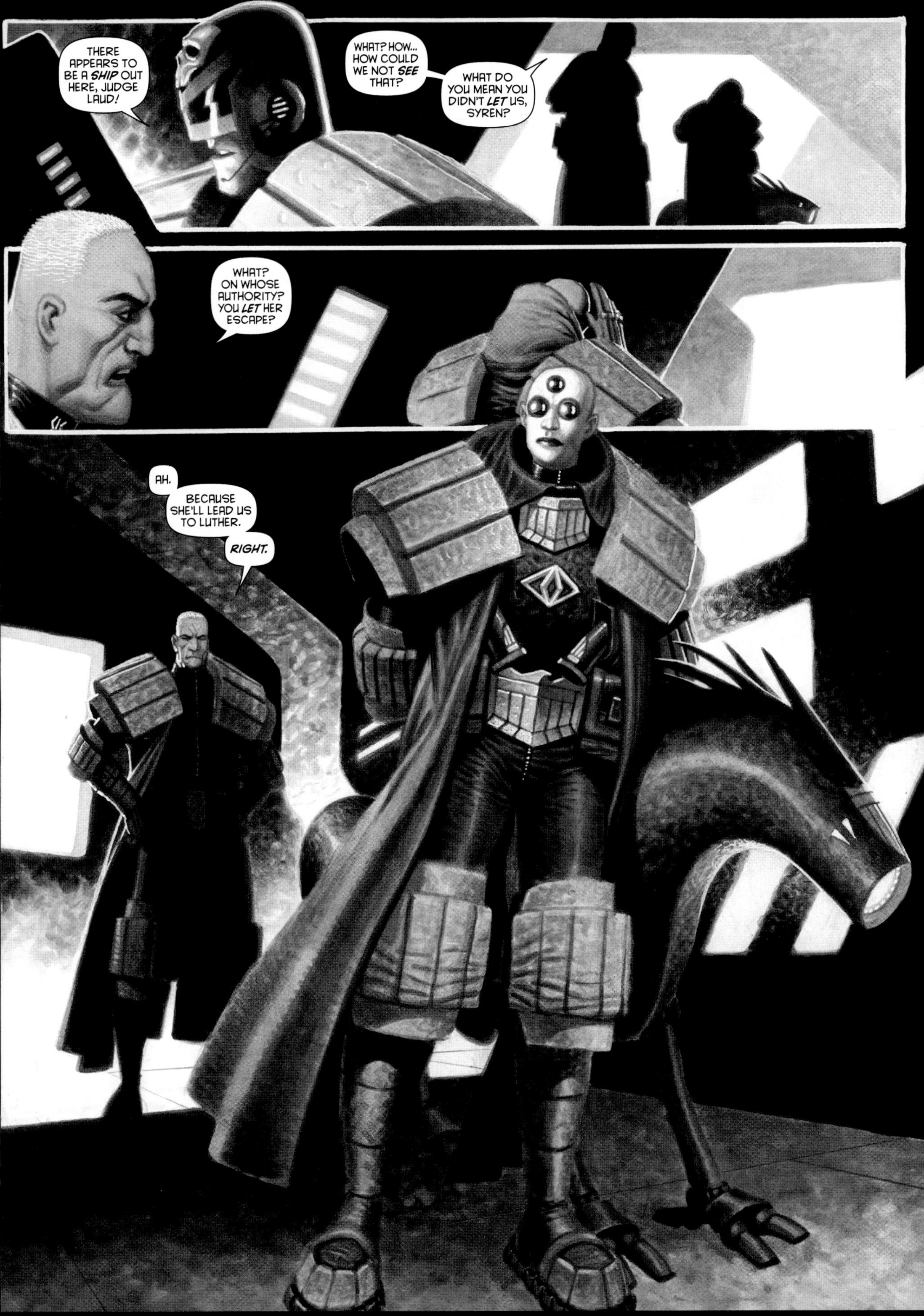
THERE APPEARS TO BE A SHIP OUT HERE, JUDGE LAUD!
WHAT? HOW... HOW COULD WE NOT SEE THAT?
WHAT DO YOU MEAN YOU DIDN'T LET US, SYREN?
WHAT? ON WHOSE AUTHORITY? YOU LET HER ESCAPE?
AH.
BECAUSE SHE'LL LEAD US TO LUTHER.
RIGHT.

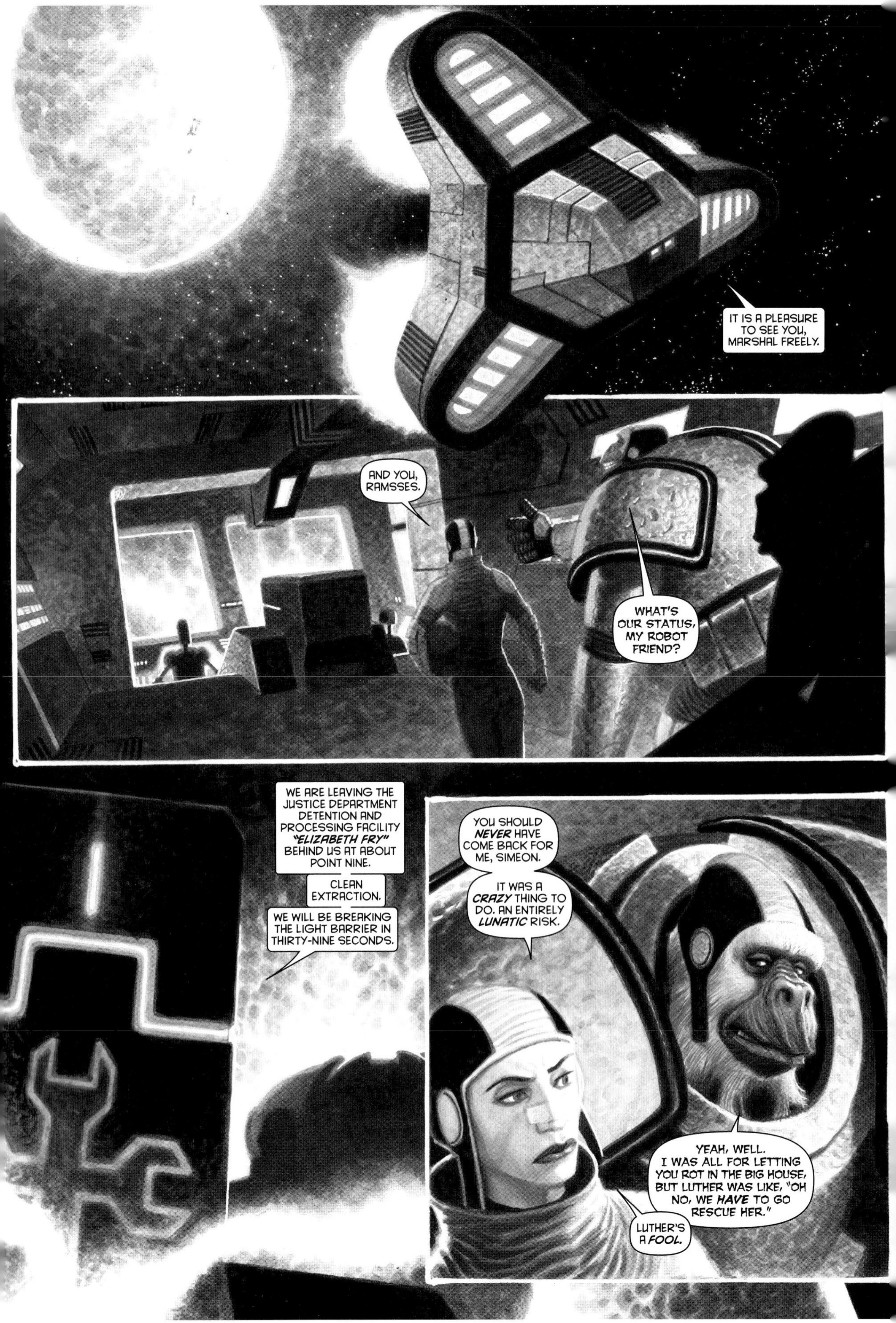
IT IS A PLEASURE TO SEE YOU, MAR'SHAL FREELY.
AND YOU, RAMSSES.
WHAT'S OUR STATUS, MY ROBOT FRIEND?
WE ARE LEAVING THE JUSTICE DEPARTMENT DETENTION AND PROCESSING FACILITY ***"ELIZABETH FRY"*** BEHIND US AT ABOUT POINT NINE.
CLEAN EXTRACTION.
WE WILL BE BREAKING THE LIGHT BARRIER IN THIRTY-NINE SECONDS.
YOU SHOULD ***NEVER*** HAVE COME BACK FOR ME, SIMEON.
IT WAS A ***CRAZY*** THING TO DO. AN ENTIRELY ***LUNATIC*** RISK.
YEAH, WELL. I WAS ALL FOR LETTING YOU ROT IN THE BIG HOUSE, BUT LUTHER WAS LIKE, "OH NO, WE ***HAVE*** TO GO RESCUE HER."
LUTHER'S A ***FOOL.***

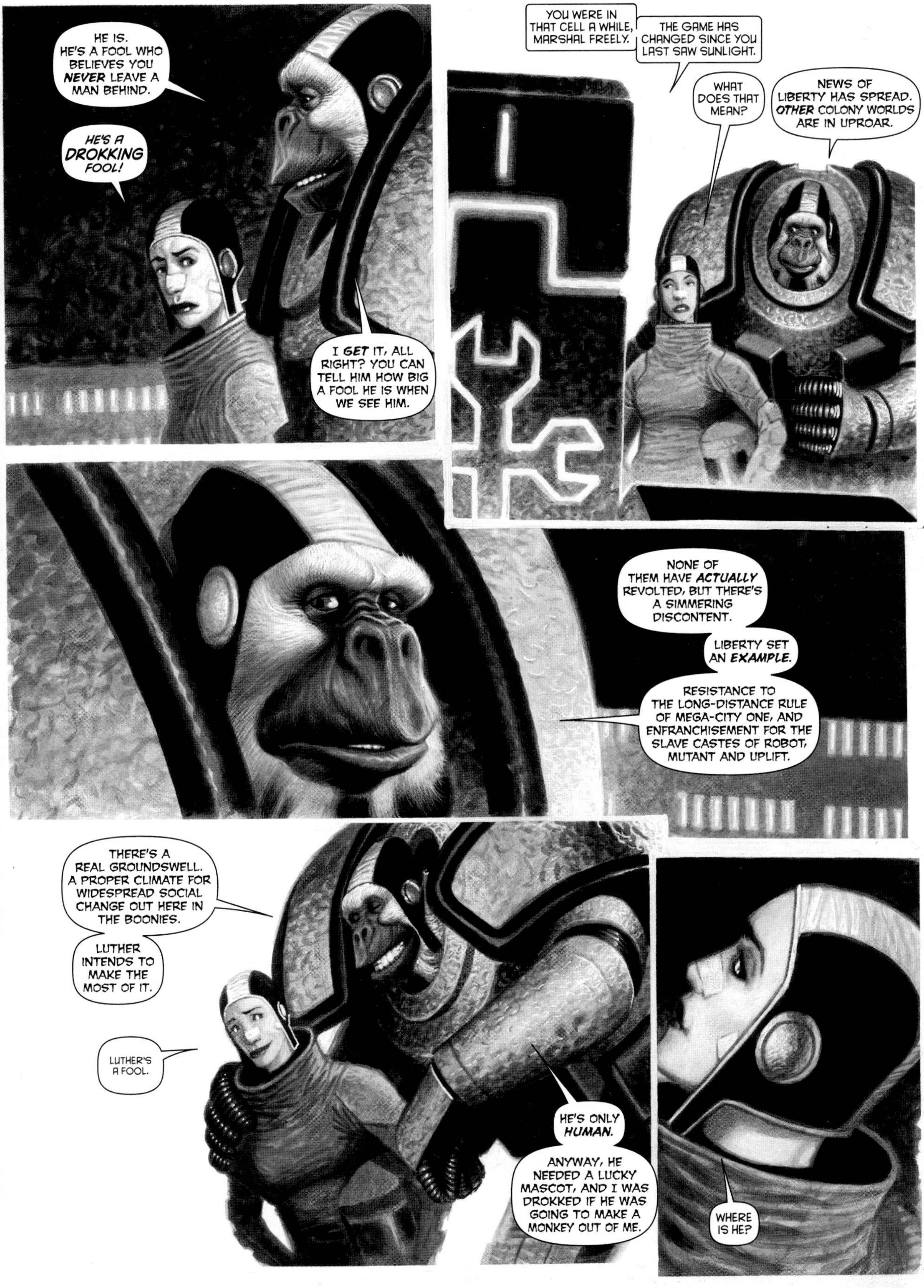

HE IS.
HE'S A FOOL WHO BELIEVES YOU **NEVER** LEAVE A MAN BEHIND.
*HE'S A* ***DROKKING*** *FOOL!*
I **GET** IT, ALL RIGHT? YOU CAN TELL HIM HOW BIG A FOOL HE IS WHEN WE SEE HIM.
YOU WERE IN THAT CELL A WHILE, MARSHAL FREELY.
THE GAME HAS CHANGED SINCE YOU LAST SAW SUNLIGHT.
WHAT DOES THAT MEAN?
NEWS OF LIBERTY HAS SPREAD. **OTHER** COLONY WORLDS ARE IN UPROAR.
NONE OF THEM HAVE **ACTUALLY** REVOLTED, BUT THERE'S A SIMMERING DISCONTENT.
LIBERTY SET AN **EXAMPLE.**
RESISTANCE TO THE LONG-DISTANCE RULE OF MEGA-CITY ONE, AND ENFRANCHISEMENT FOR THE SLAVE CASTES OF ROBOT, MUTANT AND UPLIFT.
THERE'S A REAL GROUNDSWELL. A PROPER CLIMATE FOR WIDESPREAD SOCIAL CHANGE OUT HERE IN THE BOONIES.
LUTHER INTENDS TO MAKE THE MOST OF IT.
LUTHER'S A FOOL.
HE'S ONLY **HUMAN.**
ANYWAY, HE NEEDED A LUCKY MASCOT, AND I WAS DROKKED IF HE WAS GOING TO MAKE A MONKEY OUT OF ME.
WHERE IS HE?

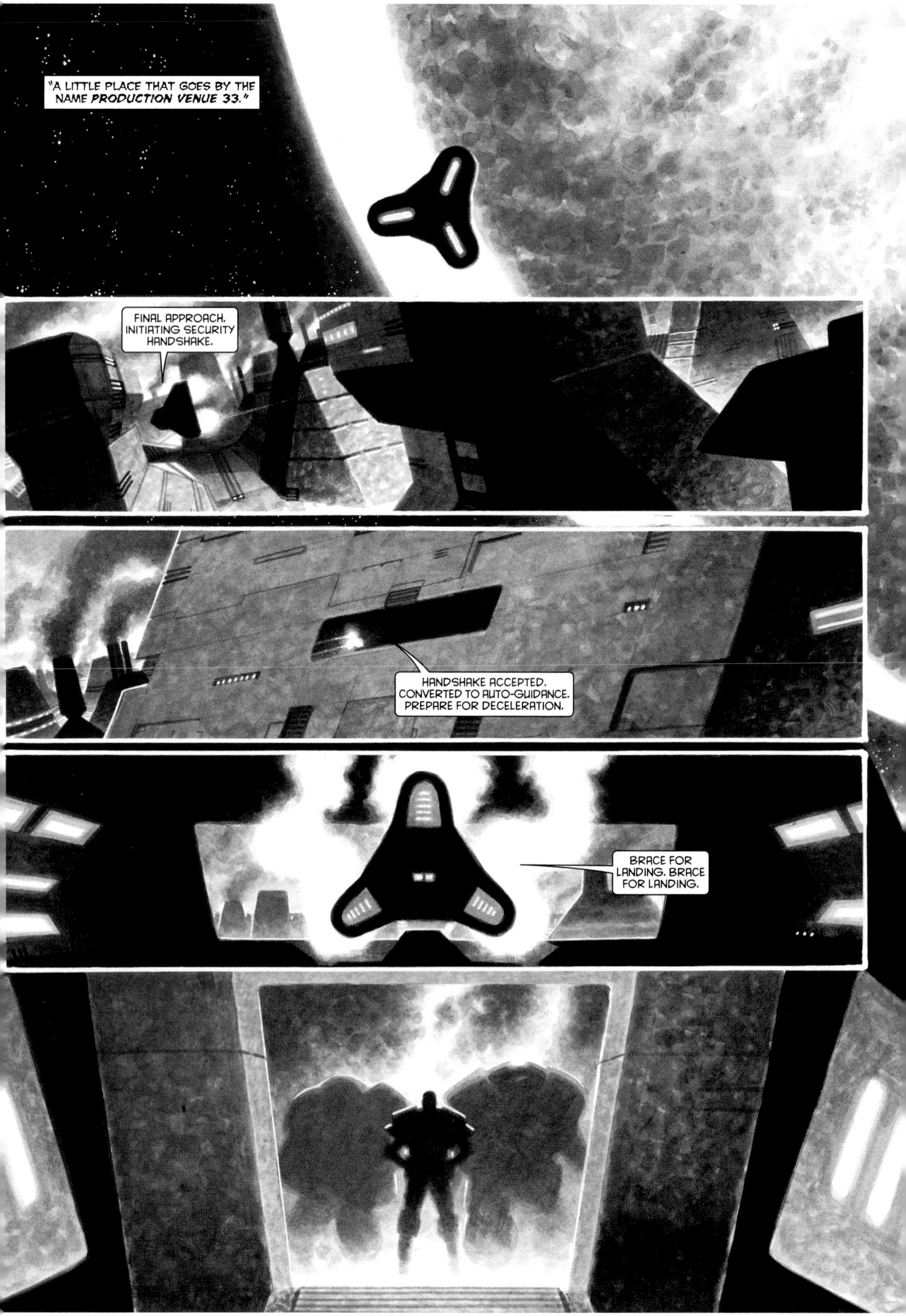
"A LITTLE PLACE THAT GOES BY THE NAME PRODUCTION VENUE 33."
FINAL APPROACH. INITIATING SECURITY HANDSHAKE.
HANDSHAKE ACCEPTED. CONVERTED TO AUTO-GUIDANCE. PREPARE FOR DECELERATION.
BRACE FOR LANDING. BRACE FOR LANDING.

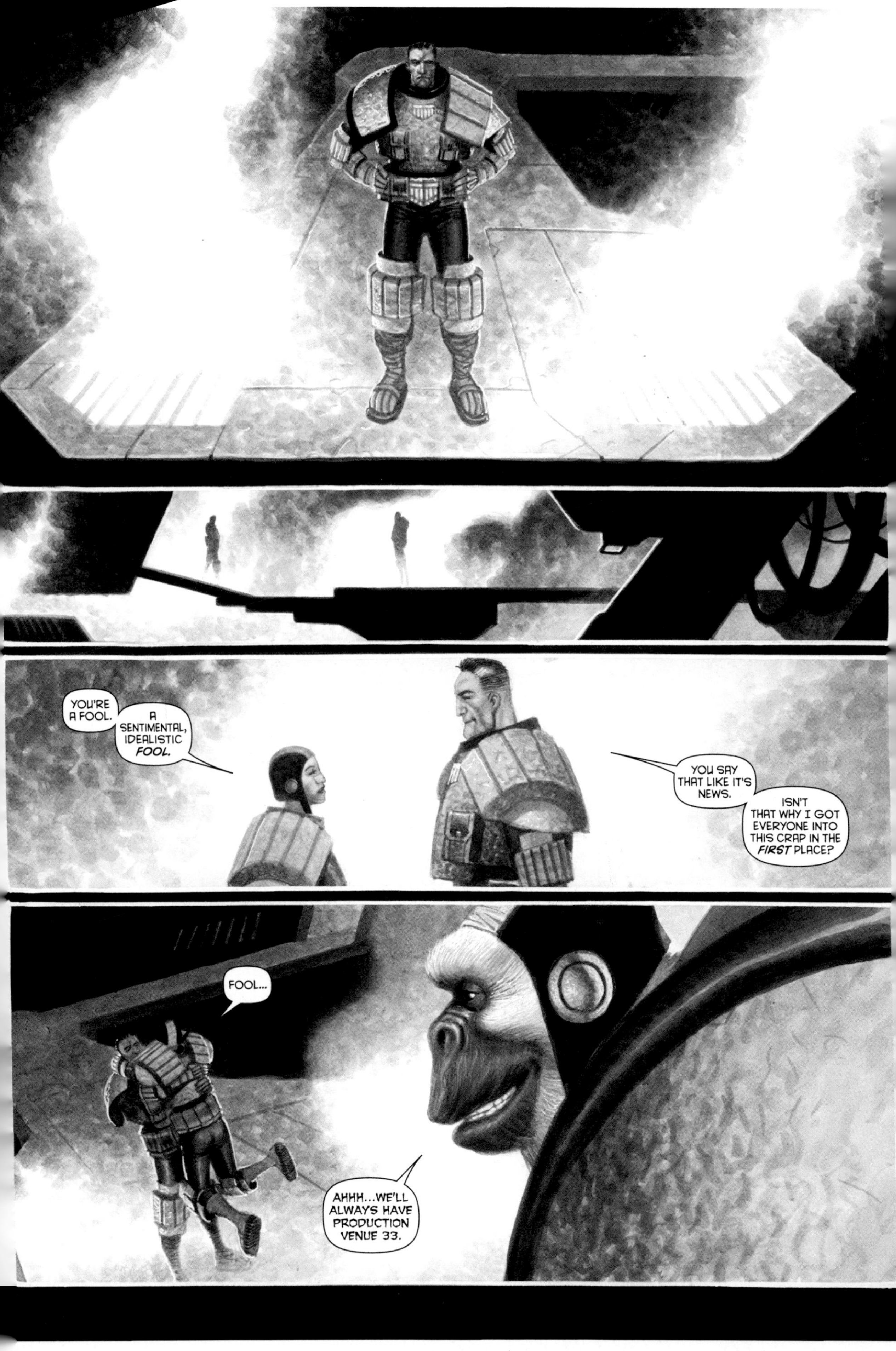
YOU'RE A FOOL.
A SENTIMENTAL, IDEALISTIC *FOOL.*
YOU SAY THAT LIKE IT'S NEWS.
ISN'T THAT WHY I GOT EVERYONE INTO THIS CRAP IN THE *FIRST* PLACE?
FOOL...
AHHH...WE'LL ALWAYS HAVE PRODUCTION VENUE 33.

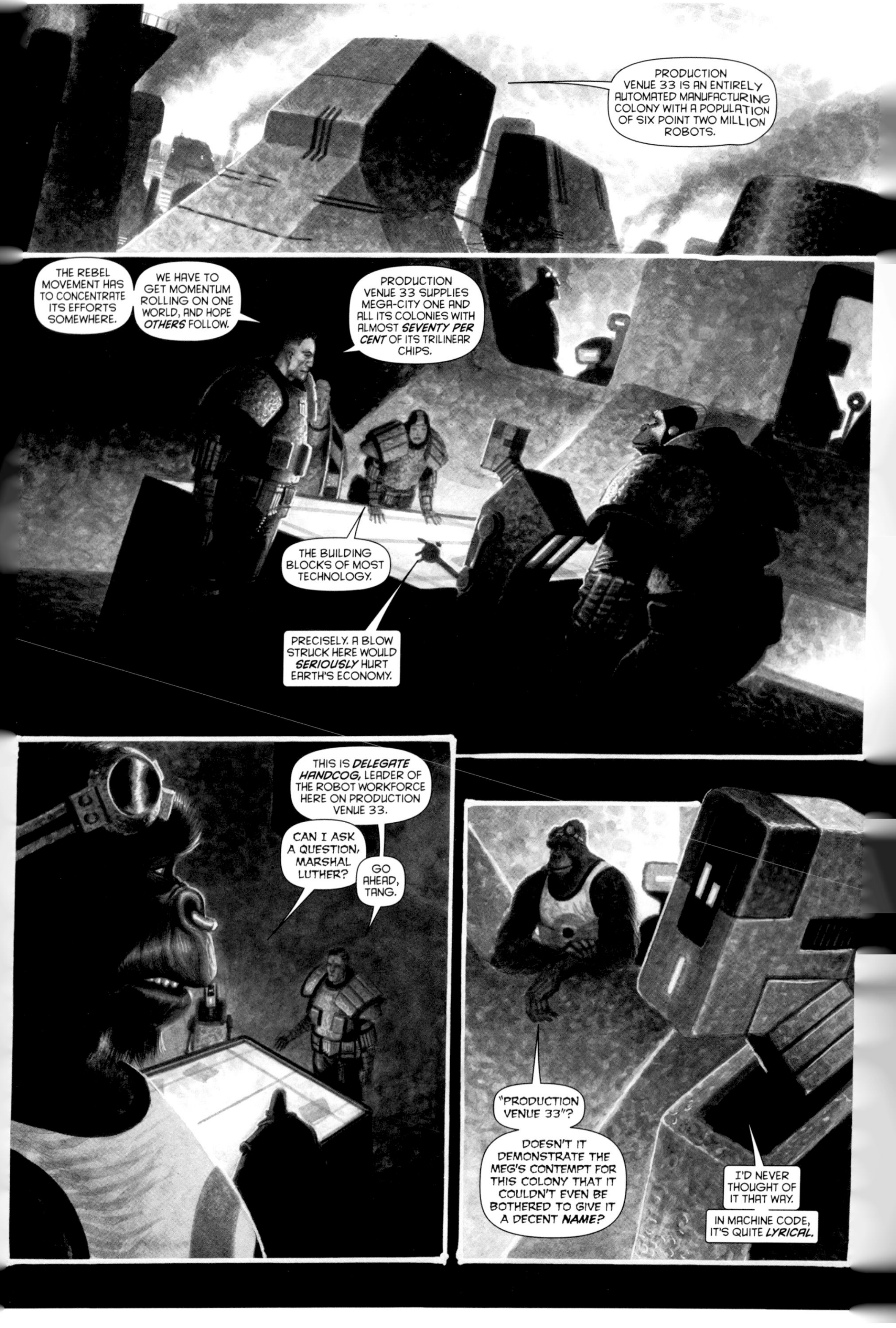
PRODUCTION VENUE 33 IS AN ENTIRELY AUTOMATED MANUFACTURING COLONY WITH A POPULATION OF SIX POINT TWO MILLION ROBOTS.
THE REBEL MOVEMENT HAS TO CONCENTRATE ITS EFFORTS SOMEWHERE.
WE HAVE TO GET MOMENTUM ROLLING ON ONE WORLD, AND HOPE OTHERS FOLLOW.
PRODUCTION VENUE 33 SUPPLIES MEGA-CITY ONE AND ALL ITS COLONIES WITH ALMOST SEVENTY PER CENT OF ITS TRILINEAR CHIPS.
THE BUILDING BLOCKS OF MOST TECHNOLOGY.
PRECISELY. A BLOW STRUCK HERE WOULD SERIOUSLY HURT EARTH'S ECONOMY.
THIS IS DELEGATE HANDCOG, LEADER OF THE ROBOT WORKFORCE HERE ON PRODUCTION VENUE 33.
CAN I ASK A QUESTION, MARSHAL LUTHER?
GO AHEAD, TANG.
"PRODUCTION VENUE 33"?
DOESN'T IT DEMONSTRATE THE MEG'S CONTEMPT FOR THIS COLONY THAT IT COULDN'T EVEN BE BOTHERED TO GIVE IT A DECENT NAME?
I'D NEVER THOUGHT OF IT THAT WAY.
IN MACHINE CODE, IT'S QUITE LYRICAL.

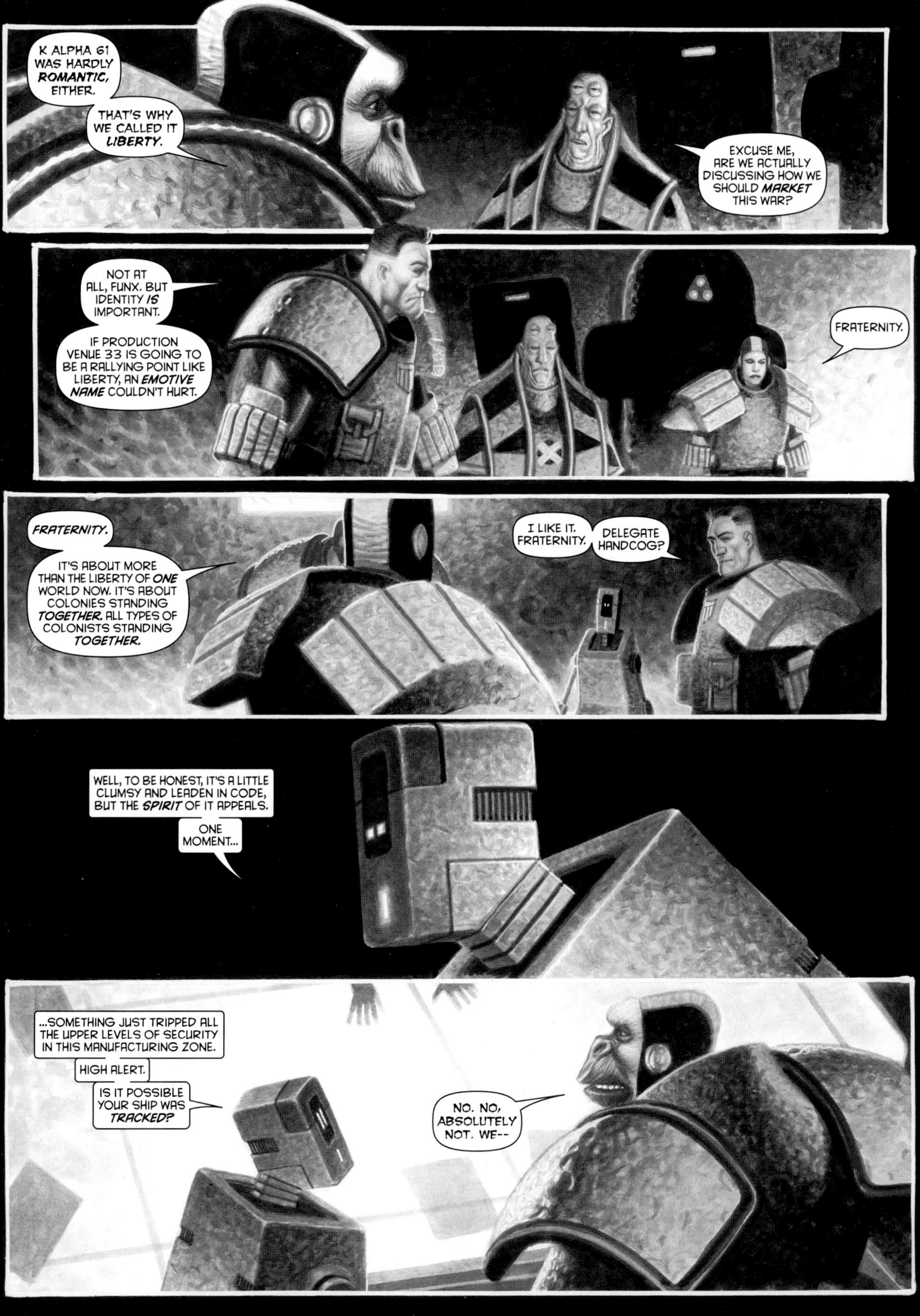
K ALPHA 61 WAS HARDLY ROMANTIC, EITHER.
THAT'S WHY WE CALLED IT LIBERTY.
EXCUSE ME, ARE WE ACTUALLY DISCUSSING HOW WE SHOULD MARKET THIS WAR?
NOT AT ALL, FUNX. BUT IDENTITY IS IMPORTANT.
IF PRODUCTION VENUE 33 IS GOING TO BE A RALLYING POINT LIKE LIBERTY, AN EMOTIVE NAME COULDN'T HURT.
FRATERNITY.
FRATERNITY.
IT'S ABOUT MORE THAN THE LIBERTY OF ONE WORLD NOW. IT'S ABOUT COLONIES STANDING TOGETHER. ALL TYPES OF COLONISTS STANDING TOGETHER.
I LIKE IT. FRATERNITY.
DELEGATE HANDCOG?
WELL, TO BE HONEST, IT'S A LITTLE CLUMSY AND LEADEN IN CODE, BUT THE SPIRIT OF IT APPEALS.
ONE MOMENT...
...SOMETHING JUST TRIPPED ALL THE UPPER LEVELS OF SECURITY IN THIS MANUFACTURING ZONE.
HIGH ALERT.
IS IT POSSIBLE YOUR SHIP WAS TRACKED?
NO. NO, ABSOLUTELY NOT. WE--

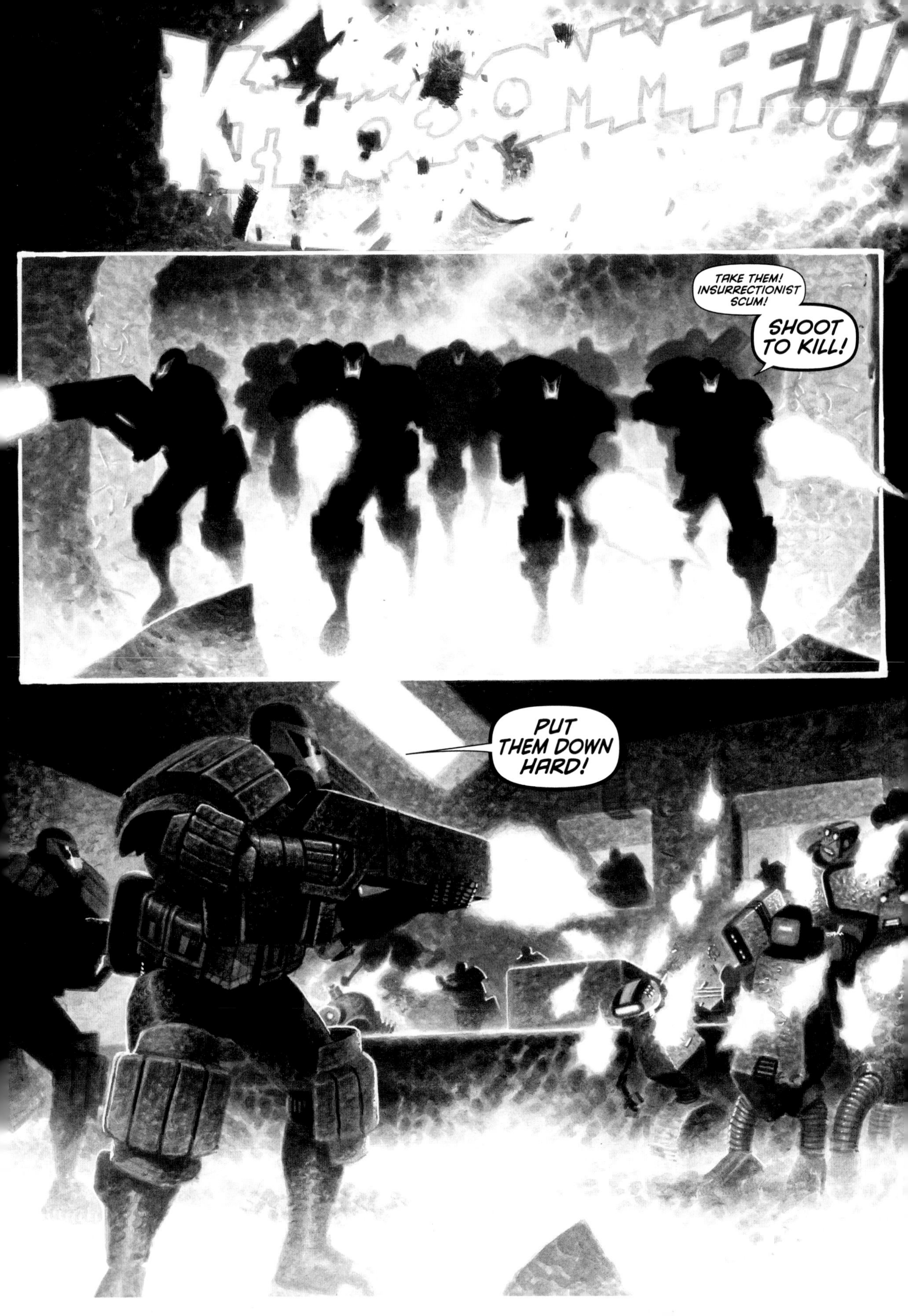
KHOOOMMFF!!
TAKE THEM! INSURRECTIONIST SCUM!
SHOOT TO KILL!
PUT THEM DOWN HARD!

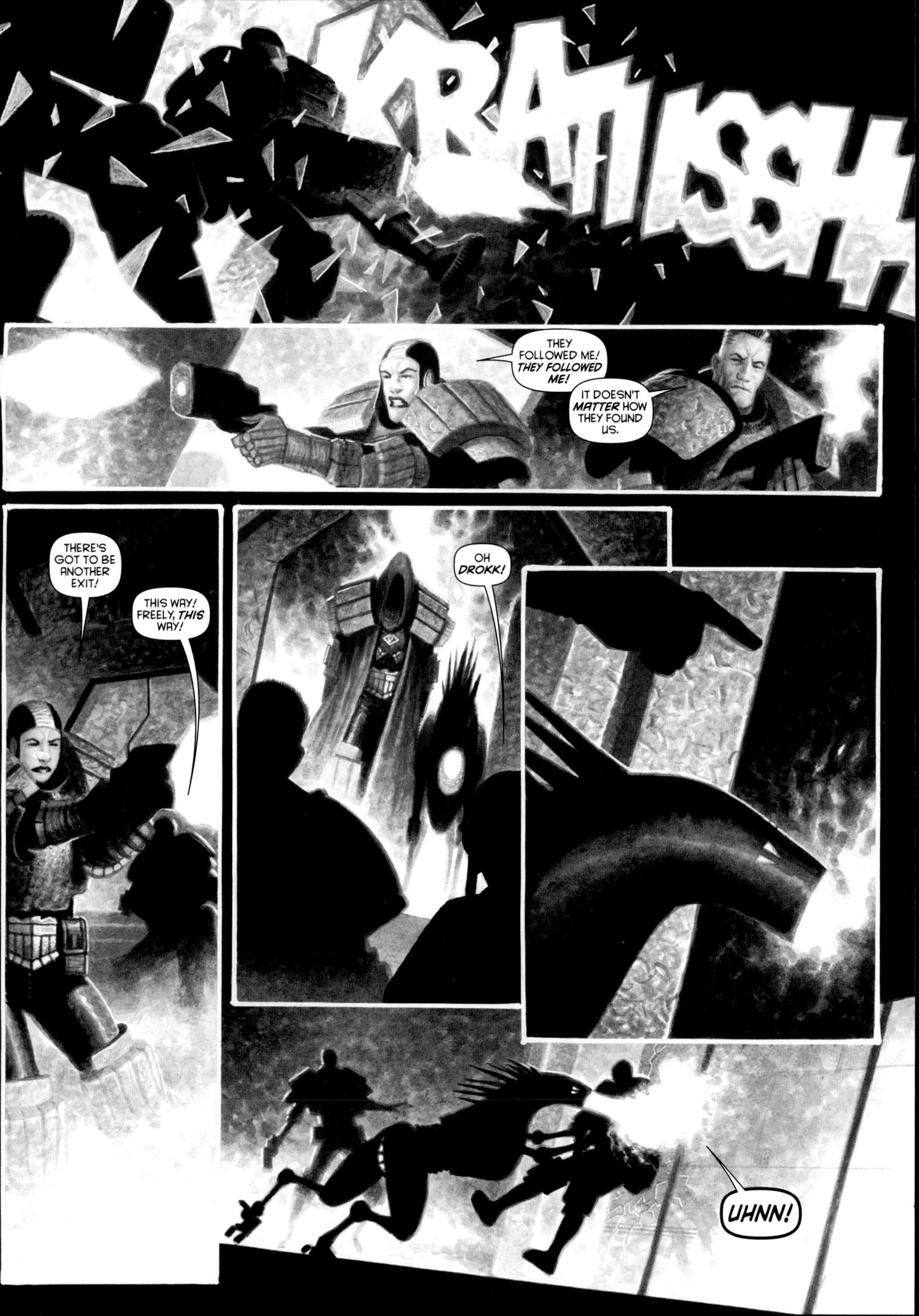
KRAASSH
THEY FOLLOWED ME! THEY FOLLOWED ME!
IT DOESN'T MATTER HOW THEY FOUND US.
THERE'S GOT TO BE ANOTHER EXIT!
THIS WAY! FREELY, THIS WAY!
OH DROKK!
UHNN!

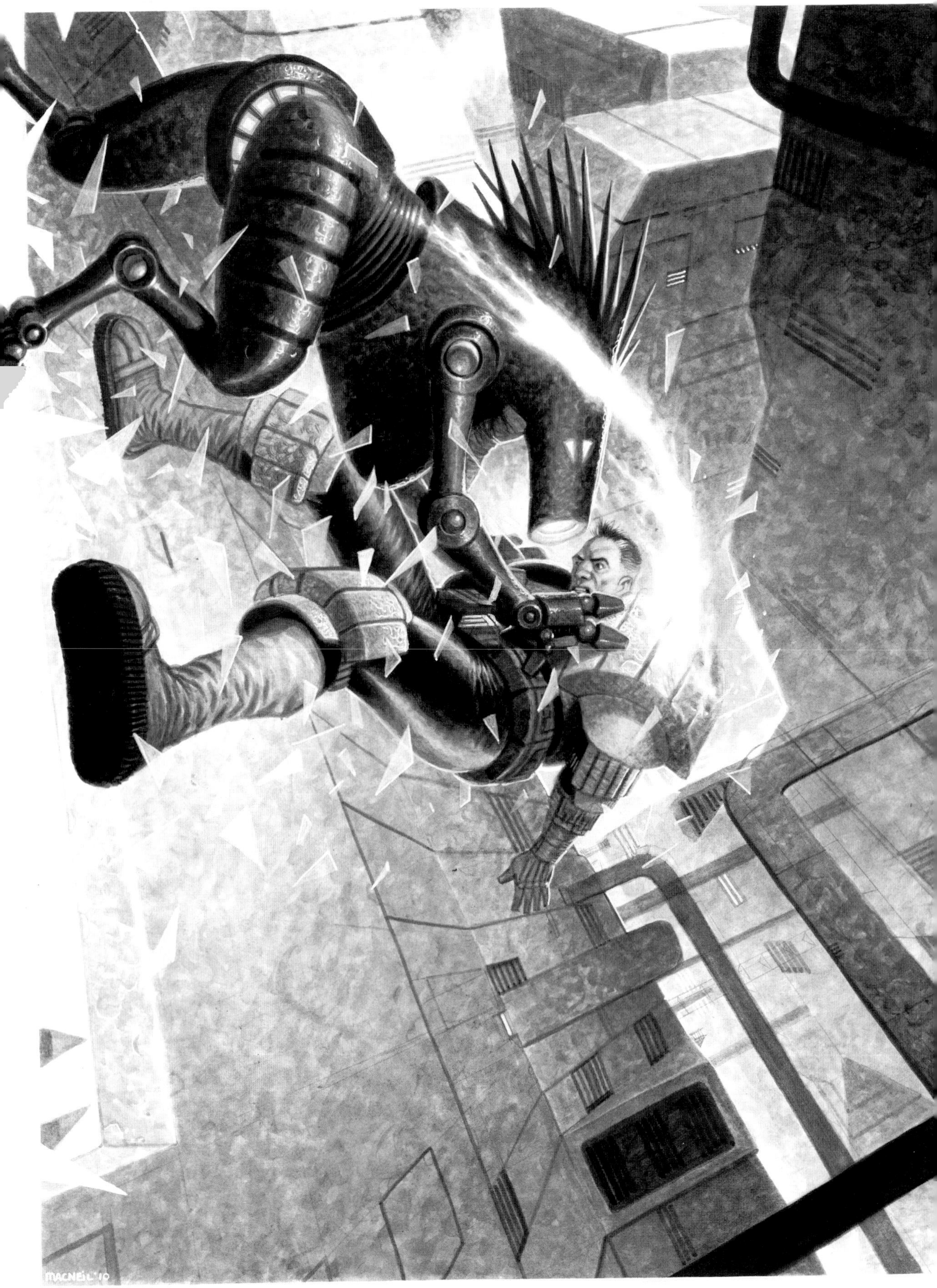
MACNEIL '10

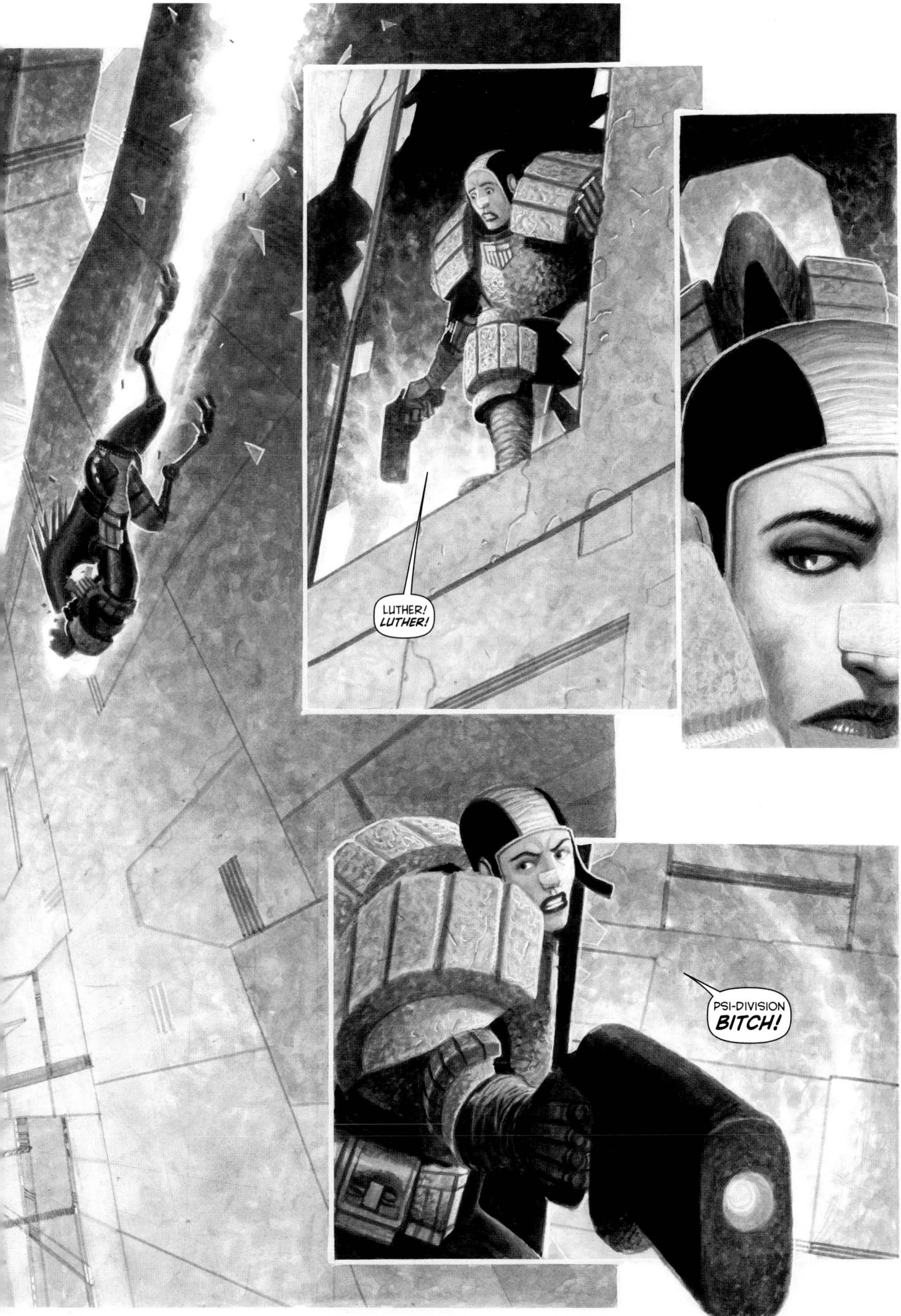
LUTHER! LUTHER!
PSI-DIVISION BITCH!

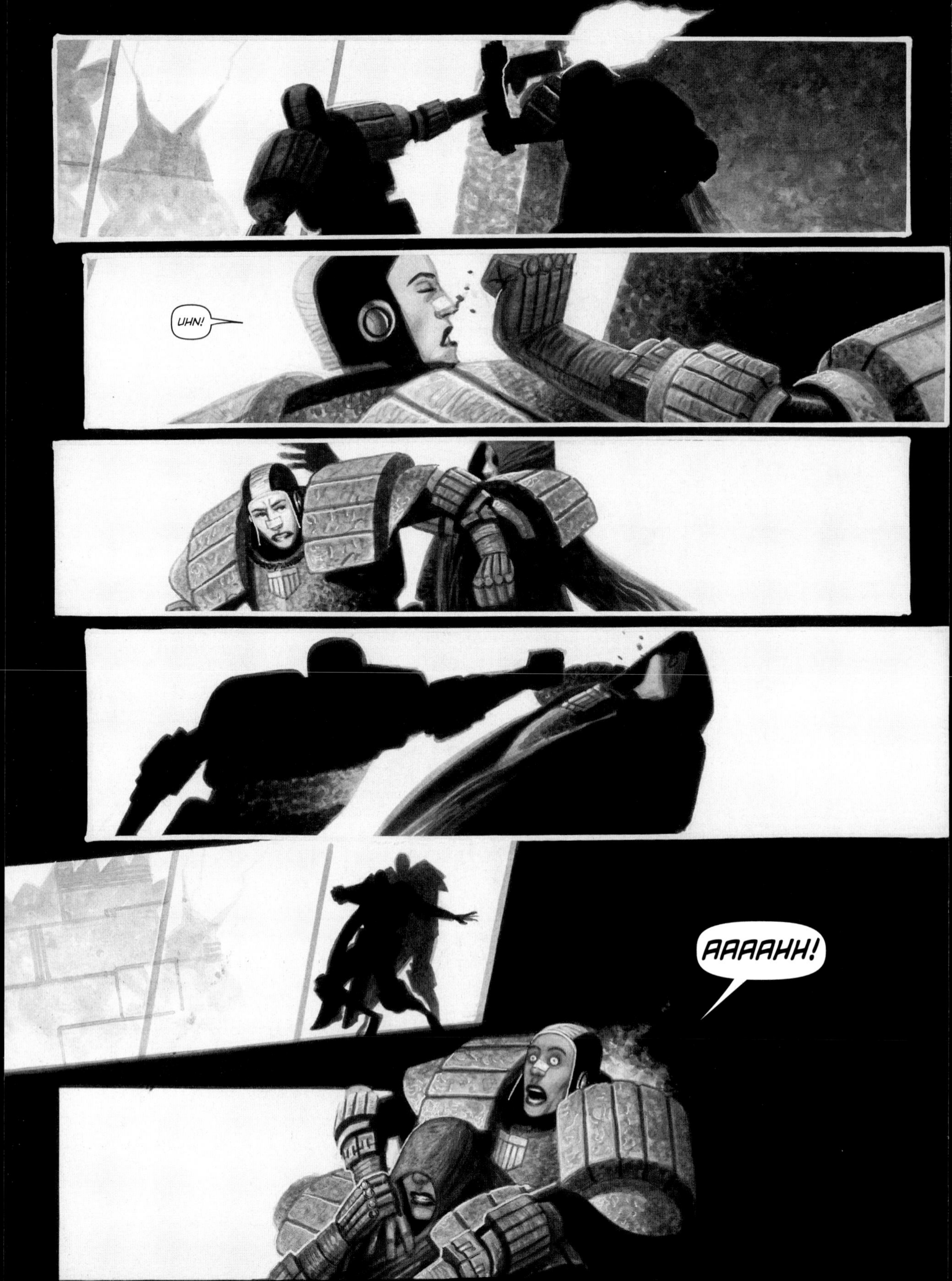
UHN!
AAAAHH!

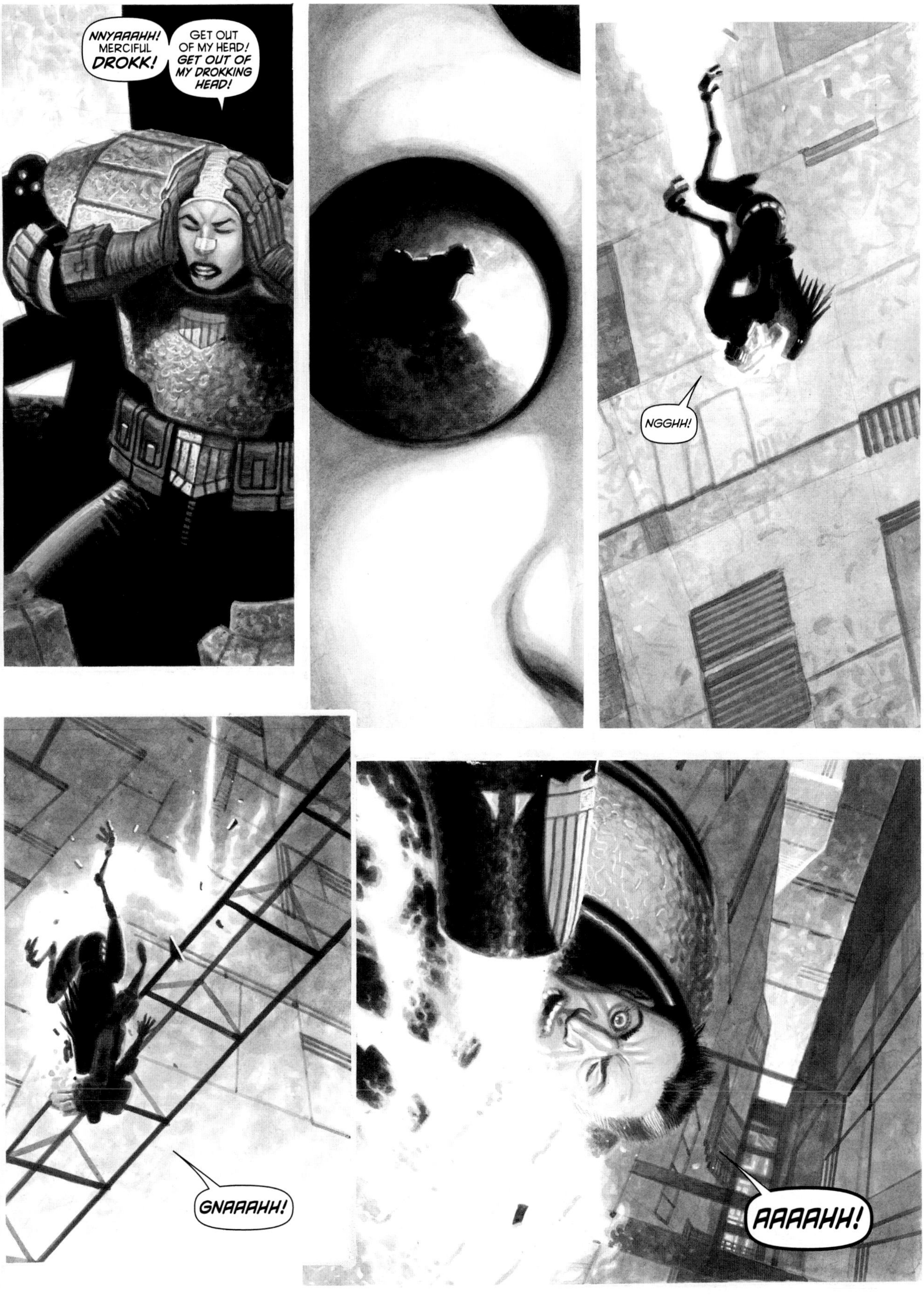
NNYAAAHH! MERCIFUL DROKK!
GET OUT OF MY HEAD! GET OUT OF MY DROKKING HEAD!
NGGHH!
GNAAAAHH!
AAAAHH!

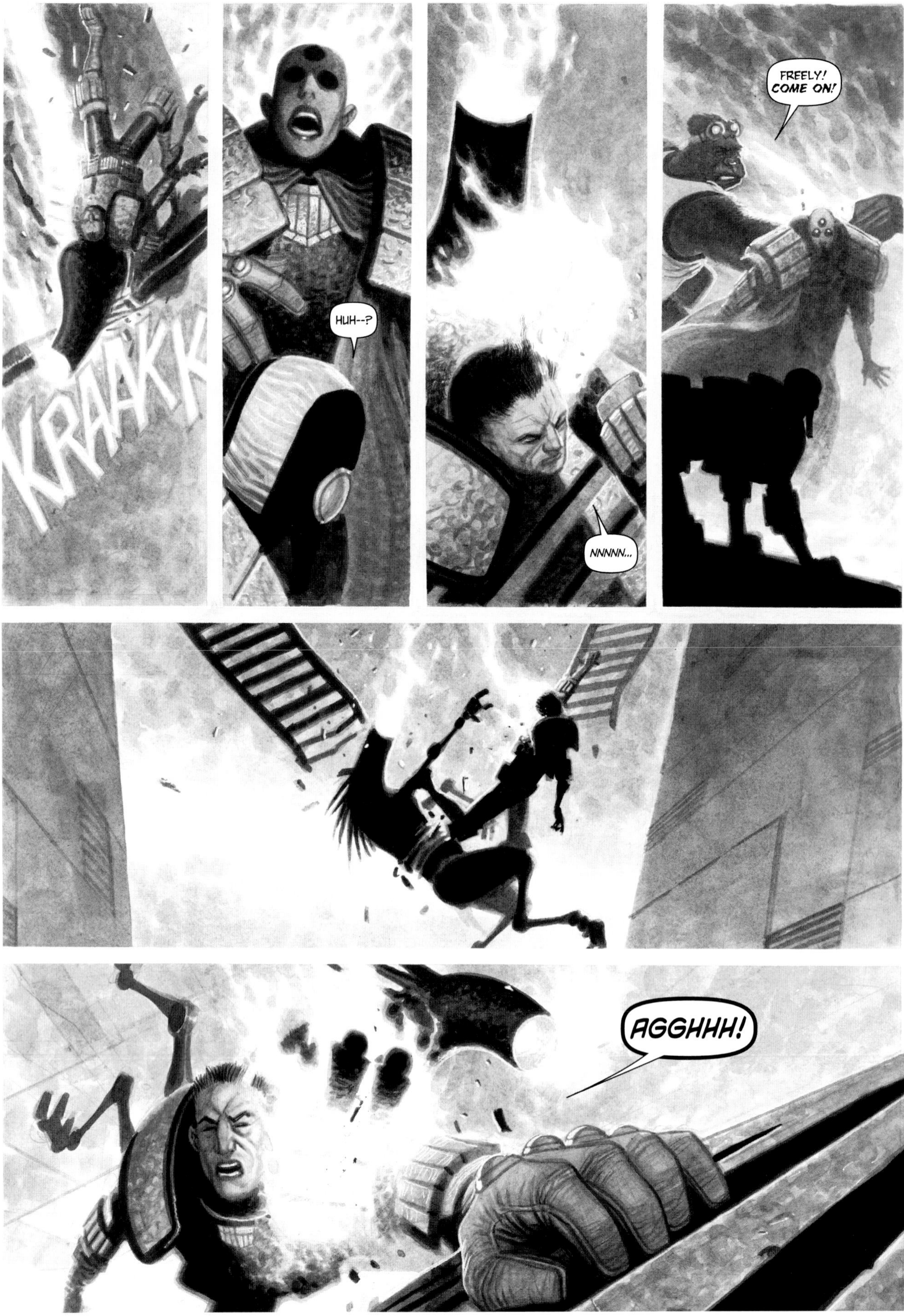
KRAAKK
HUH--?
NNNNN...
FREELY! COME ON!
AGGHHH!

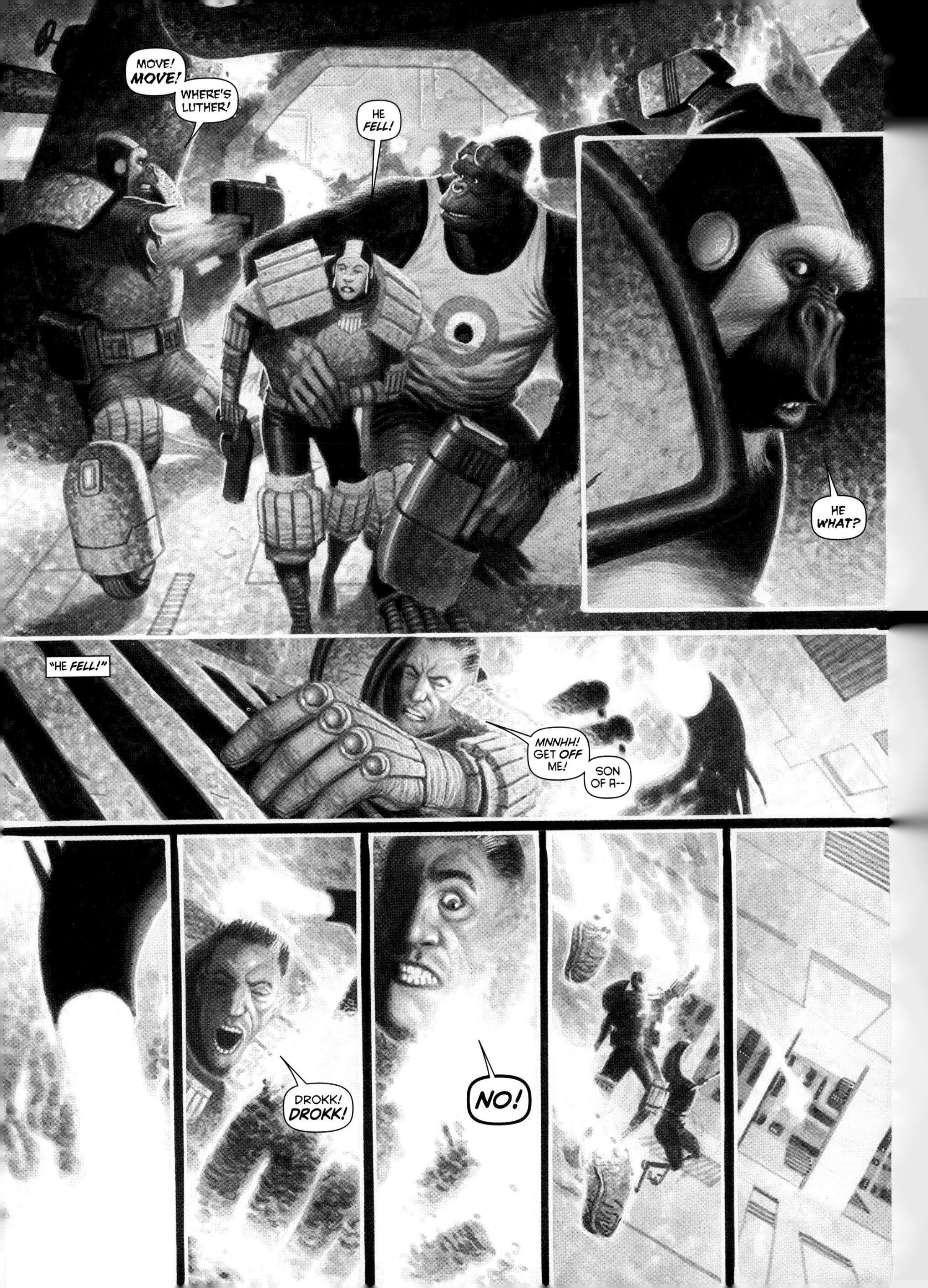
MOVE! MOVE!
WHERE'S LUTHER!
HE FELL!
HE WHAT?
"HE FELL!"
MNNHH! GET OFF ME!
SON OF A--
DROKK! DROKK!
NO!

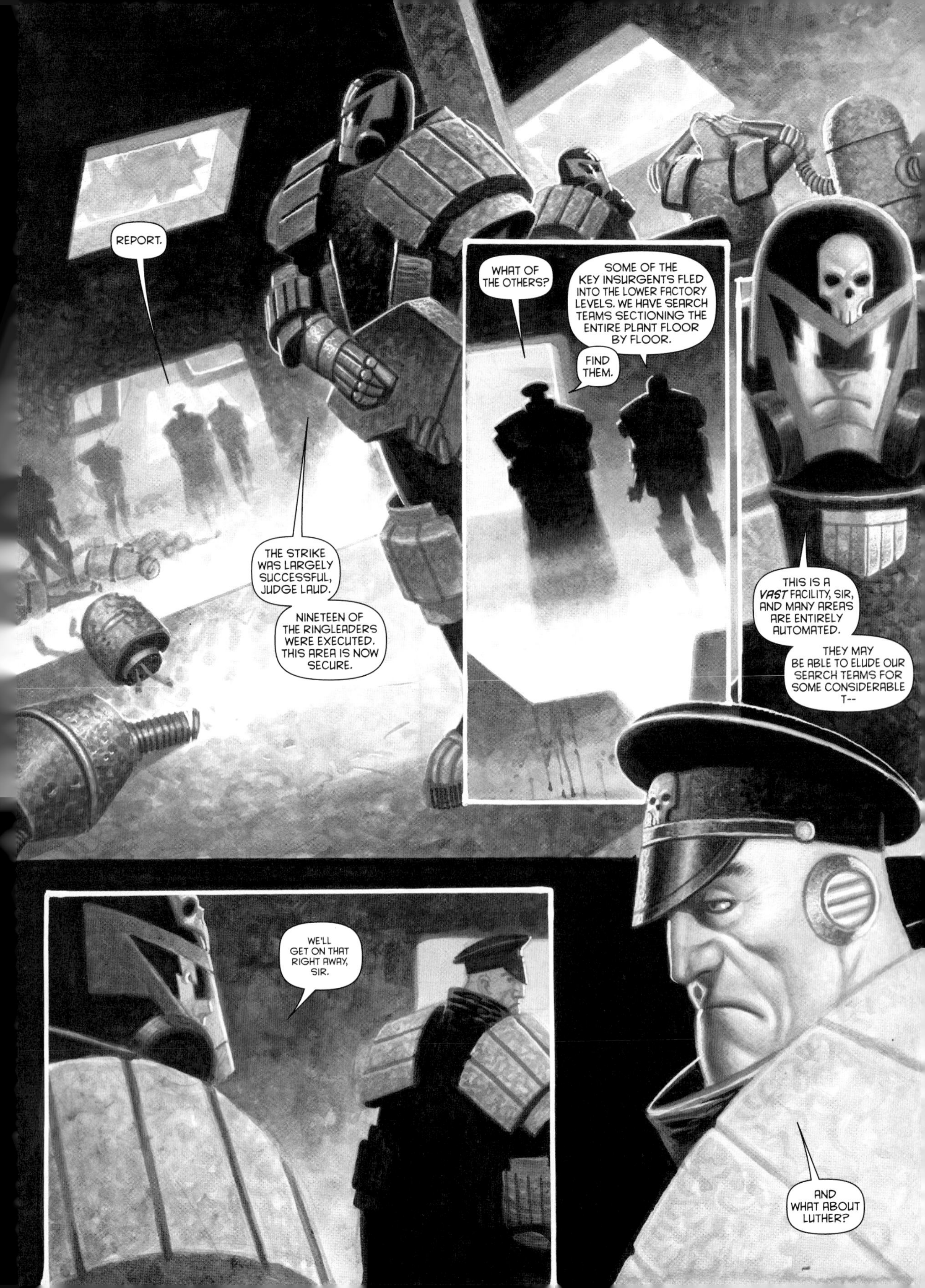
REPORT.
THE STRIKE WAS LARGELY SUCCESSFUL, JUDGE LAUD.
NINETEEN OF THE RINGLEADERS WERE EXECUTED. THIS AREA IS NOW SECURE.
WHAT OF THE OTHERS?
SOME OF THE KEY INSURGENTS FLED INTO THE LOWER FACTORY LEVELS. WE HAVE SEARCH TEAMS SECTIONING THE ENTIRE PLANT FLOOR BY FLOOR.
FIND THEM.
THIS IS A VAST FACILITY, SIR, AND MANY AREAS ARE ENTIRELY AUTOMATED.
THEY MAY BE ABLE TO ELUDE OUR SEARCH TEAMS FOR SOME CONSIDERABLE T--
AND WHAT ABOUT LUTHER?
WE'LL GET ON THAT RIGHT AWAY, SIR.

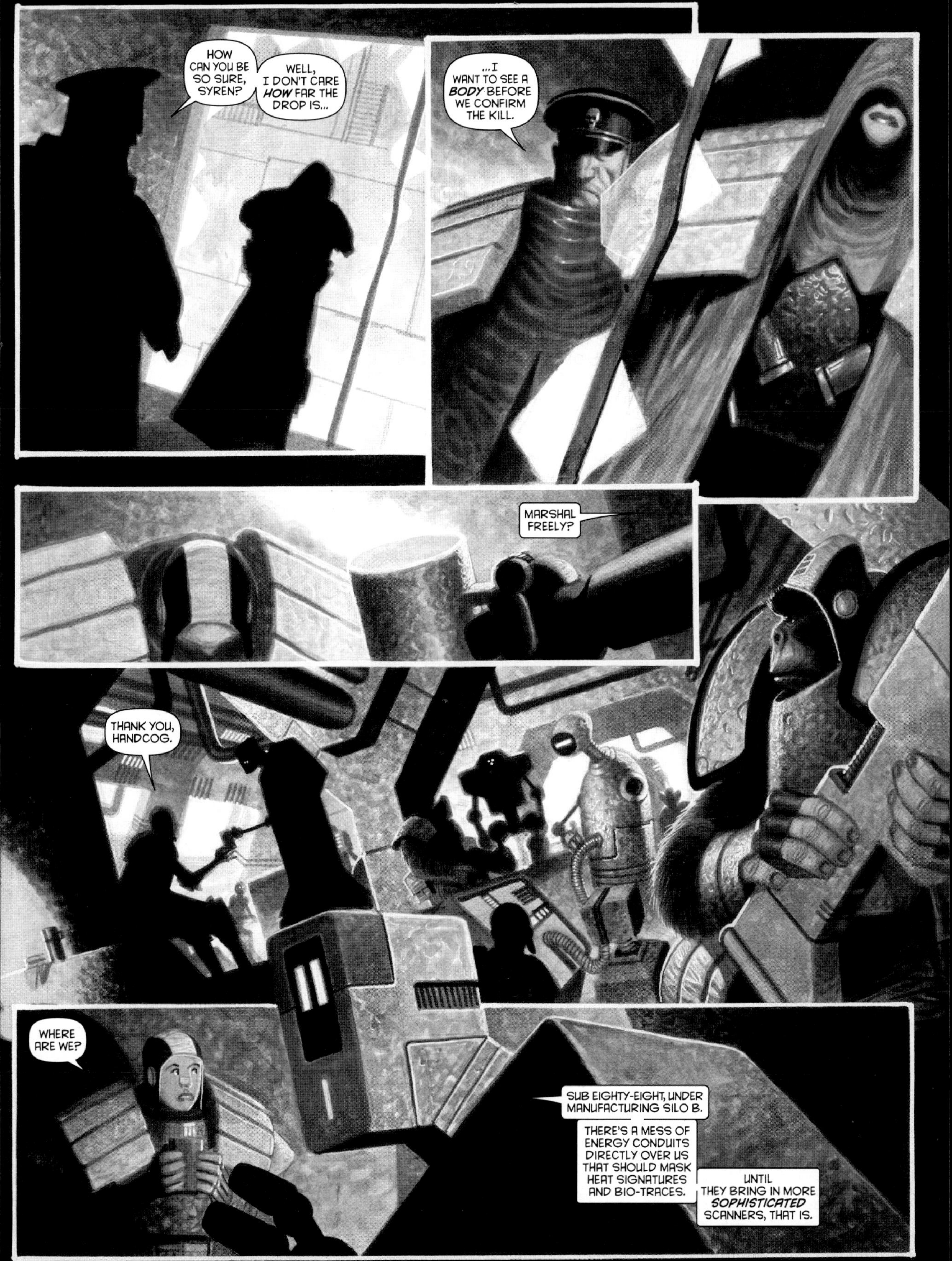

HOW CAN YOU BE SO SURE, SYREN?
WELL, I DON'T CARE *HOW* FAR THE DROP IS...
...I WANT TO SEE A *BODY* BEFORE WE CONFIRM THE KILL.
MARSHAL FREELY?
THANK YOU, HANDCOG.
WHERE ARE WE?
SUB EIGHTY-EIGHT, UNDER MANUFACTURING SILO B.
THERE'S A MESS OF ENERGY CONDUITS DIRECTLY OVER US THAT SHOULD MASK HEAT SIGNATURES AND BIO-TRACES.
UNTIL THEY BRING IN MORE *SOPHISTICATED* SCANNERS, THAT IS.

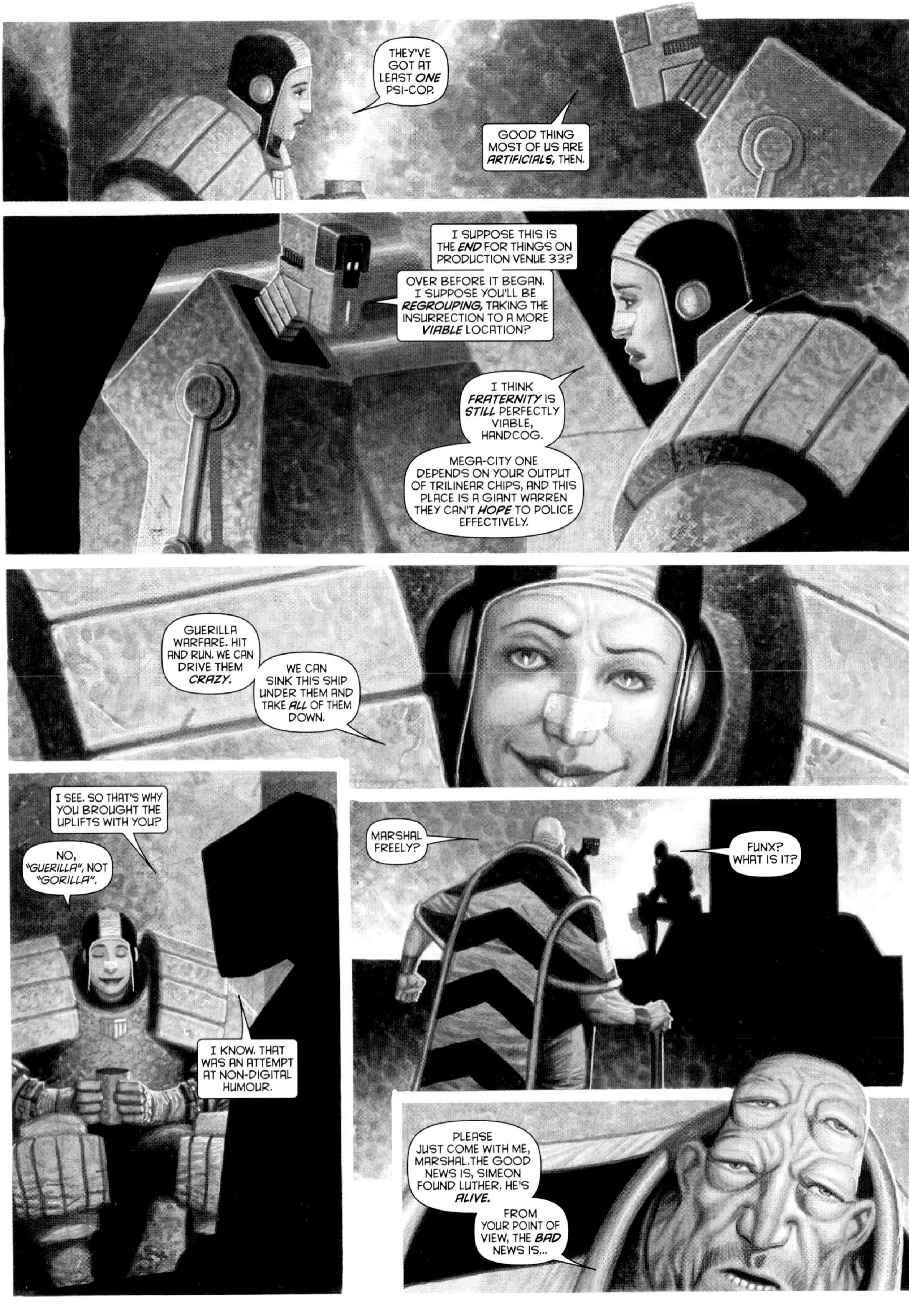
THEY'VE GOT AT LEAST ONE PSI-COP.
GOOD THING MOST OF US ARE ARTIFICIALS, THEN.
I SUPPOSE THIS IS THE END FOR THINGS ON PRODUCTION VENUE 33?
OVER BEFORE IT BEGAN. I SUPPOSE YOU'LL BE REGROUPING, TAKING THE INSURRECTION TO A MORE VIABLE LOCATION?
I THINK FRATERNITY IS STILL PERFECTLY VIABLE, HANDCOG.
MEGA-CITY ONE DEPENDS ON YOUR OUTPUT OF TRILINEAR CHIPS, AND THIS PLACE IS A GIANT WARREN THEY CAN'T HOPE TO POLICE EFFECTIVELY.
GUERILLA WARFARE. HIT AND RUN. WE CAN DRIVE THEM CRAZY.
WE CAN SINK THIS SHIP UNDER THEM AND TAKE ALL OF THEM DOWN.
I SEE. SO THAT'S WHY YOU BROUGHT THE UPLIFTS WITH YOU?
NO, "GUERILLA", NOT "GORILLA".
I KNOW. THAT WAS AN ATTEMPT AT NON-DIGITAL HUMOUR.
MARSHAL FREELY?
FUNX? WHAT IS IT?
PLEASE JUST COME WITH ME, MARSHAL. THE GOOD NEWS IS, SIMEON FOUND LUTHER. HE'S ALIVE.
FROM YOUR POINT OF VIEW, THE BAD NEWS IS...

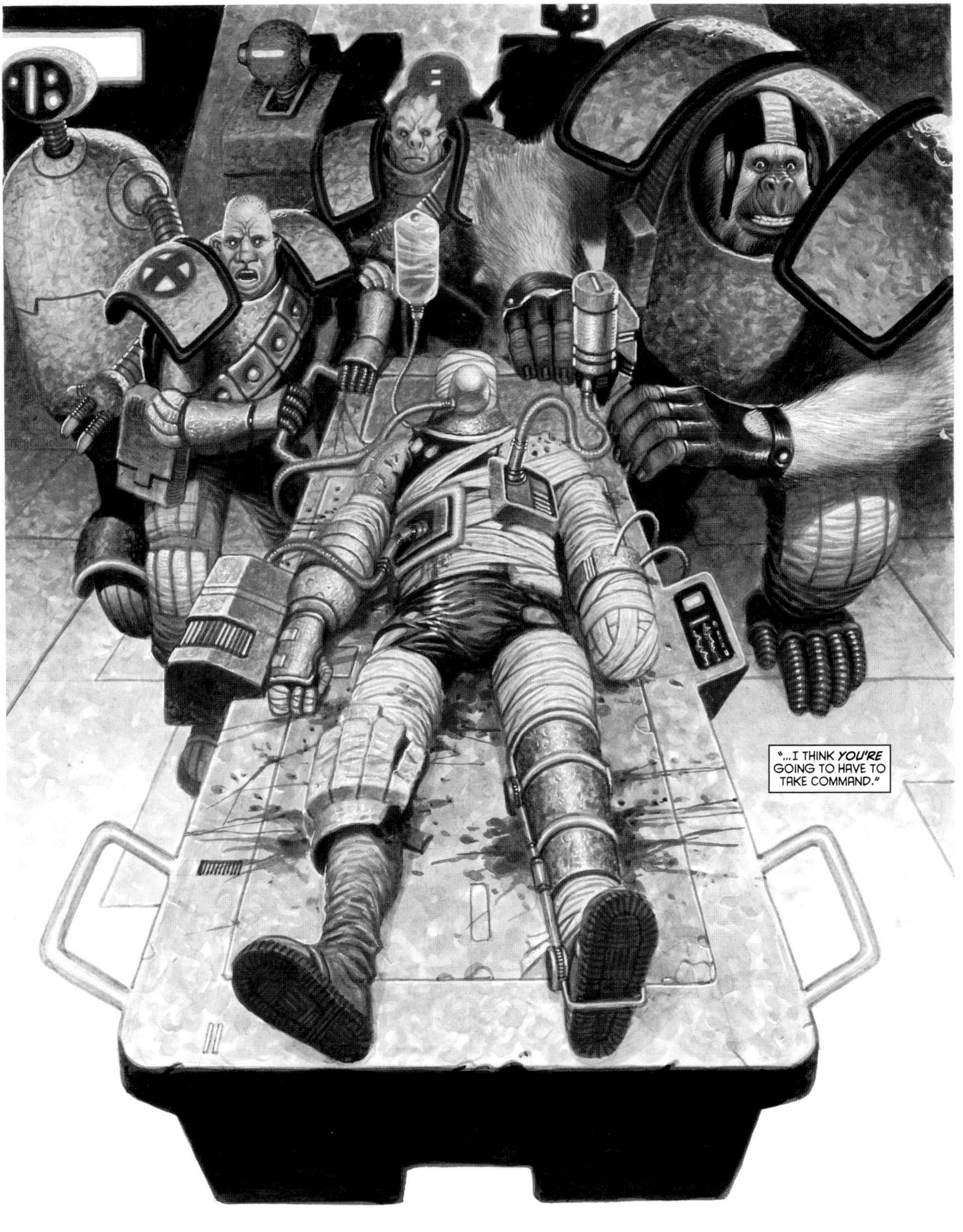
"...I THINK *YOU'RE* GOING TO HAVE TO TAKE COMMAND."

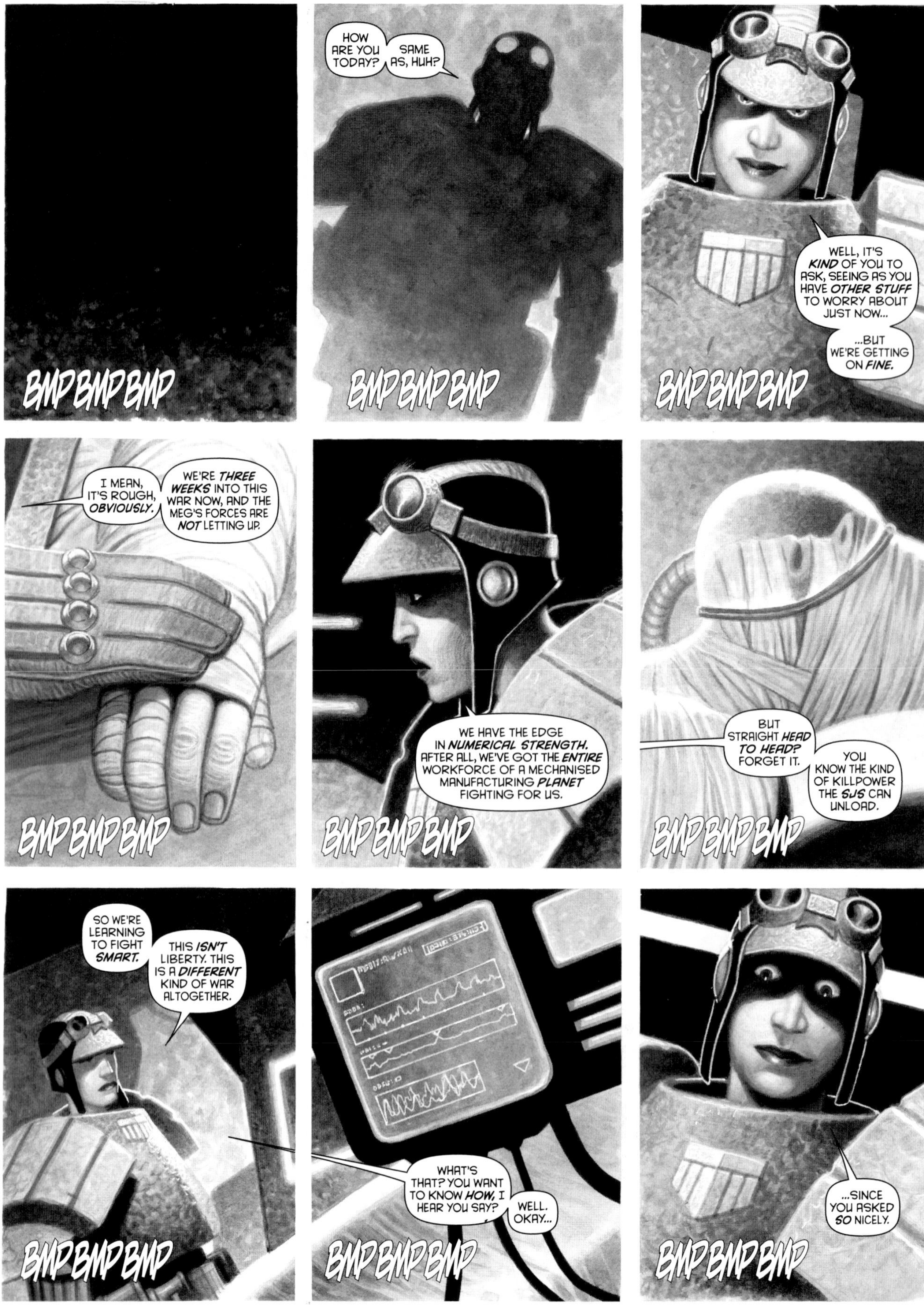
BMP BMP BMP
HOW ARE YOU TODAY?
SAME AS, HUH?
BMP BMP BMP
WELL, IT'S KIND OF YOU TO ASK, SEEING AS YOU HAVE OTHER STUFF TO WORRY ABOUT JUST NOW...
...BUT WE'RE GETTING ON FINE.
BMP BMP BMP
I MEAN, IT'S ROUGH, OBVIOUSLY.
WE'RE THREE WEEKS INTO THIS WAR NOW, AND THE MEG'S FORCES ARE NOT LETTING UP.
BMP BMP BMP
WE HAVE THE EDGE IN NUMERICAL STRENGTH. AFTER ALL, WE'VE GOT THE ENTIRE WORKFORCE OF A MECHANISED MANUFACTURING PLANET FIGHTING FOR US.
BMP BMP BMP
BUT STRAIGHT HEAD TO HEAD? FORGET IT.
YOU KNOW THE KIND OF KILLPOWER THE SJS CAN UNLOAD.
BMP BMP BMP
SO WE'RE LEARNING TO FIGHT SMART.
THIS ISN'T LIBERTY. THIS IS A DIFFERENT KIND OF WAR ALTOGETHER.
BMP BMP BMP
WHAT'S THAT? YOU WANT TO KNOW HOW, I HEAR YOU SAY?
WELL. OKAY...
BMP BMP BMP
...SINCE YOU ASKED SO NICELY.
BMP BMP BMP

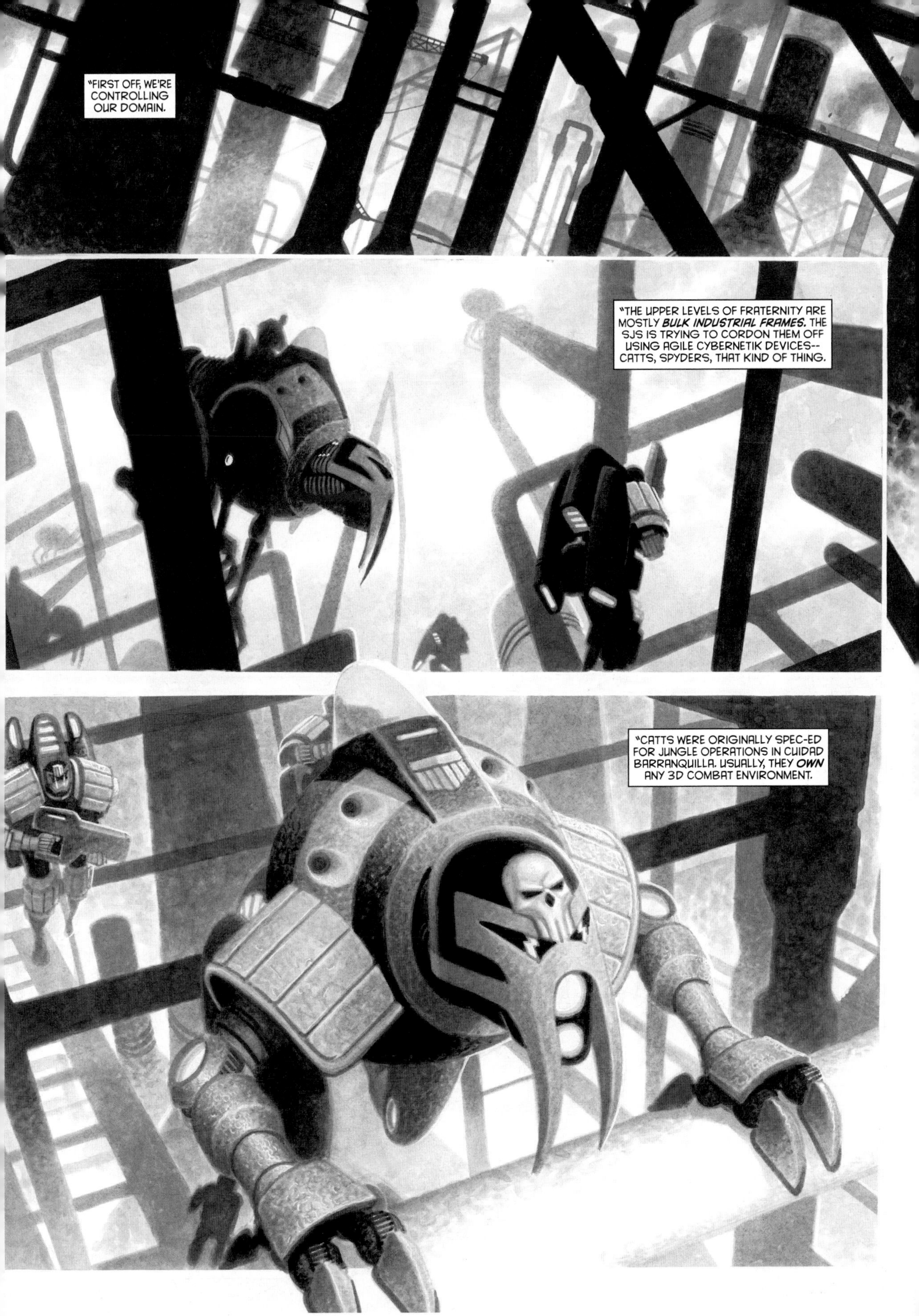
"FIRST OFF, WE'RE CONTROLLING OUR DOMAIN.
"THE UPPER LEVELS OF FRATERNITY ARE MOSTLY BULK INDUSTRIAL FRAMES. THE SJS IS TRYING TO CORDON THEM OFF USING AGILE CYBERNETIK DEVICES--CATTS, SPYDERS, THAT KIND OF THING.
"CATTS WERE ORIGINALLY SPEC-ED FOR JUNGLE OPERATIONS IN CUIDAD BARRANQUILLA. USUALLY, THEY OWN ANY 3D COMBAT ENVIRONMENT.

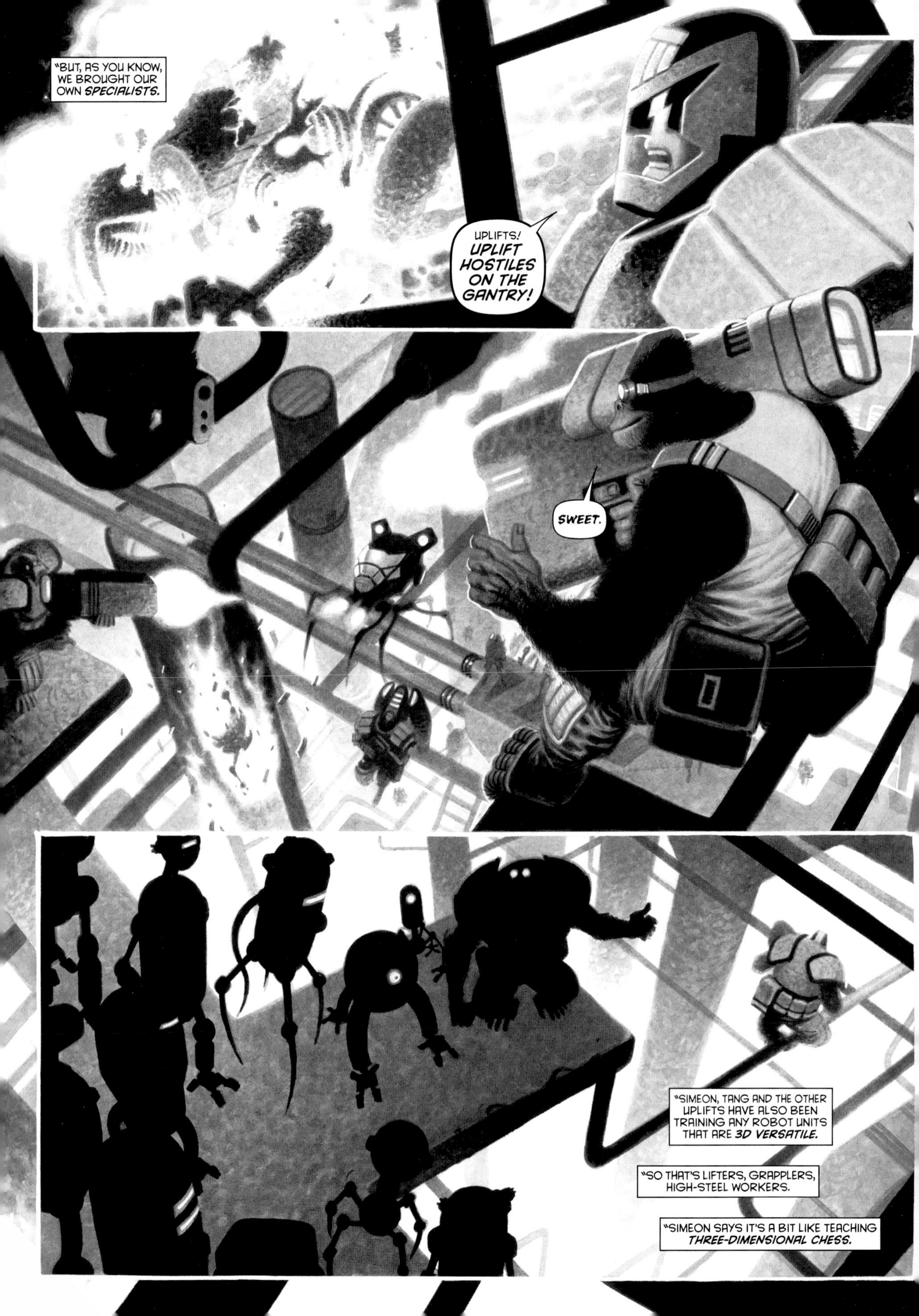
"BUT, AS YOU KNOW, WE BROUGHT OUR OWN SPECIALISTS.
UPLIFTS! UPLIFT HOSTILES ON THE GANTRY!
SWEET.
"SIMEON, TANG AND THE OTHER UPLIFTS HAVE ALSO BEEN TRAINING ANY ROBOT UNITS THAT ARE 3D VERSATILE.
"SO THAT'S LIFTERS, GRAPPLERS, HIGH-STEEL WORKERS.
"SIMEON SAYS IT'S A BIT LIKE TEACHING THREE-DIMENSIONAL CHESS.

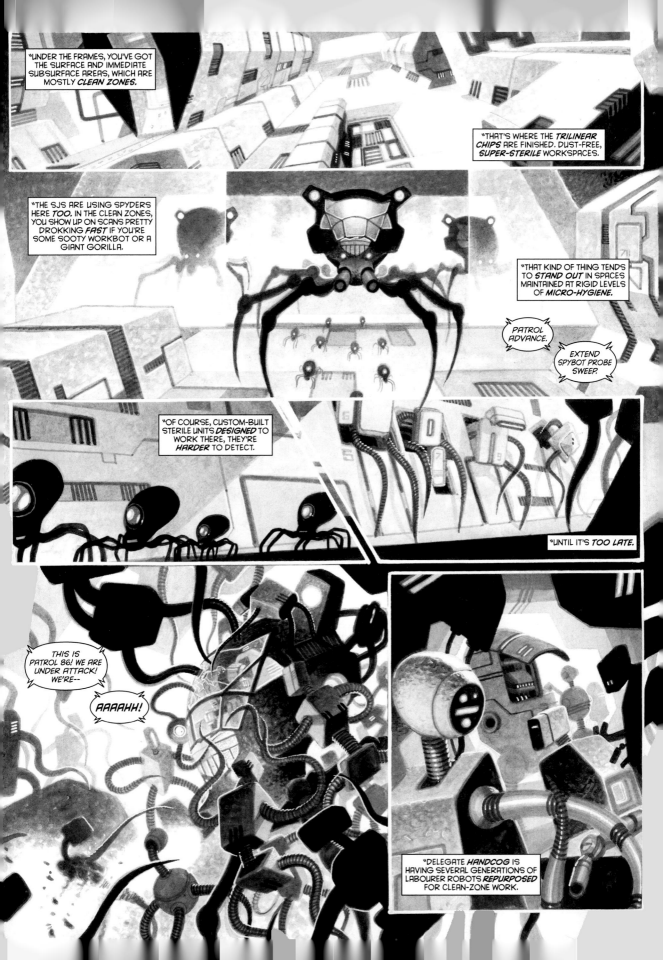

"UNDER THE FRAMES, YOU'VE GOT THE SURFACE AND IMMEDIATE SUBSURFACE AREAS, WHICH ARE MOSTLY *CLEAN ZONES*.

"THAT'S WHERE THE *TRILINEAR CHIPS* ARE FINISHED. DUST-FREE, *SUPER-STERILE* WORKSPACES.

"THE SJS ARE USING SPYDERS HERE *TOO*. IN THE CLEAN ZONES, YOU SHOW UP ON SCANS PRETTY DROKKING *FAST* IF YOU'RE SOME SOOTY WORKBOT OR A GIANT GORILLA.

"THAT KIND OF THING TENDS TO *STAND OUT* IN SPACES MAINTAINED AT RIGID LEVELS OF *MICRO-HYGIENE*.

PATROL ADVANCE.

EXTEND SPYBOT PROBE SWEEP.

"OF COURSE, CUSTOM-BUILT STERILE UNITS *DESIGNED* TO WORK THERE, THEY'RE *HARDER* TO DETECT.

"UNTIL IT'S *TOO LATE*.

THIS IS PATROL 86! WE ARE UNDER ATTACK! WE'RE--

AAAAHH!

"DELEGATE *HANDCOG* IS HAVING SEVERAL GENERATIONS OF LABOURER ROBOTS *REPURPOSED* FOR CLEAN-ZONE WORK.

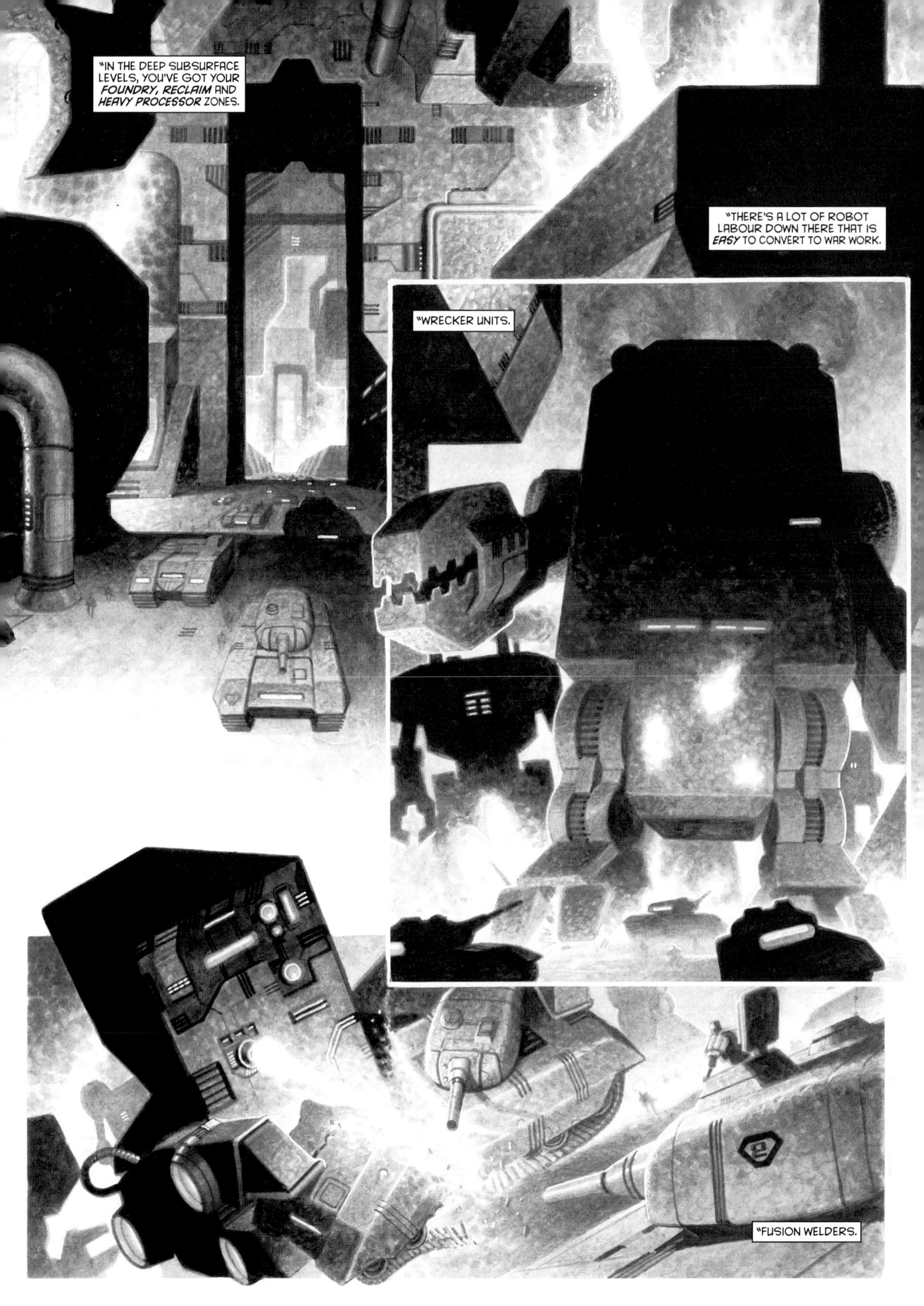
"IN THE DEEP SUBSURFACE LEVELS, YOU'VE GOT YOUR *FOUNDRY, RECLAIM* AND *HEAVY PROCESSOR* ZONES.
"THERE'S A LOT OF ROBOT LABOUR DOWN THERE THAT IS *EASY* TO CONVERT TO WAR WORK.
"WRECKER UNITS.
"FUSION WELDERS.

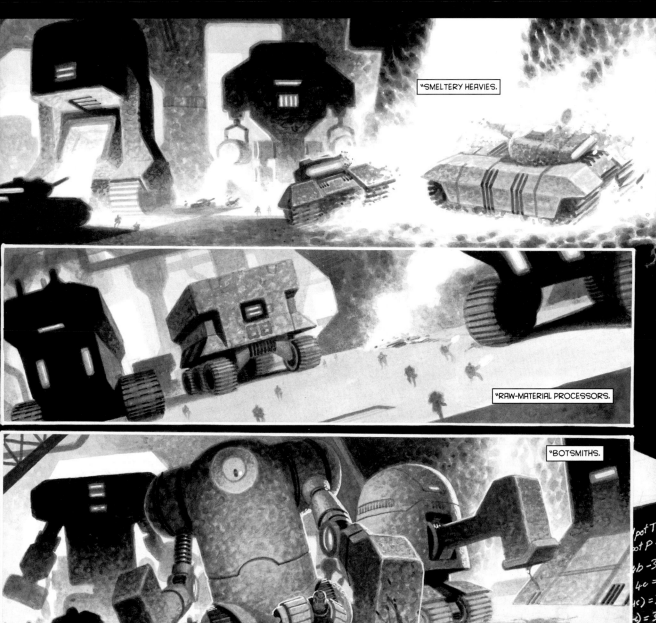

"SMELTERY HEAVIES.
"RAW-MATERIAL PROCESSORS.
"BOTSMITHS.
a^2 - b^2 = b(a-b)
(a+b)(a-b) = b(a-b)
a+b = b
a = 0
c://dos
c://dos.run
run.dos.run
"FUNX IS SHARING ALL THE TACTICS WE LEARNED ON LIBERTY WITH THE ROBOT WORKERS.

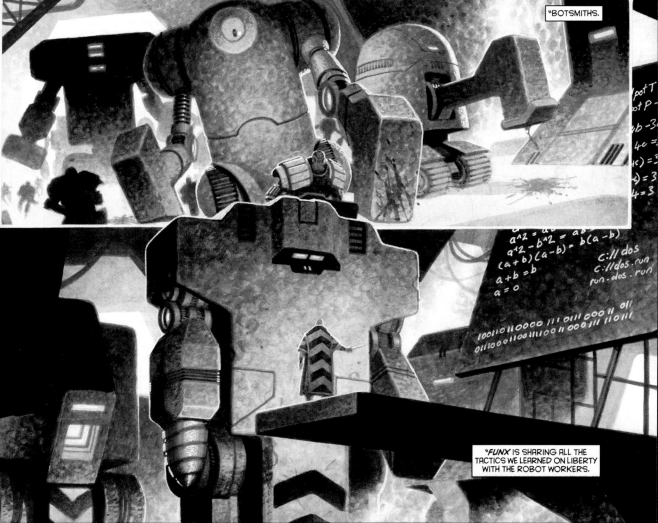

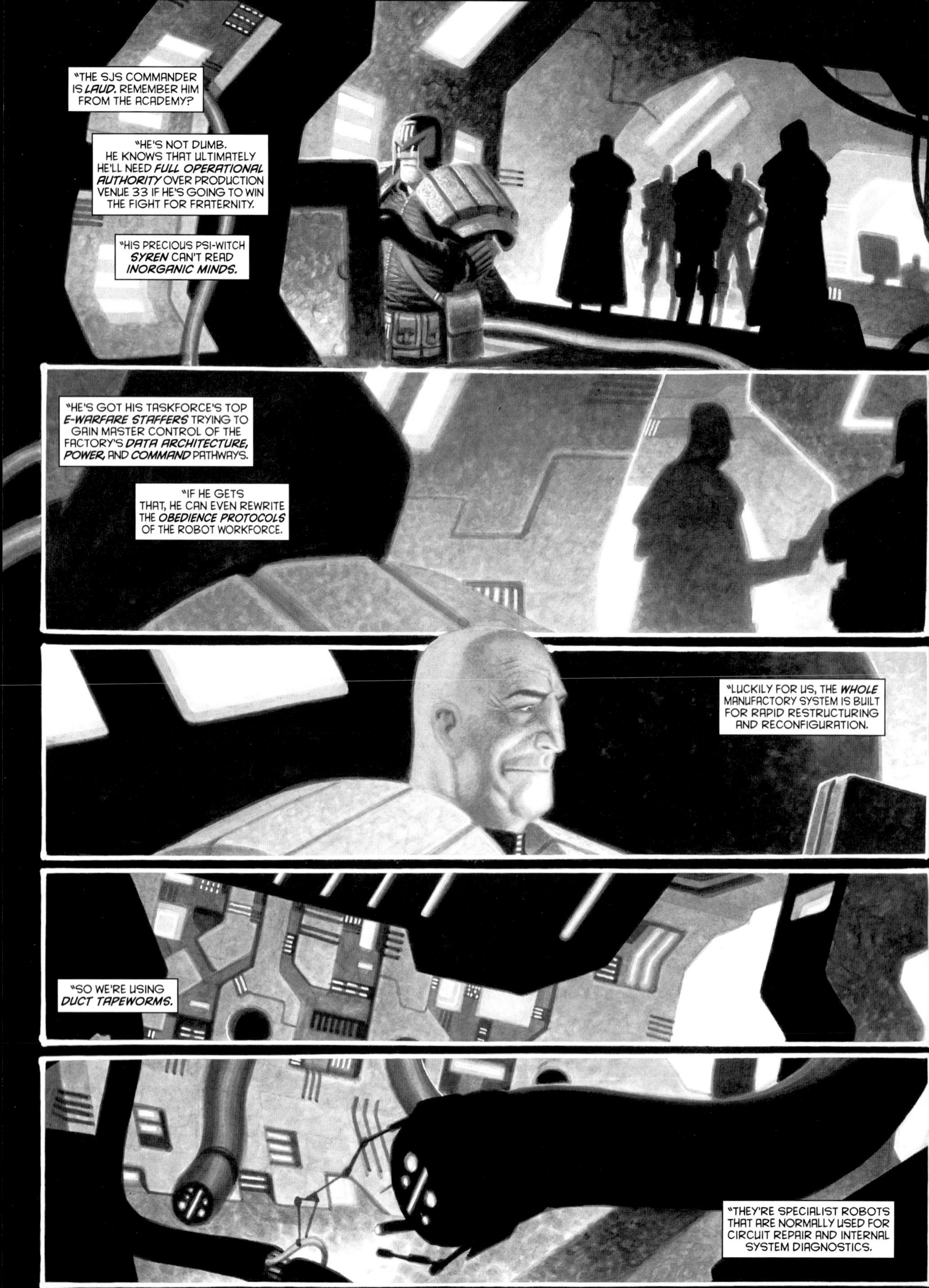
"THE SJS COMMANDER IS LAUD. REMEMBER HIM FROM THE ACADEMY?
"HE'S NOT DUMB. HE KNOWS THAT ULTIMATELY HE'LL NEED FULL OPERATIONAL AUTHORITY OVER PRODUCTION VENUE 33 IF HE'S GOING TO WIN THE FIGHT FOR FRATERNITY.
"HIS PRECIOUS PSI-WITCH SYREN CAN'T READ INORGANIC MINDS.
"HE'S GOT HIS TASKFORCE'S TOP E-WARFARE STAFFERS TRYING TO GAIN MASTER CONTROL OF THE FACTORY'S DATA ARCHITECTURE, POWER, AND COMMAND PATHWAYS.
"IF HE GETS THAT, HE CAN EVEN REWRITE THE OBEDIENCE PROTOCOLS OF THE ROBOT WORKFORCE.
"LUCKILY FOR US, THE WHOLE MANUFACTORY SYSTEM IS BUILT FOR RAPID RESTRUCTURING AND RECONFIGURATION.
"SO WE'RE USING DUCT TAPEWORMS.
"THEY'RE SPECIALIST ROBOTS THAT ARE NORMALLY USED FOR CIRCUIT REPAIR AND INTERNAL SYSTEM DIAGNOSTICS.

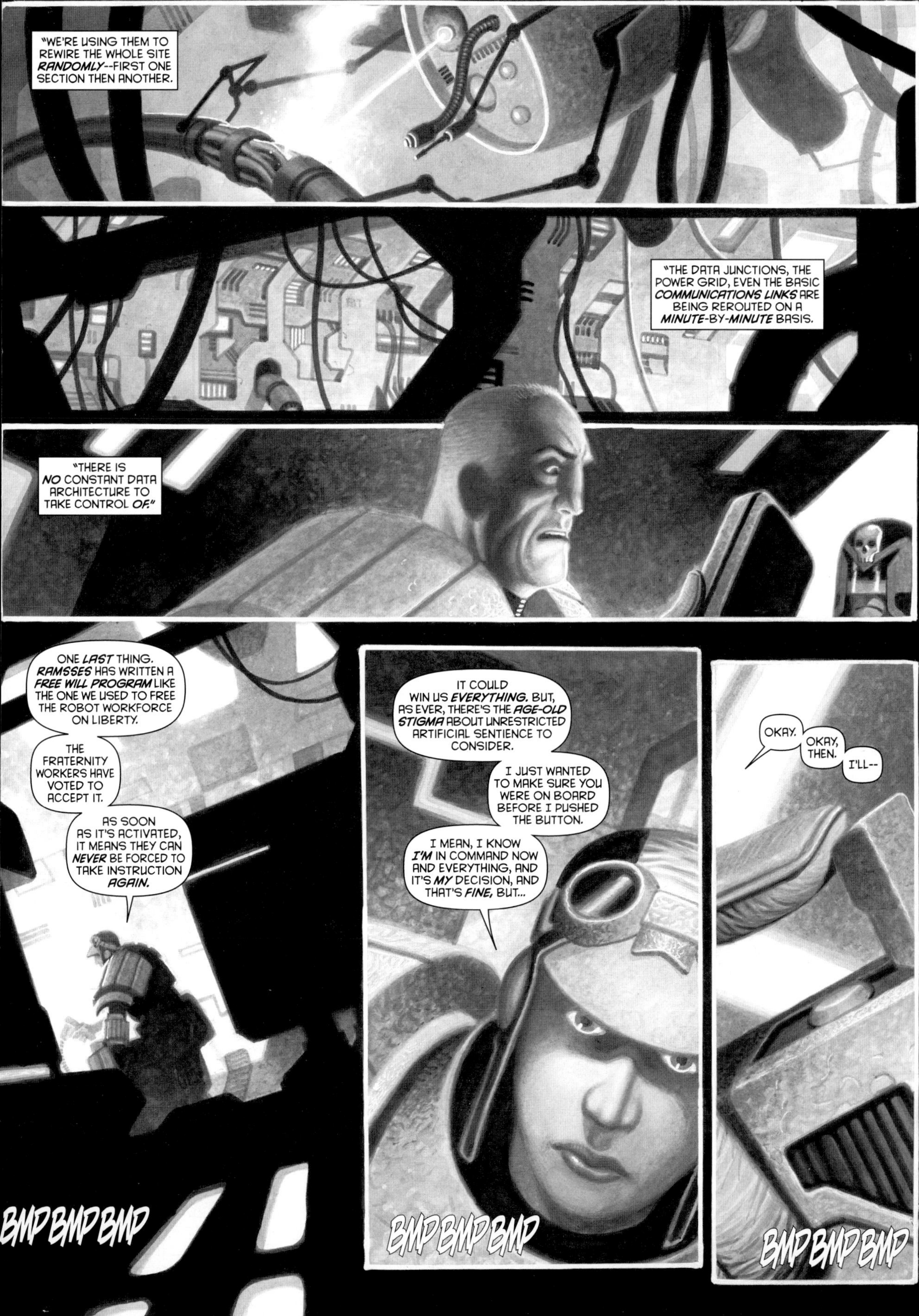
"WE'RE USING THEM TO REWIRE THE WHOLE SITE *RANDOMLY*--FIRST ONE SECTION THEN ANOTHER.
"THE DATA JUNCTIONS, THE POWER GRID, EVEN THE BASIC *COMMUNICATIONS LINKS* ARE BEING REROUTED ON A *MINUTE*-BY-*MINUTE* BASIS.
"THERE IS *NO* CONSTANT DATA ARCHITECTURE TO TAKE CONTROL *OF.*"
ONE *LAST* THING. *RAMSSES* HAS WRITTEN A *FREE WILL PROGRAM* LIKE THE ONE WE USED TO FREE THE ROBOT WORKFORCE ON LIBERTY.
THE FRATERNITY WORKERS HAVE VOTED TO ACCEPT IT.
AS SOON AS IT'S ACTIVATED, IT MEANS THEY CAN *NEVER* BE FORCED TO TAKE INSTRUCTION *AGAIN.*
BMP BMP BMP
IT COULD WIN US *EVERYTHING.* BUT, AS EVER, THERE'S THE *AGE-OLD STIGMA* ABOUT UNRESTRICTED ARTIFICIAL SENTIENCE TO CONSIDER.
I JUST WANTED TO MAKE SURE YOU WERE ON BOARD BEFORE I PUSHED THE BUTTON.
I MEAN, I KNOW *I'M* IN COMMAND NOW AND EVERYTHING, AND IT'S *MY* DECISION, AND THAT'S *FINE,* BUT...
BMP BMP BMP
OKAY.
OKAY, THEN.
I'LL--
BMP BMP BMP

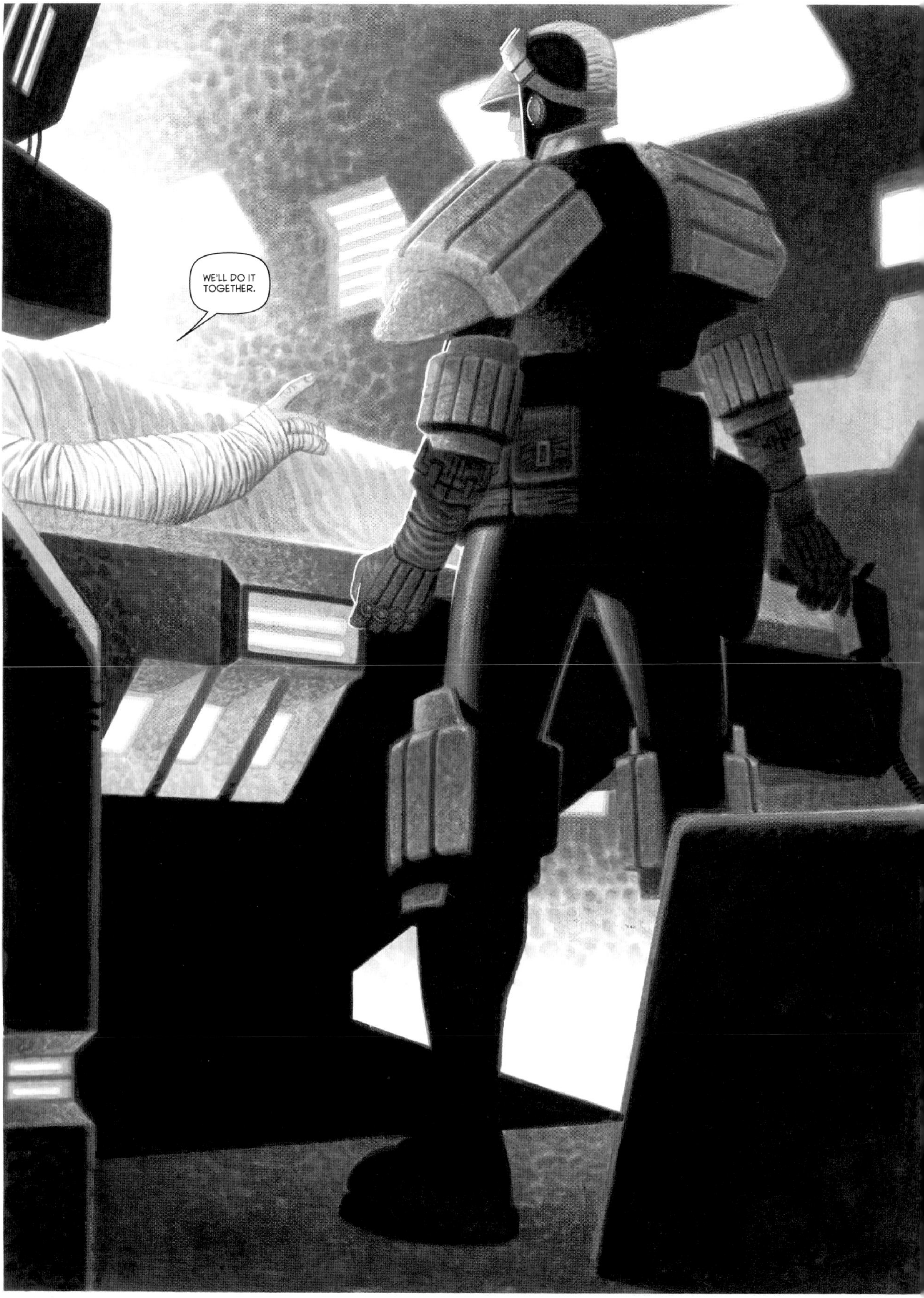
WE'LL DO IT TOGETHER.

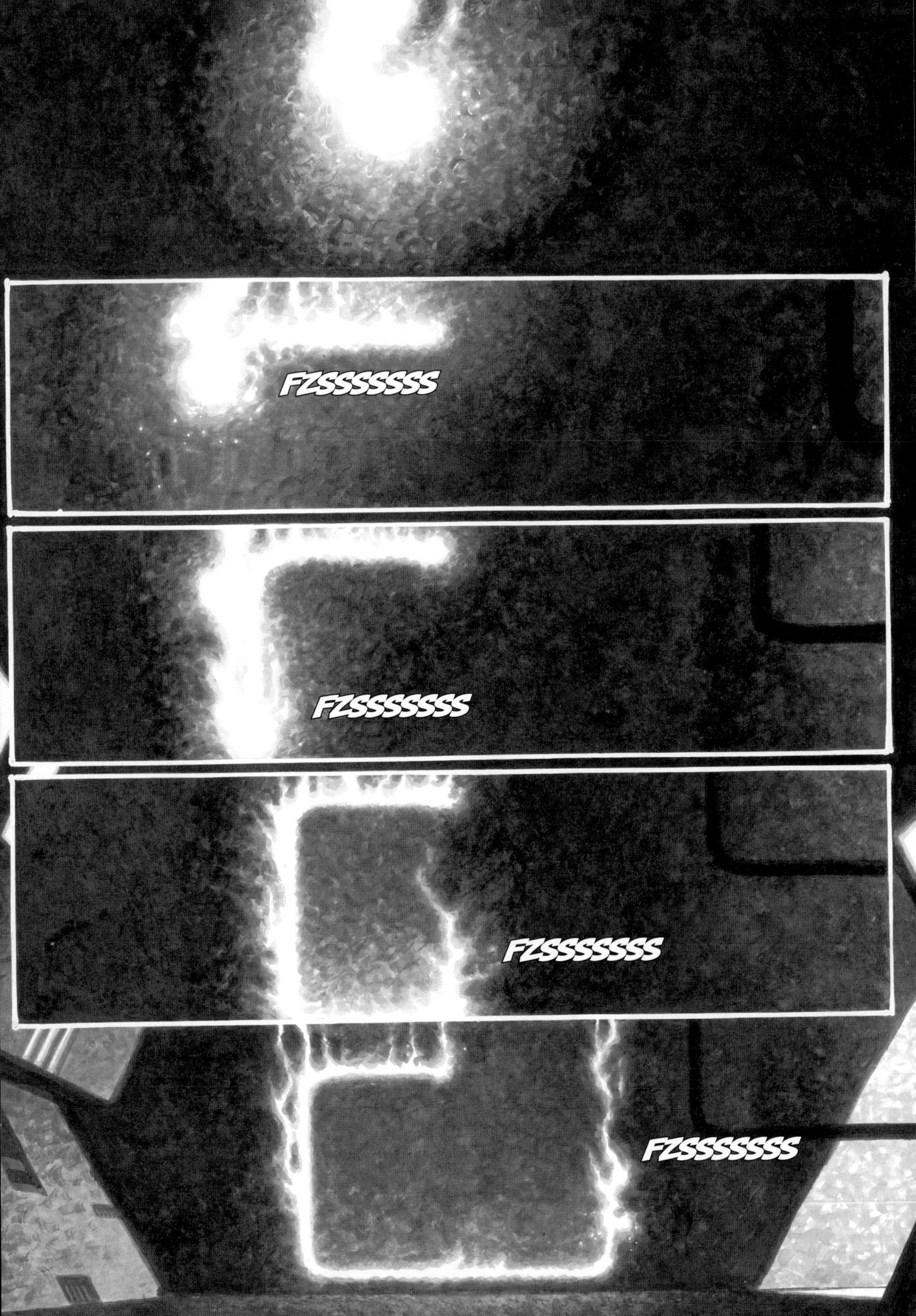
FZSSSSSSS
FZSSSSSSS
FZSSSSSSS
FZSSSSSSS

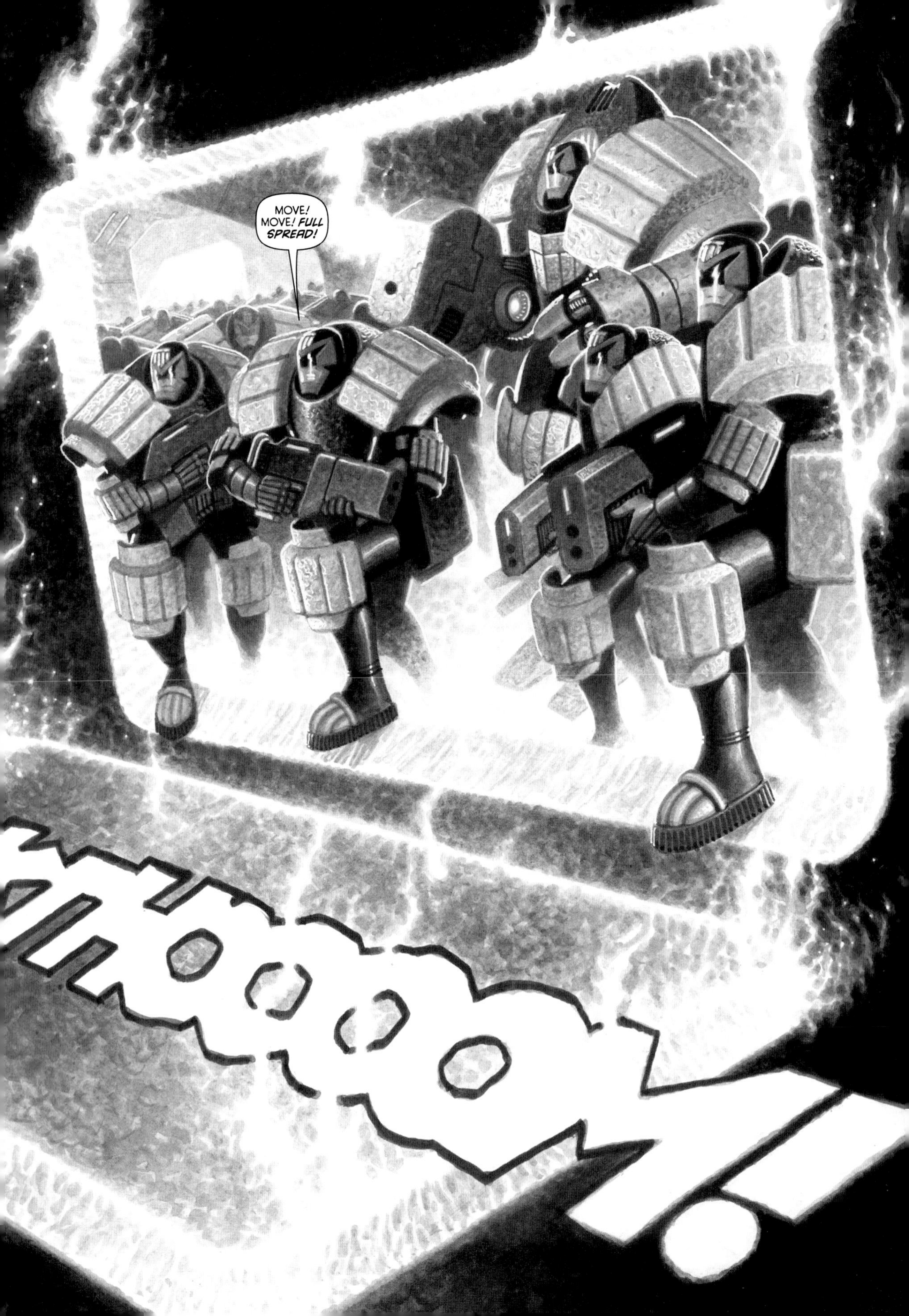
MOVE! MOVE! FULL SPREAD!

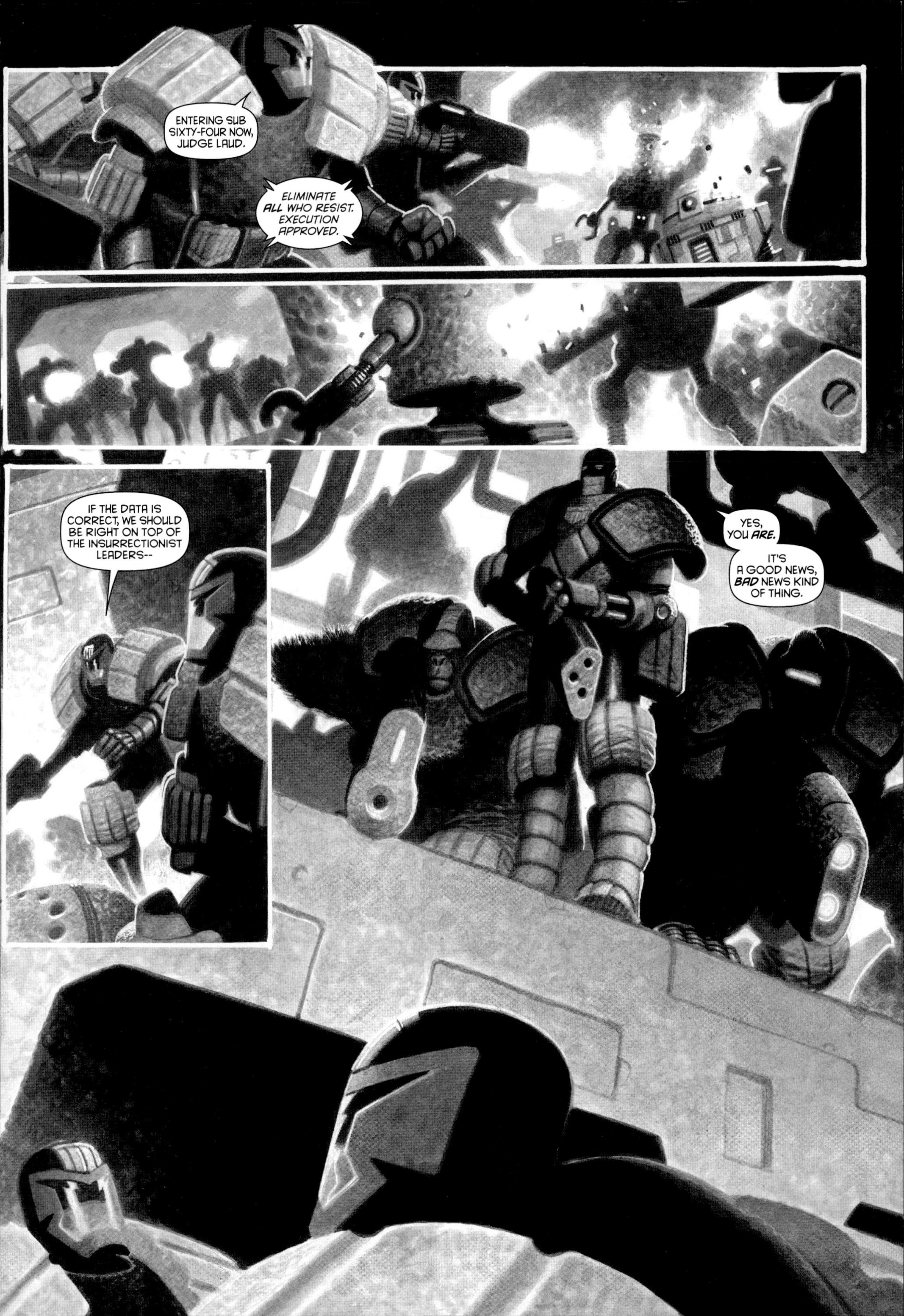
ENTERING SUB SIXTY-FOUR NOW, JUDGE LAUD.
ELIMINATE **ALL** WHO RESIST. EXECUTION APPROVED.
IF THE DATA IS CORRECT, WE SHOULD BE RIGHT ON TOP OF THE INSURRECTIONIST LEADERS--
YES, YOU **ARE.**
IT'S A GOOD NEWS, **BAD** NEWS KIND OF THING.

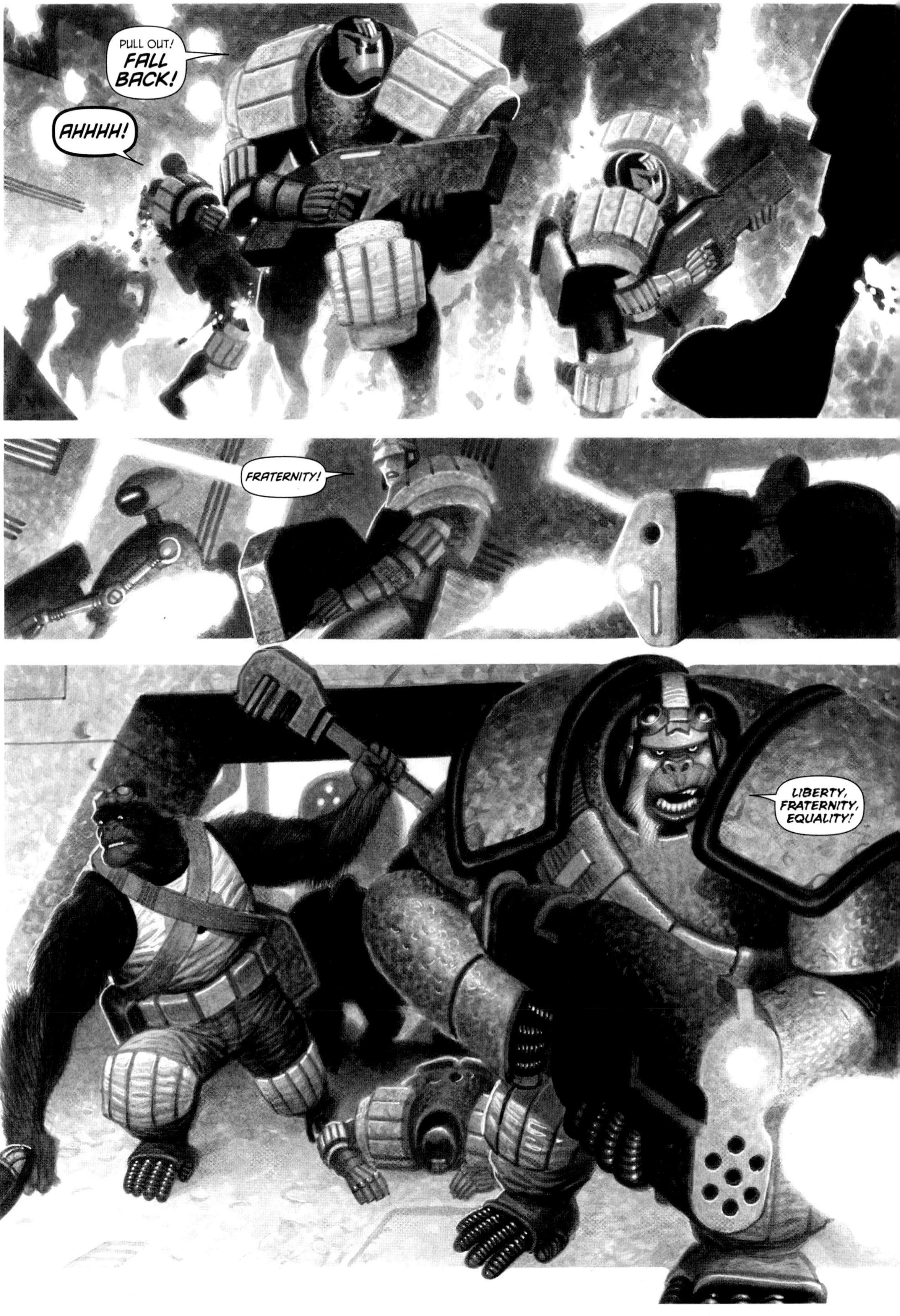
PULL OUT! FALL BACK!
AHHHH!
FRATERNITY!
LIBERTY, FRATERNITY, EQUALITY!

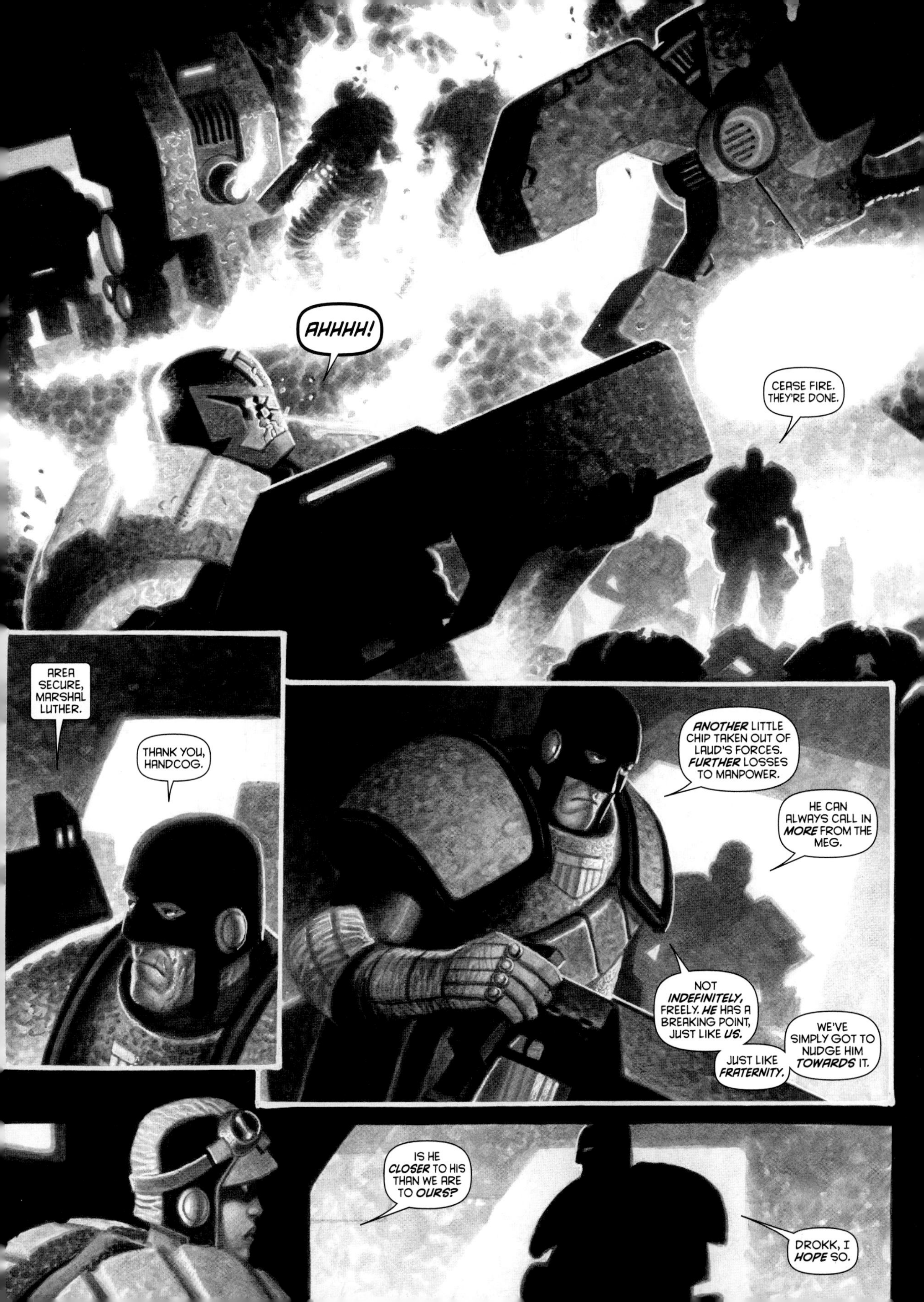
AHHHH!
CEASE FIRE. THEY'RE DONE.
AREA SECURE, MARSHAL LUTHER.
THANK YOU, HANDCOG.
ANOTHER LITTLE CHIP TAKEN OUT OF LAUD'S FORCES. FURTHER LOSSES TO MANPOWER.
HE CAN ALWAYS CALL IN MORE FROM THE MEG.
NOT INDEFINITELY, FREELY. HE HAS A BREAKING POINT, JUST LIKE US.
JUST LIKE FRATERNITY.
WE'VE SIMPLY GOT TO NUDGE HIM TOWARDS IT.
IS HE CLOSER TO HIS THAN WE ARE TO OURS?
DROKK, I HOPE SO.

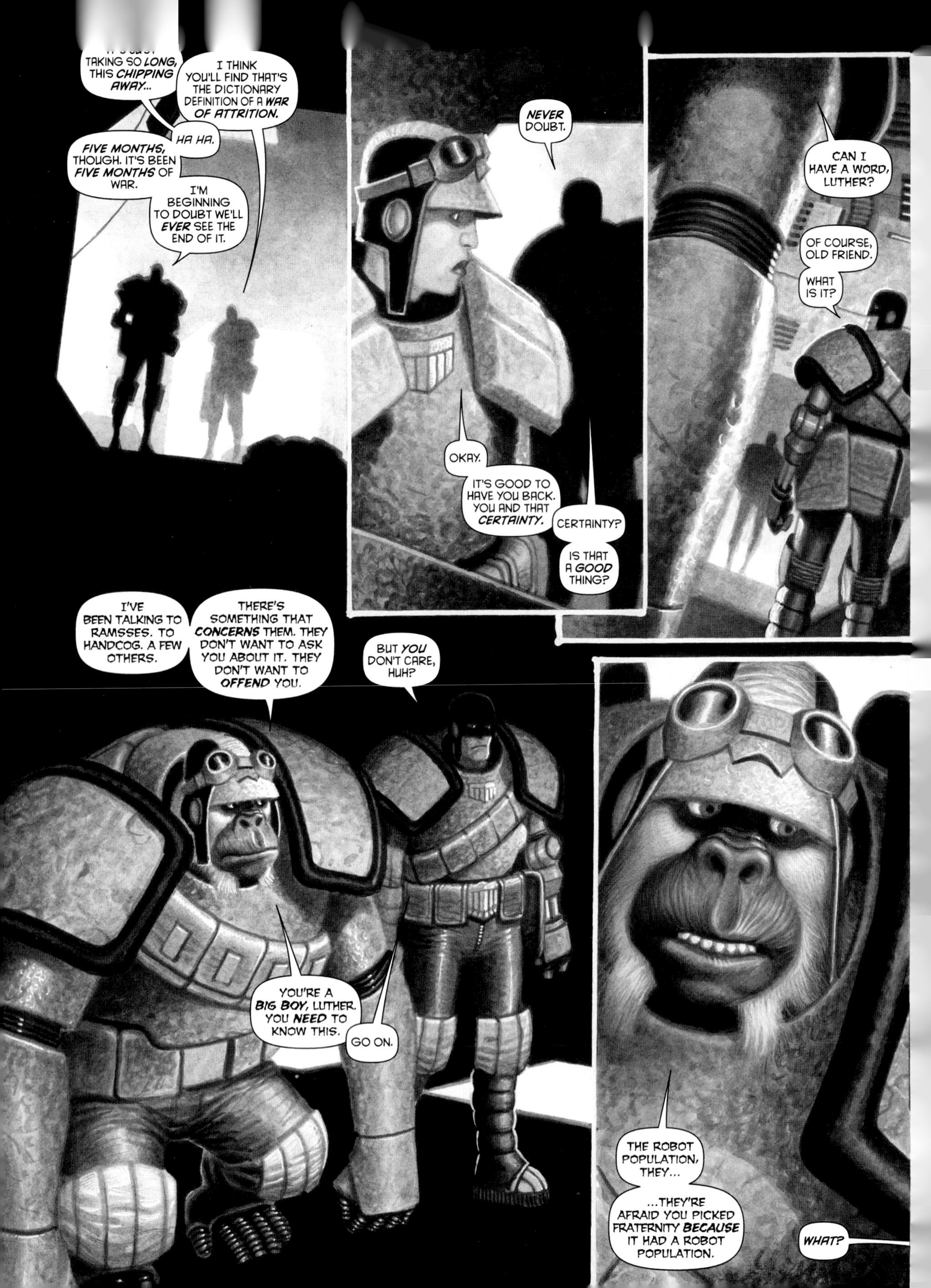
TAKING SO LONG, THIS CHIPPING AWAY...
I THINK YOU'LL FIND THAT'S THE DICTIONARY DEFINITION OF A WAR OF ATTRITION.
HA HA.
FIVE MONTHS, THOUGH. IT'S BEEN FIVE MONTHS OF WAR.
I'M BEGINNING TO DOUBT WE'LL EVER SEE THE END OF IT.
NEVER DOUBT.
OKAY.
IT'S GOOD TO HAVE YOU BACK. YOU AND THAT CERTAINTY.
CERTAINTY?
IS THAT A GOOD THING?
CAN I HAVE A WORD, LUTHER?
OF COURSE, OLD FRIEND.
WHAT IS IT?
I'VE BEEN TALKING TO RAMSSES. TO HANDCOG. A FEW OTHERS.
THERE'S SOMETHING THAT CONCERNS THEM. THEY DON'T WANT TO ASK YOU ABOUT IT. THEY DON'T WANT TO OFFEND YOU.
BUT YOU DON'T CARE, HUH?
YOU'RE A BIG BOY, LUTHER. YOU NEED TO KNOW THIS.
GO ON.
THE ROBOT POPULATION, THEY...
...THEY'RE AFRAID YOU PICKED FRATERNITY BECAUSE IT HAD A ROBOT POPULATION.
WHAT?

THEY THINK YOU'VE CHOSEN *THIS* WORLD TO MAKE A STAND AGAINST THE JUDGES BECAUSE THERE'S VIRTUALLY *ZERO HUMAN LIFE* HERE TO LOSE.

LOSSES WILL BE ALL *ROBOT FORMS.* ROBOTS ARE *EXPENDABLE.*

I KNOW.

YOU *KNOW* I DON'T THINK THAT!

IT'S HARD TO *HELP* IT, ISN'T IT?

I MEAN, ENTIRELY? ORGANICS LIKE US, NO MATTER *HOW* MUCH COMRADESHIP WE HAVE WITH THE BOTS, THEY'LL *NEVER* BE ALIVE THE SAME WAY, *WILL* THEY?

GRUD'S *SAKE,* SIMEON--

I KNOW! *I KNOW!*

I JUST NEEDED YOU TO *THINK* ABOUT THIS. I WAS PRETTY SURE YOU ALREADY *HAD.*

THERE *ARE* LIVES TO LOSE HERE. JUST NOT LIVES AS *WE* KNOW THEM.

THIS *ISN'T* A GAME. AN EXERCISE. A *RISK-FREE* WAY OF MAKING A *POINT.*

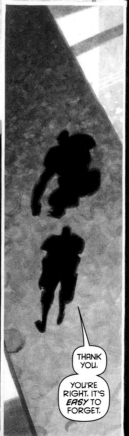

THANK YOU.

YOU'RE RIGHT. IT'S *EASY* TO FORGET.

DO THEY *REALLY* THINK I'M THAT PREJUDICED?

DO THEY *REALLY* BELIEVE I THINK THAT *LITTLE* OF THEM?

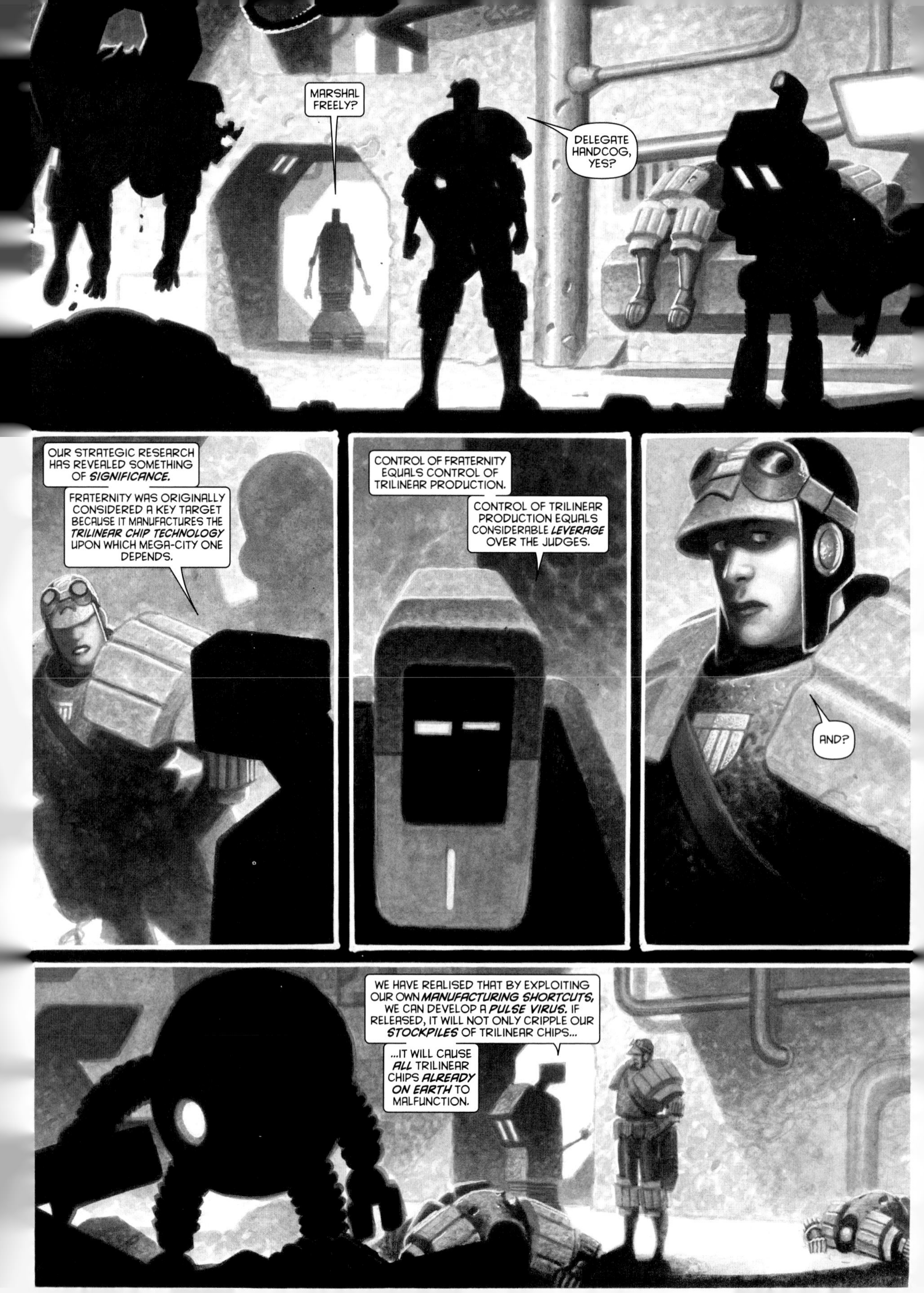
MARSHAL FREELY?
DELEGATE HANDCOG, YES?
OUR STRATEGIC RESEARCH HAS REVEALED SOMETHING OF ***SIGNIFICANCE.***
FRATERNITY WAS ORIGINALLY CONSIDERED A KEY TARGET BECAUSE IT MANUFACTURES THE ***TRILINEAR CHIP TECHNOLOGY*** UPON WHICH MEGA-CITY ONE DEPENDS.
CONTROL OF FRATERNITY EQUALS CONTROL OF TRILINEAR PRODUCTION.
CONTROL OF TRILINEAR PRODUCTION EQUALS CONSIDERABLE ***LEVERAGE*** OVER THE JUDGES.
AND?
WE HAVE REALISED THAT BY EXPLOITING OUR OWN ***MANUFACTURING SHORTCUTS,*** WE CAN DEVELOP A ***PULSE VIRUS.*** IF RELEASED, IT WILL NOT ONLY CRIPPLE OUR ***STOCKPILES*** OF TRILINEAR CHIPS...
...IT WILL CAUSE ***ALL*** TRILINEAR CHIPS ***ALREADY ON EARTH*** TO MALFUNCTION.

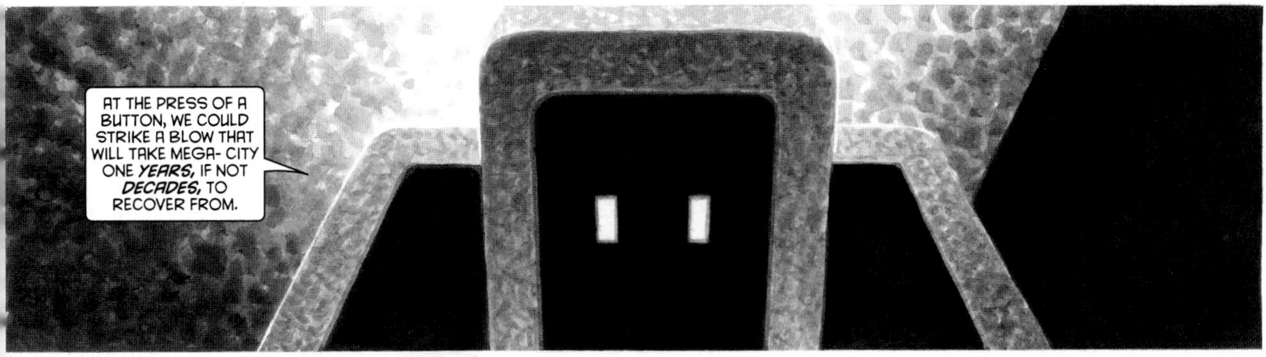
AT THE PRESS OF A BUTTON, WE COULD STRIKE A BLOW THAT WILL TAKE MEGA- CITY ONE *YEARS,* IF NOT *DECADES,* TO RECOVER FROM.

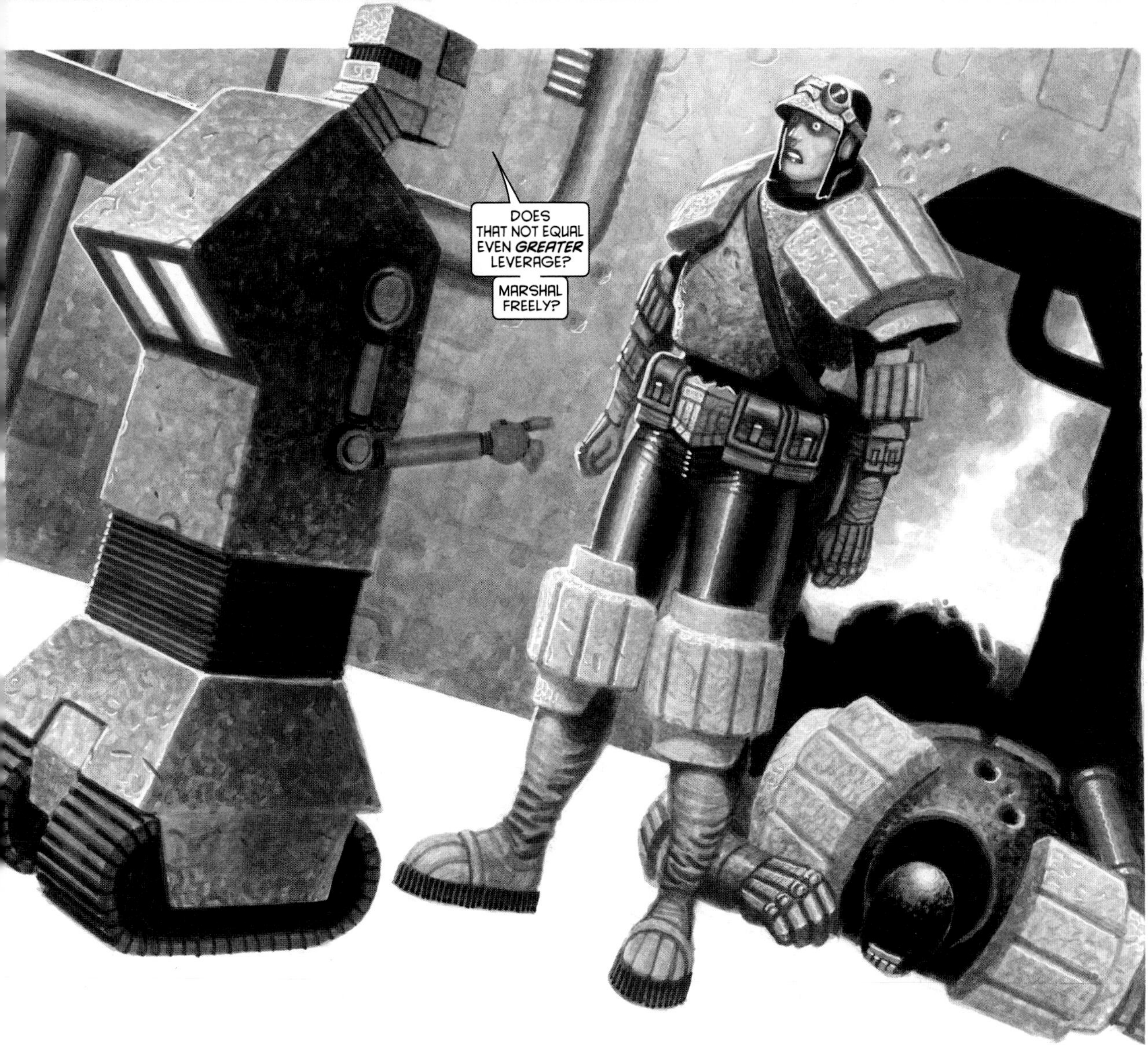
DOES THAT NOT EQUAL EVEN *GREATER* LEVERAGE?
MARSHAL FREELY?

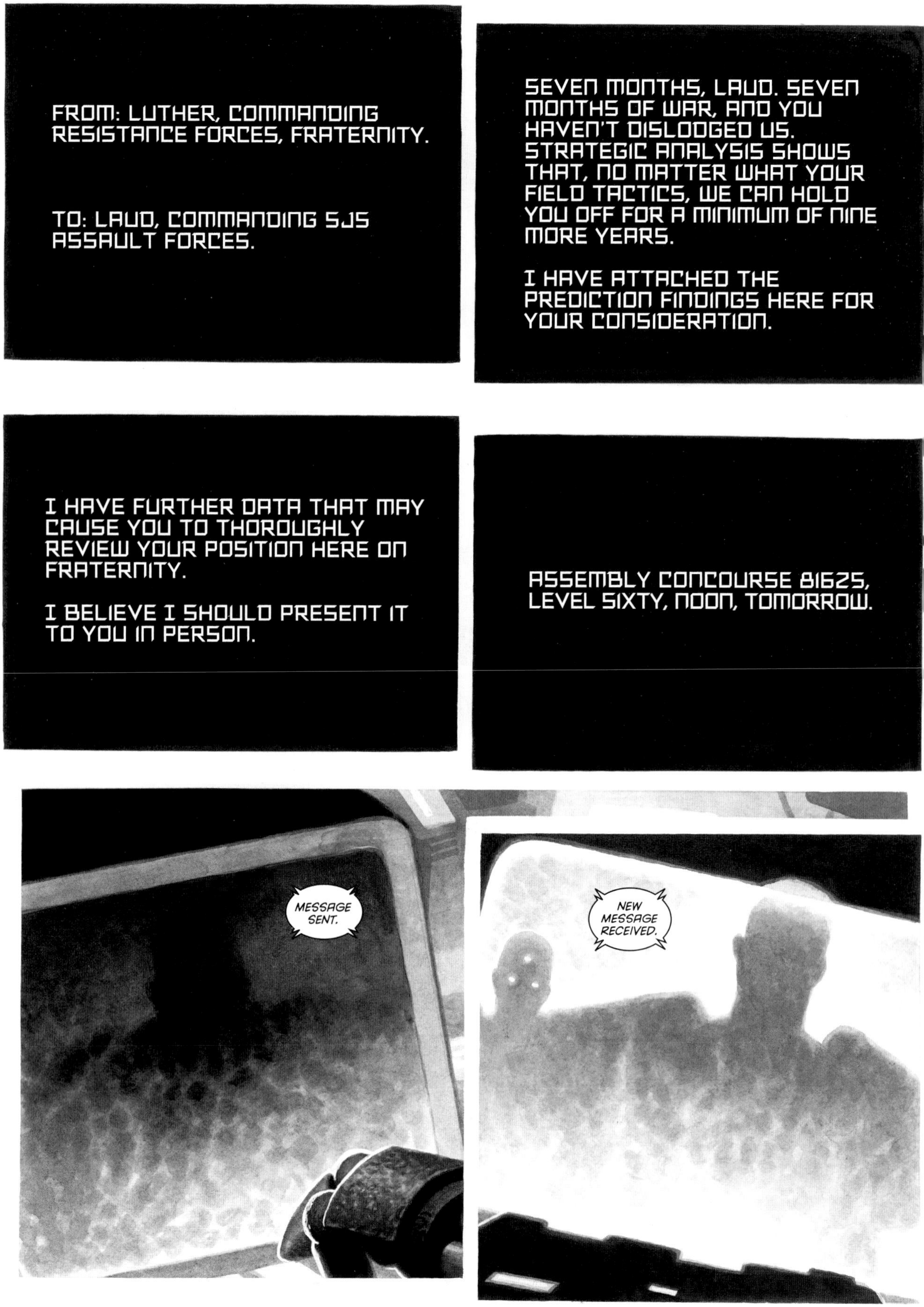
FROM: LUTHER, COMMANDING RESISTANCE FORCES, FRATERNITY.
TO: LAUD, COMMANDING SJS ASSAULT FORCES.
SEVEN MONTHS, LAUD. SEVEN MONTHS OF WAR, AND YOU HAVEN'T DISLODGED US. STRATEGIC ANALYSIS SHOWS THAT, NO MATTER WHAT YOUR FIELD TACTICS, WE CAN HOLD YOU OFF FOR A MINIMUM OF NINE MORE YEARS.
I HAVE ATTACHED THE PREDICTION FINDINGS HERE FOR YOUR CONSIDERATION.
I HAVE FURTHER DATA THAT MAY CAUSE YOU TO THOROUGHLY REVIEW YOUR POSITION HERE ON FRATERNITY.
I BELIEVE I SHOULD PRESENT IT TO YOU IN PERSON.
ASSEMBLY CONCOURSE 81625, LEVEL SIXTY, NOON, TOMORROW.
MESSAGE SENT.
NEW MESSAGE RECEIVED.

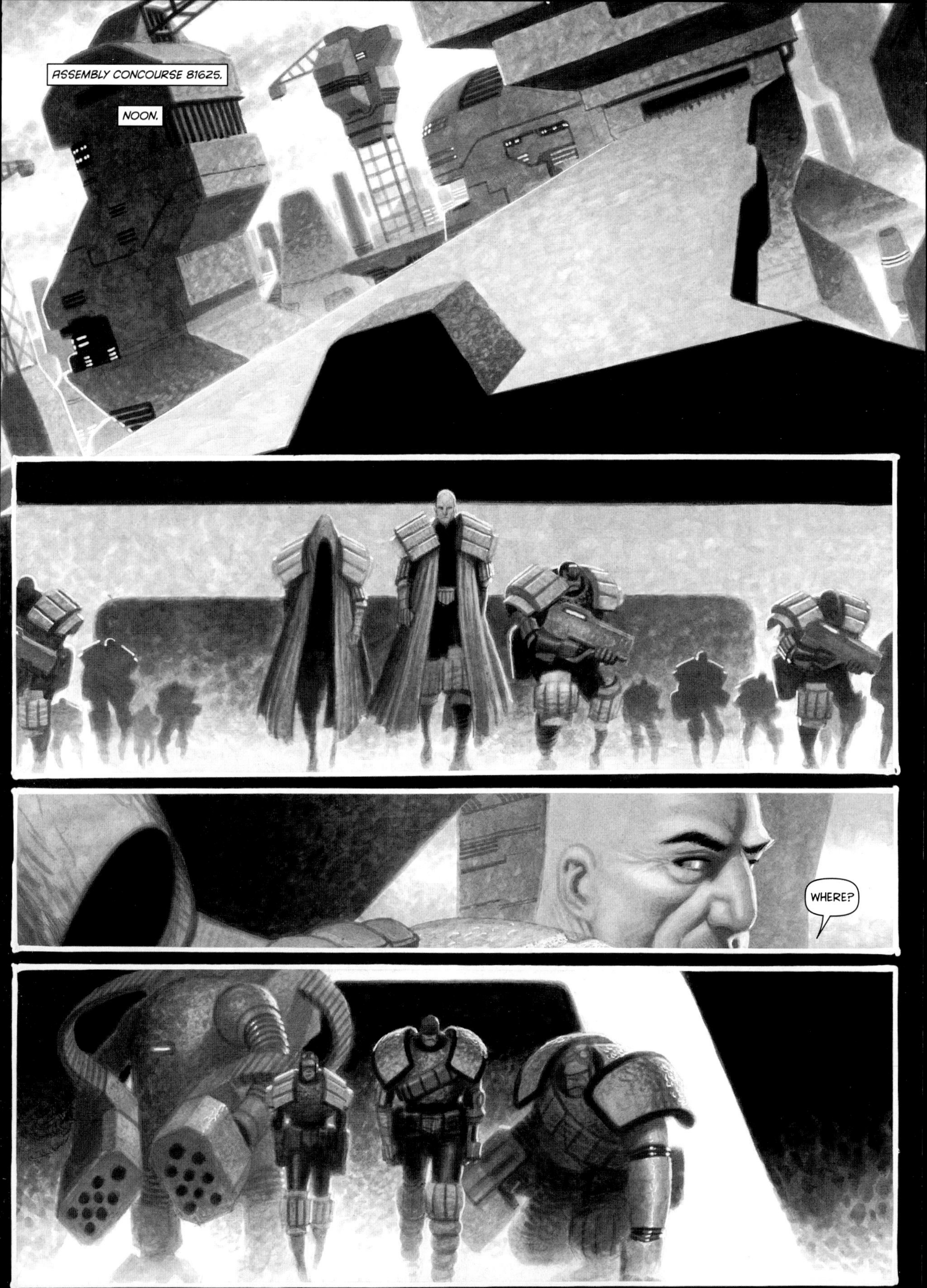
ASSEMBLY CONCOURSE 81625.
NOON.
WHERE?

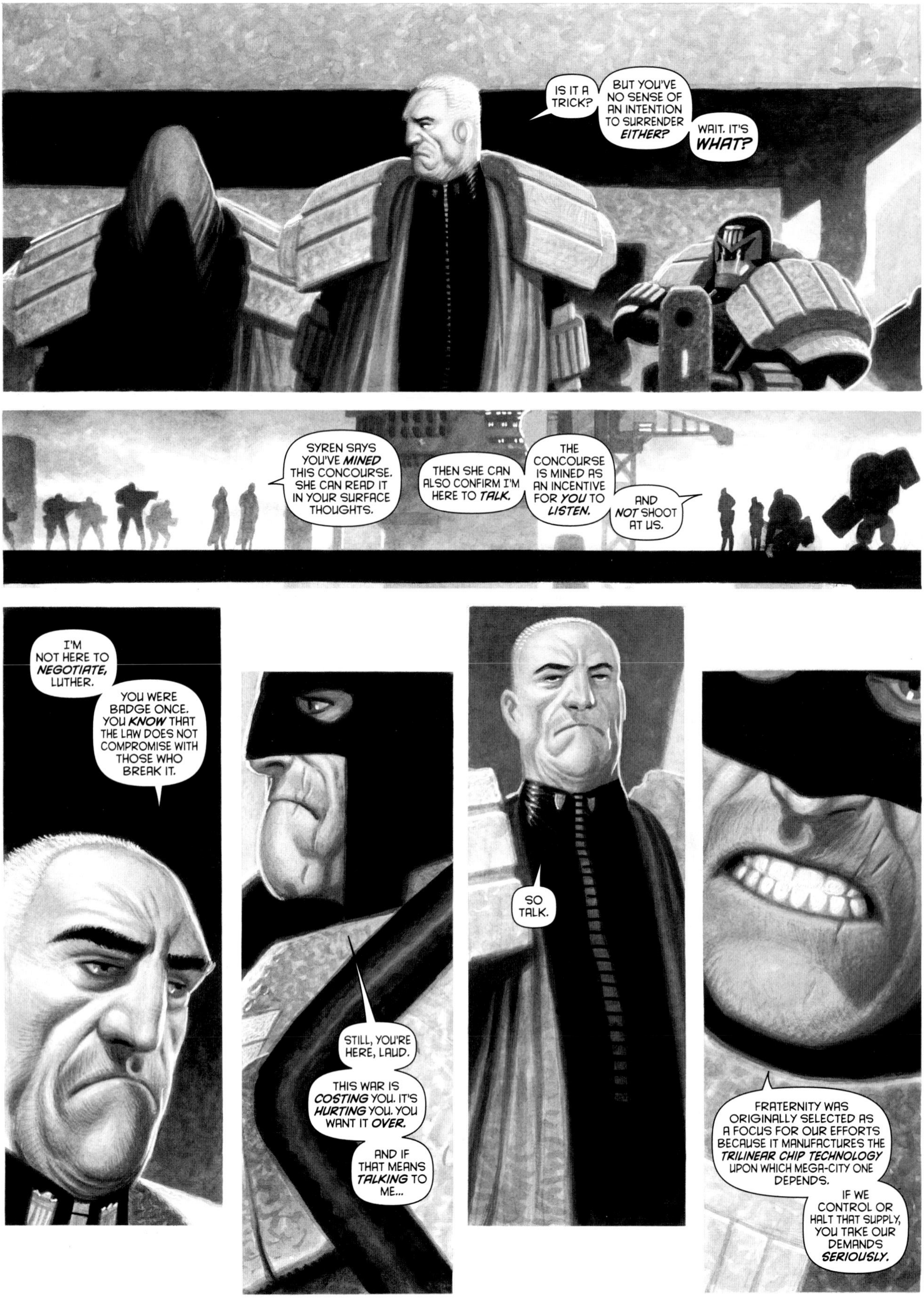

IS IT A TRICK?
BUT YOU'VE NO SENSE OF AN INTENTION TO SURRENDER EITHER?
WAIT. IT'S WHAT?
SYREN SAYS YOU'VE MINED THIS CONCOURSE. SHE CAN READ IT IN YOUR SURFACE THOUGHTS.
THEN SHE CAN ALSO CONFIRM I'M HERE TO TALK.
THE CONCOURSE IS MINED AS AN INCENTIVE FOR YOU TO LISTEN.
AND NOT SHOOT AT US.
I'M NOT HERE TO NEGOTIATE, LUTHER.
YOU WERE BADGE ONCE. YOU KNOW THAT THE LAW DOES NOT COMPROMISE WITH THOSE WHO BREAK IT.
STILL, YOU'RE HERE, LAUD.
THIS WAR IS COSTING YOU. IT'S HURTING YOU. YOU WANT IT OVER.
AND IF THAT MEANS TALKING TO ME...
SO TALK.
FRATERNITY WAS ORIGINALLY SELECTED AS A FOCUS FOR OUR EFFORTS BECAUSE IT MANUFACTURES THE TRILINEAR CHIP TECHNOLOGY UPON WHICH MEGA-CITY ONE DEPENDS.
IF WE CONTROL OR HALT THAT SUPPLY, YOU TAKE OUR DEMANDS SERIOUSLY.

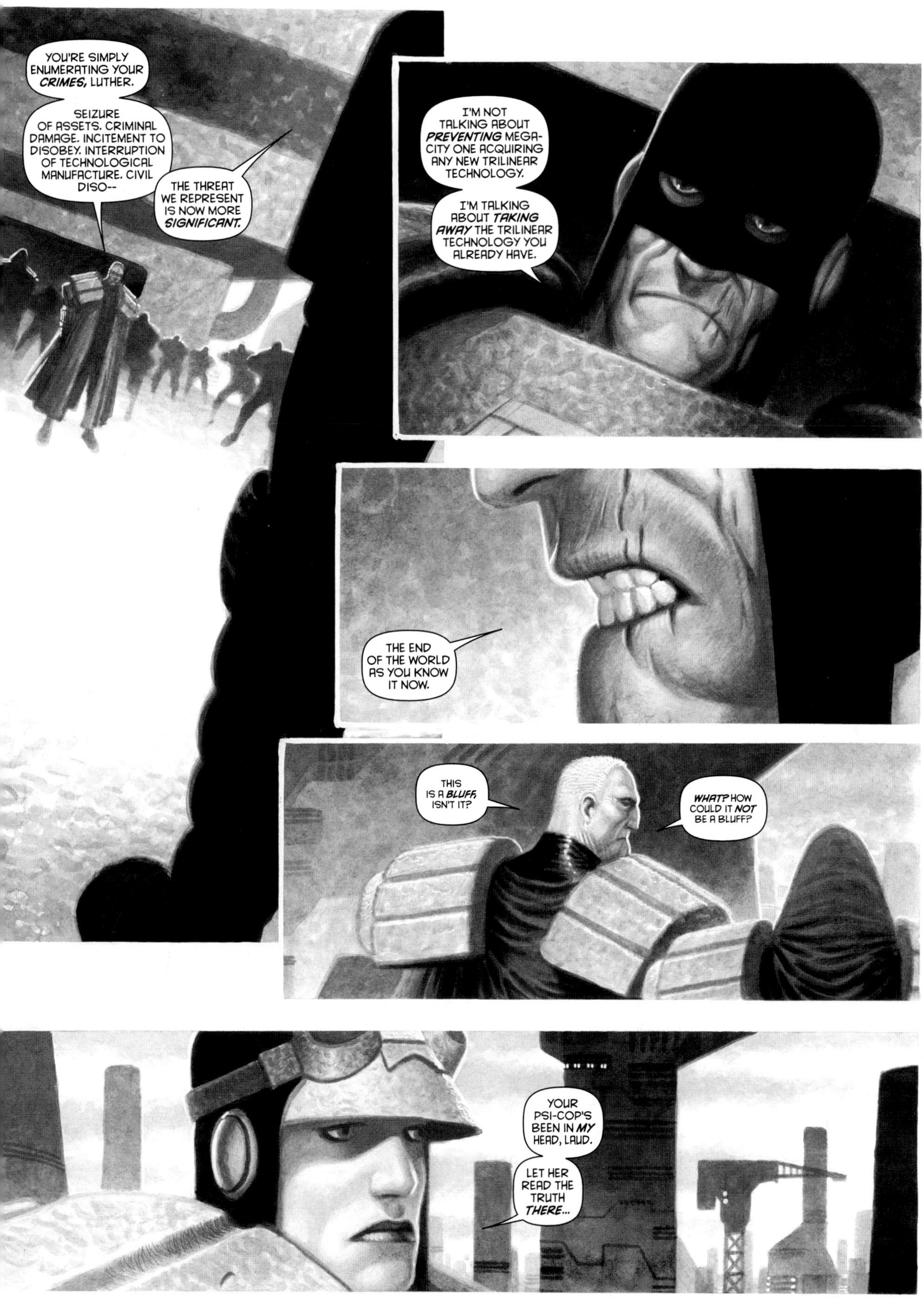
YOU'RE SIMPLY ENUMERATING YOUR *CRIMES,* LUTHER.
SEIZURE OF ASSETS. CRIMINAL DAMAGE. INCITEMENT TO DISOBEY. INTERRUPTION OF TECHNOLOGICAL MANUFACTURE. CIVIL DISO--
THE THREAT WE REPRESENT IS NOW MORE *SIGNIFICANT.*
I'M NOT TALKING ABOUT *PREVENTING* MEGA-CITY ONE ACQUIRING ANY NEW TRILINEAR TECHNOLOGY.
I'M TALKING ABOUT *TAKING AWAY* THE TRILINEAR TECHNOLOGY YOU ALREADY HAVE.
THE END OF THE WORLD AS YOU KNOW IT NOW.
THIS IS A *BLUFF,* ISN'T IT?
*WHAT?* HOW COULD IT *NOT* BE A BLUFF?
YOUR PSI-COP'S BEEN IN *MY* HEAD, LAUD.
LET HER READ THE TRUTH *THERE...*

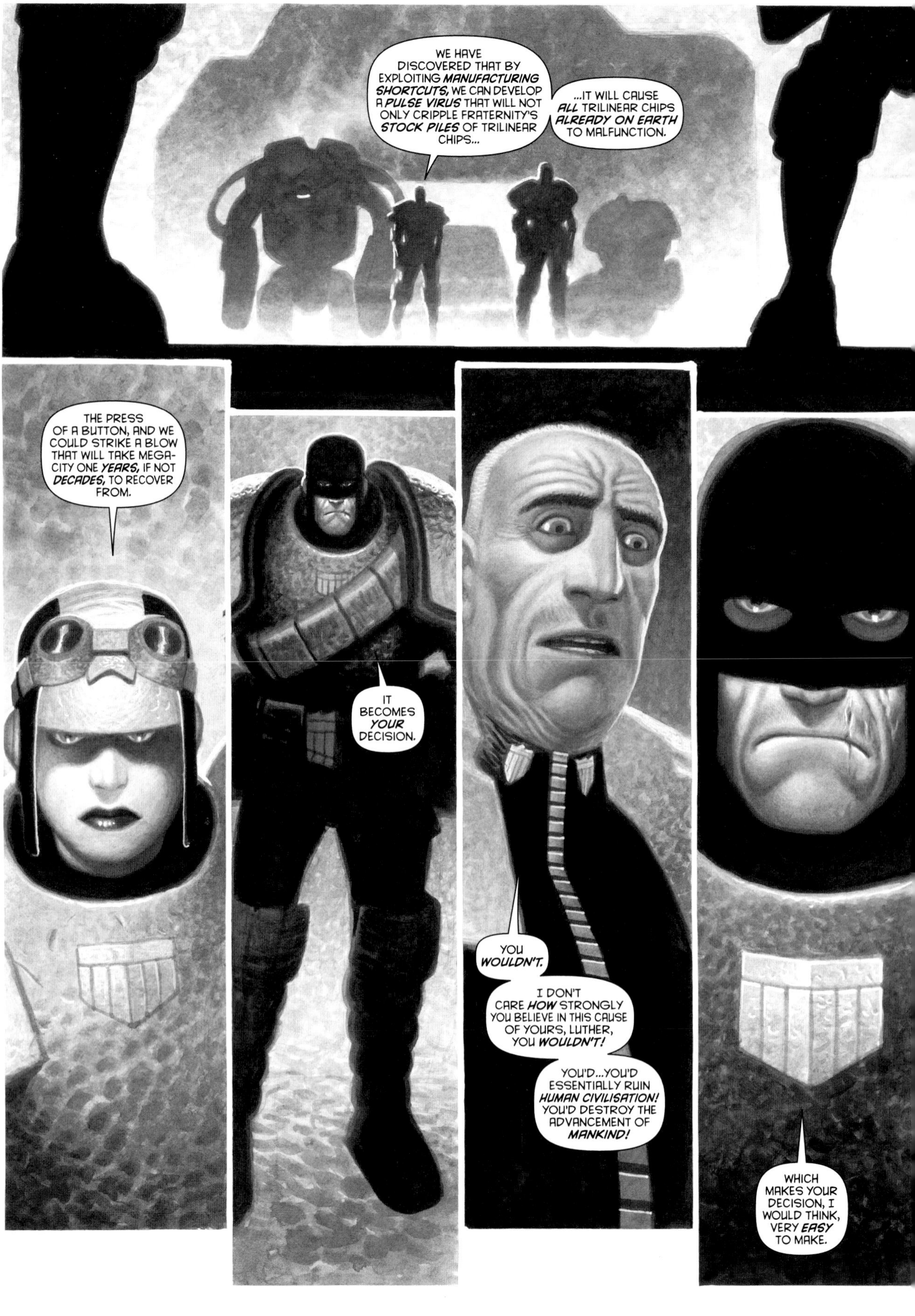

WE HAVE DISCOVERED THAT BY EXPLOITING *MANUFACTURING SHORTCUTS,* WE CAN DEVELOP A *PULSE VIRUS* THAT WILL NOT ONLY CRIPPLE FRATERNITY'S *STOCK PILES* OF TRILINEAR CHIPS...
...IT WILL CAUSE *ALL* TRILINEAR CHIPS *ALREADY ON EARTH* TO MALFUNCTION.
THE PRESS OF A BUTTON, AND WE COULD STRIKE A BLOW THAT WILL TAKE MEGA-CITY ONE *YEARS,* IF NOT *DECADES,* TO RECOVER FROM.
IT BECOMES *YOUR* DECISION.
YOU *WOULDN'T.*
I DON'T CARE *HOW* STRONGLY YOU BELIEVE IN THIS CAUSE OF YOURS, LUTHER, YOU *WOULDN'T!*
YOU'D...YOU'D ESSENTIALLY RUIN *HUMAN CIVILISATION!* YOU'D DESTROY THE ADVANCEMENT OF *MANKIND!*
WHICH MAKES YOUR DECISION, I WOULD THINK, VERY *EASY* TO MAKE.

NO. *NO!*

THIS *ISN'T* A GAME OF WHO'LL BLINK FIRST!

*DROKK'S SAKE,* MAN! YOU'RE NOT *STUPID!* CONSIDER WHAT YOU'RE *SAYING!*

ARE YOU GOING TO DOOM THE HUMAN RACE JUST TO MAKE SOME KIND OF *INSANE MORAL POINT?*

IT'S DIFFICULT, *ISN'T* IT, WHEN YOU'RE CONFRONTED BY AN *IMPLACABLE ATTITUDE?*

YOU CAN'T *ARGUE* WITH THIS THREAT. IT'S TOO *BIG* TO ARGUE WITH.

YOU'RE ACTUALLY GOING TO HAVE TO *DEAL* WITH IT INSTEAD.

OH, YOU *CHILD!* HOW MUCH CONTEXT DO YOU *NEED?*

THIS LAST DECADE HAS SEEN THE HUMAN RACE MOVE TOWARDS A POINT WHERE IT CEASES TO BE A *POST-GLOBAL* CULTURE AND BECOMES A TRUE *INTERSTELLAR* SOCIETY.

THIS IS A *PRECARIOUS POINT* IN OUR EVOLUTION!

THAT'S THE *REAL* REASON MEGA-CITY ONE DIDN'T HELP K ALPHA 61 DURING THE ZHIND WAR, BUT *HAPPILY* SENT A FLEET TO DEAL WITH THE COLONY WHEN *YOU* STEPPED OUT OF LINE!

WE DIDN'T *WANT* A WAR WITH *ALIENS!*

WE'RE TOO *VULNERABLE!* WE CAN'T *AFFORD* TO FIGHT AN ALIEN WAR!

WE CAN'T *AFFORD* TO *LOSE* VITAL RESOURCE COLONIES LIKE K ALPHA 61 AND PRODUCTION VENUE 33!

FOR THE NEXT FEW DECADES, *EVERYTHING* IS ABOUT *TRANSITION!*

*EVERYTHING* IS ABOUT *GRADUATING* AS A SPECIES!

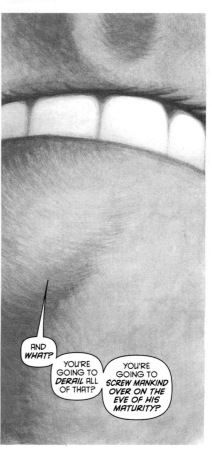

AND *WHAT?*

YOU'RE GOING TO *DERAIL* ALL OF THAT?

YOU'RE GOING TO *SCREW MANKIND OVER* ON THE EVE OF HIS *MATURITY?*

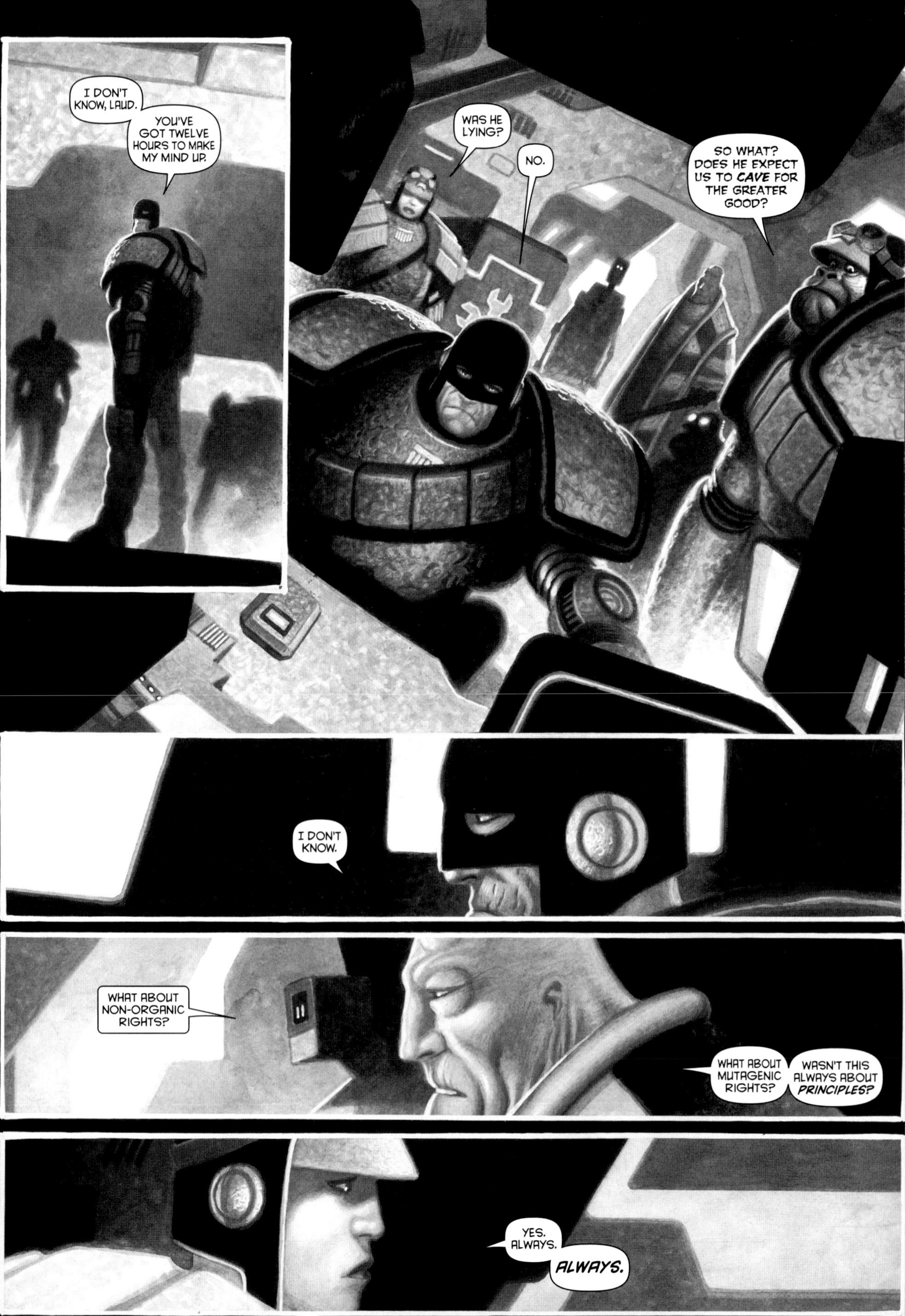
I DON'T KNOW, LAUD.
YOU'VE GOT TWELVE HOURS TO MAKE MY MIND UP.
WAS HE LYING?
NO.
SO WHAT? DOES HE EXPECT US TO CAVE FOR THE GREATER GOOD?
I DON'T KNOW.
WHAT ABOUT NON-ORGANIC RIGHTS?
WHAT ABOUT MUTAGENIC RIGHTS?
WASN'T THIS ALWAYS ABOUT PRINCIPLES?
YES. ALWAYS.
ALWAYS.

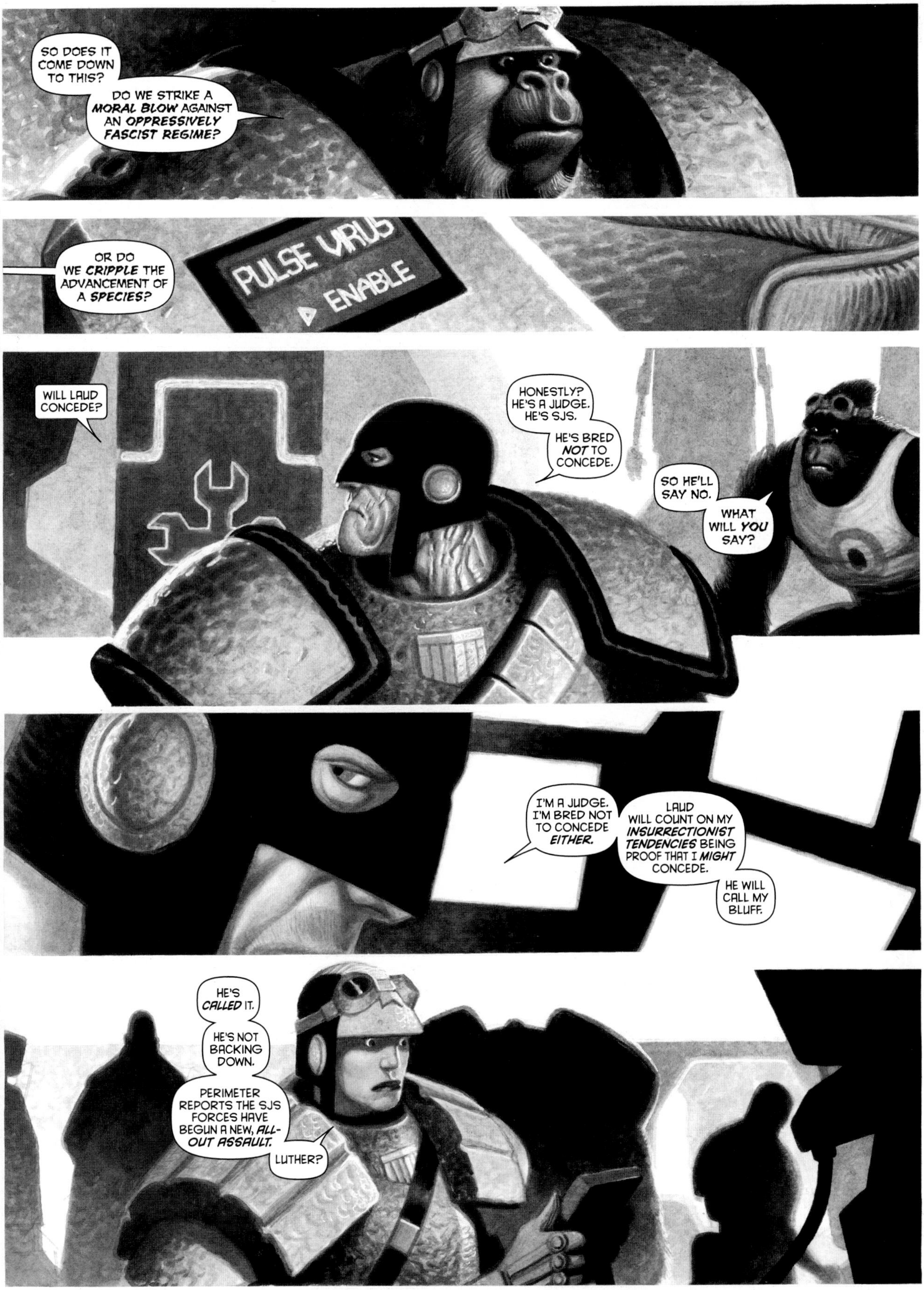

SO DOES IT COME DOWN TO THIS?
DO WE STRIKE A MORAL BLOW AGAINST AN OPPRESSIVELY FASCIST REGIME?
OR DO WE CRIPPLE THE ADVANCEMENT OF A SPECIES?
PULSE VIRUS
ENABLE
WILL LAUD CONCEDE?
HONESTLY? HE'S A JUDGE. HE'S SJS.
HE'S BRED NOT TO CONCEDE.
SO HE'LL SAY NO.
WHAT WILL YOU SAY?
I'M A JUDGE. I'M BRED NOT TO CONCEDE EITHER.
LAUD WILL COUNT ON MY INSURRECTIONIST TENDENCIES BEING PROOF THAT I MIGHT CONCEDE.
HE WILL CALL MY BLUFF.
HE'S CALLED IT.
HE'S NOT BACKING DOWN.
PERIMETER REPORTS THE SJS FORCES HAVE BEGUN A NEW, ALL-OUT ASSAULT.
LUTHER?

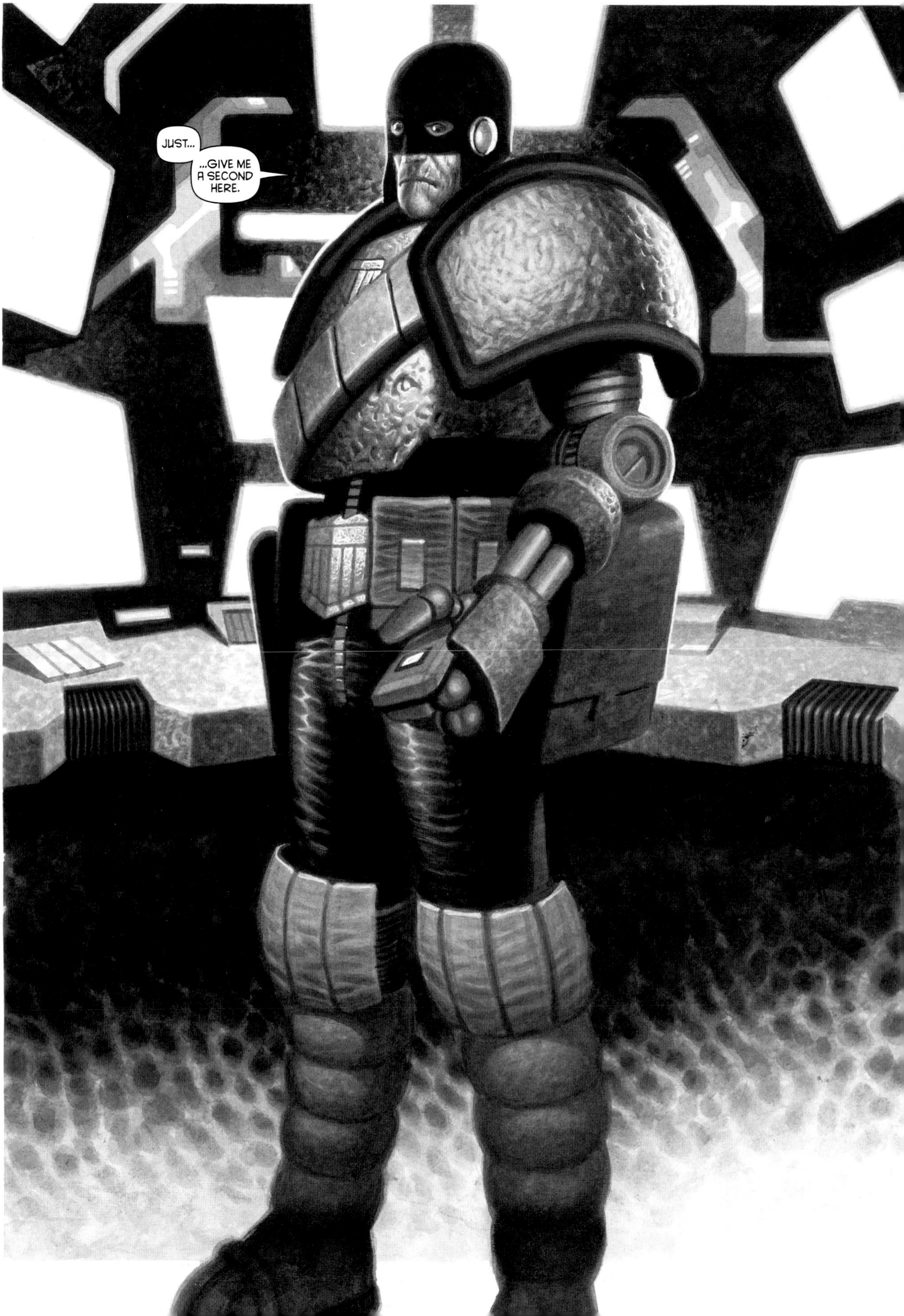
JUST...
...GIVE ME A SECOND HERE.

# EXTRAS

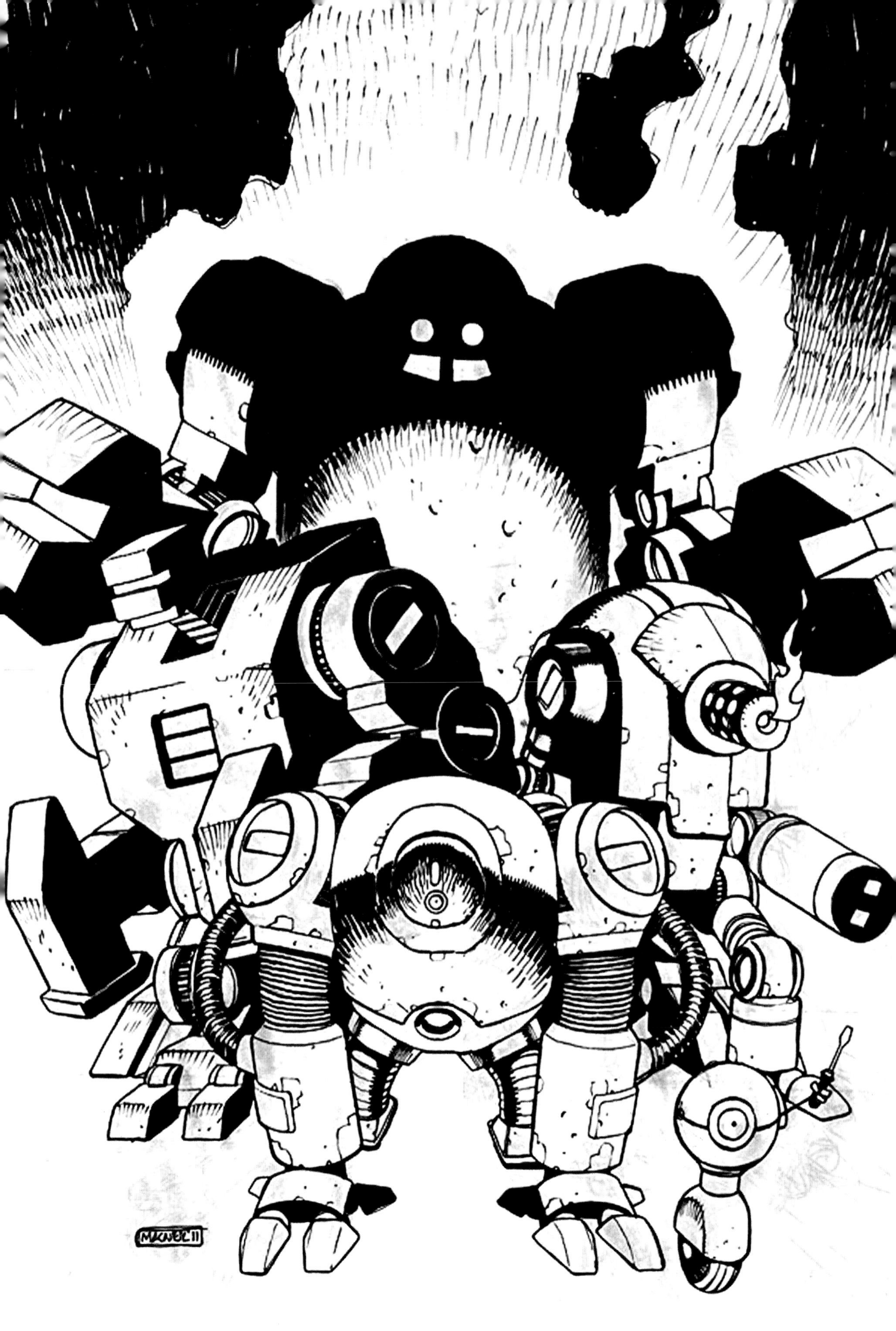

Hi Matt, here's the sketches I sent to Dan re: Judges spacewar thing. Hope you like'm too.

Cheers

Colin

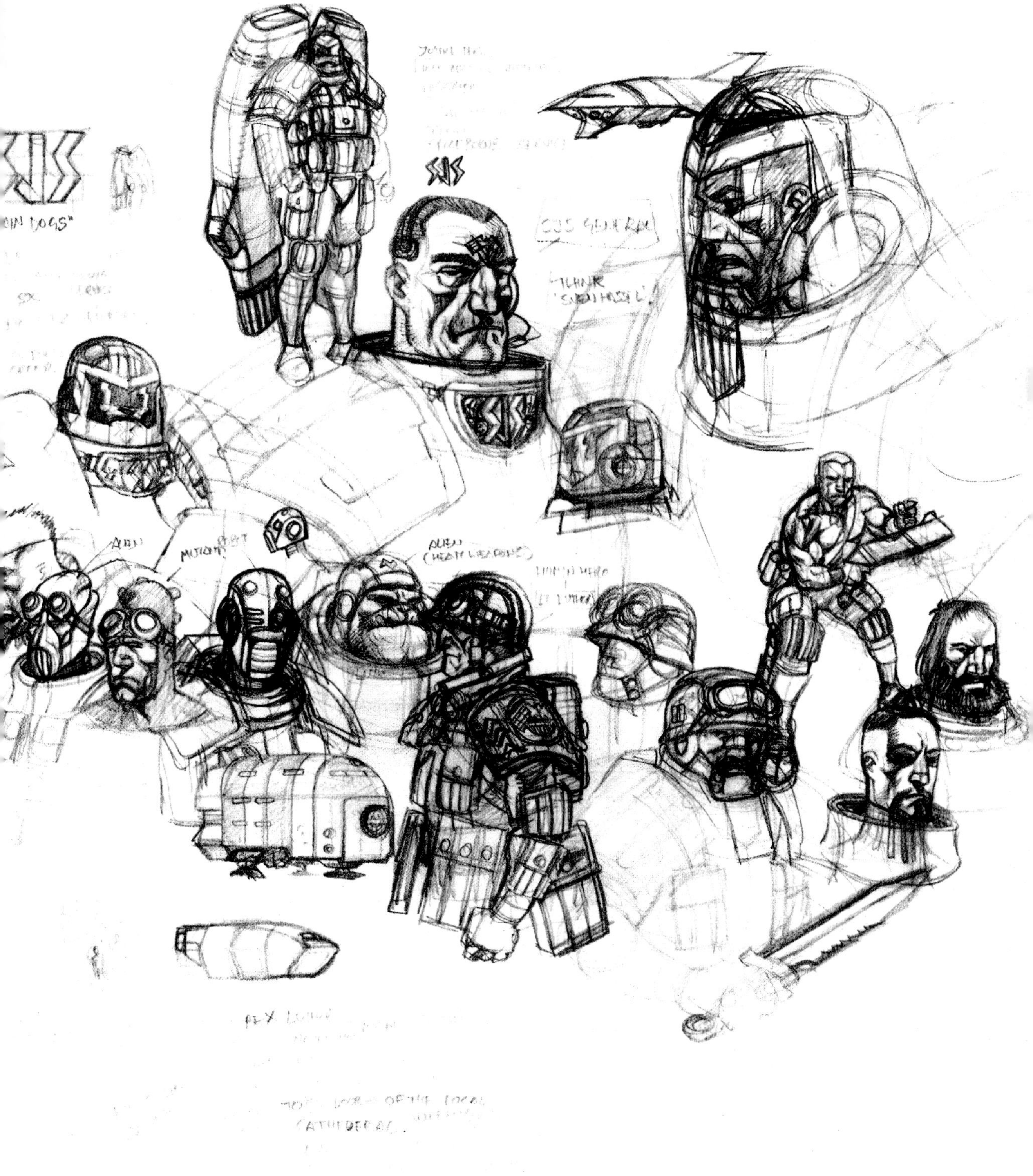
SJS GENERAL
MUTANT
ALIEN (HEAVY WEAPONS)

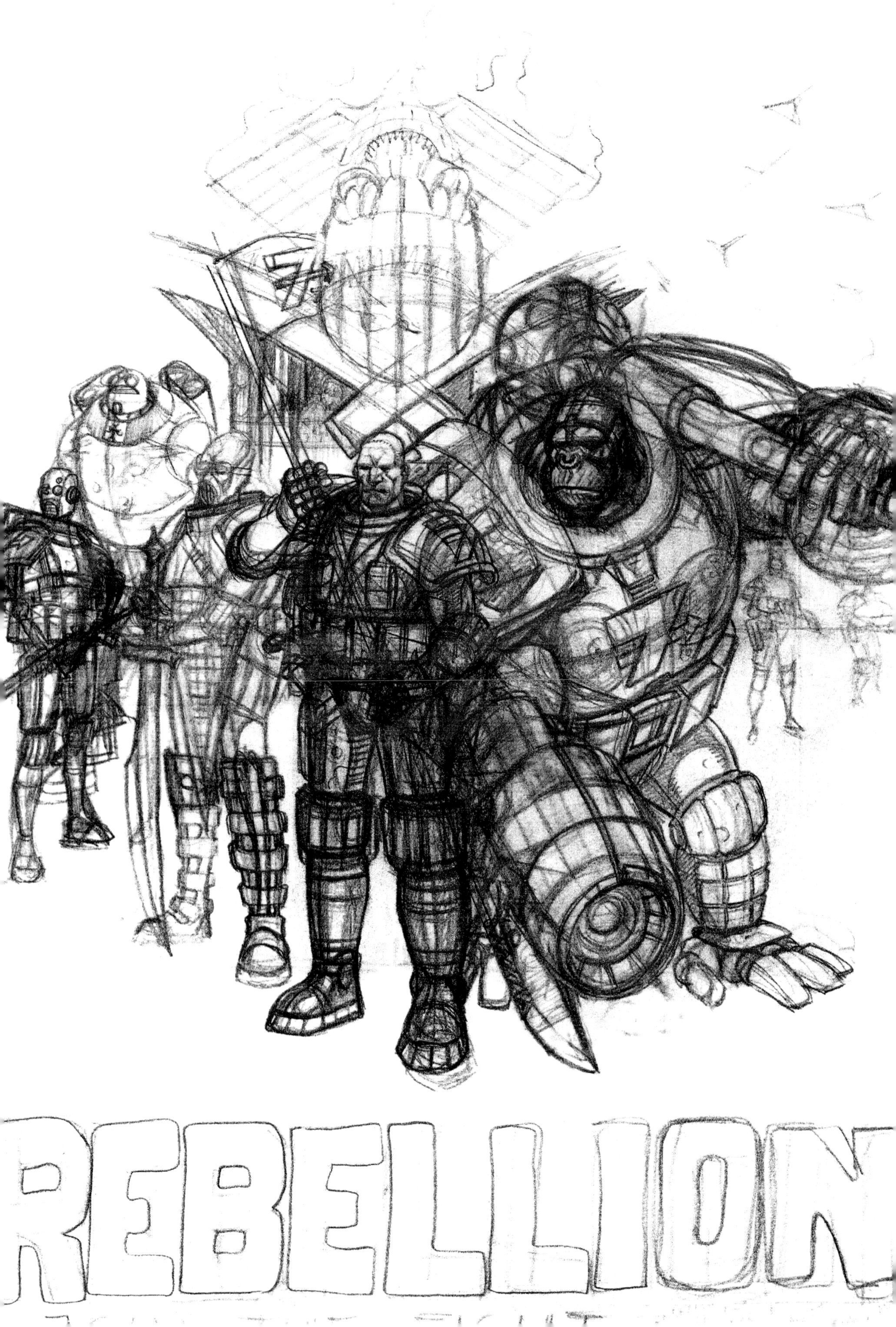
REBELLION

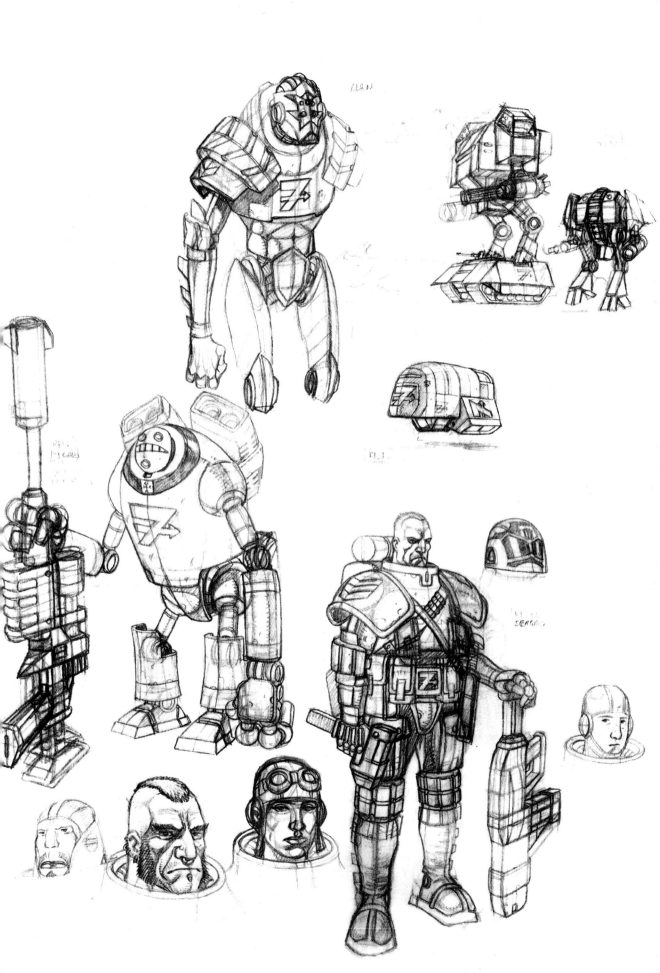

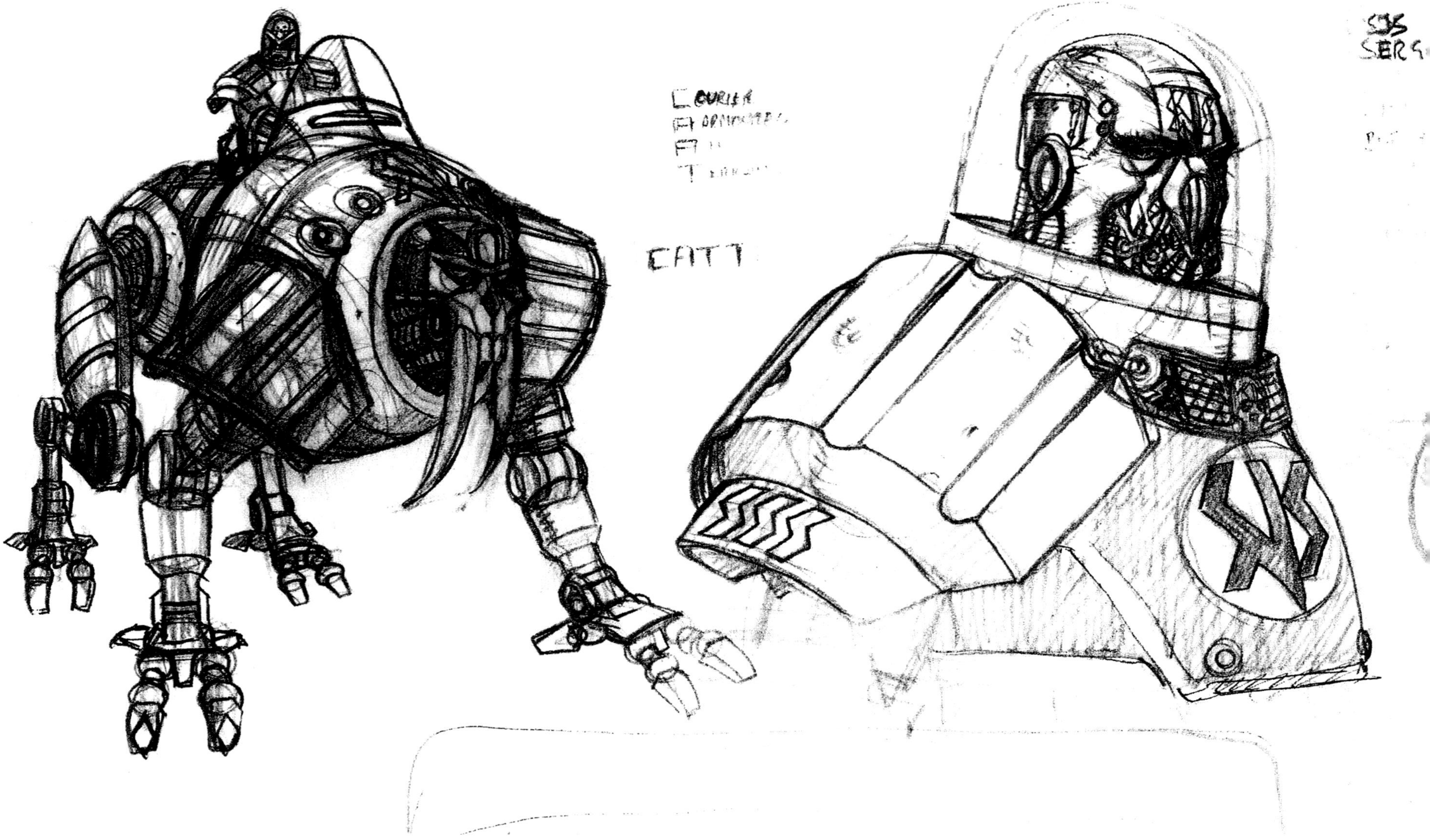
COURIER
CATT

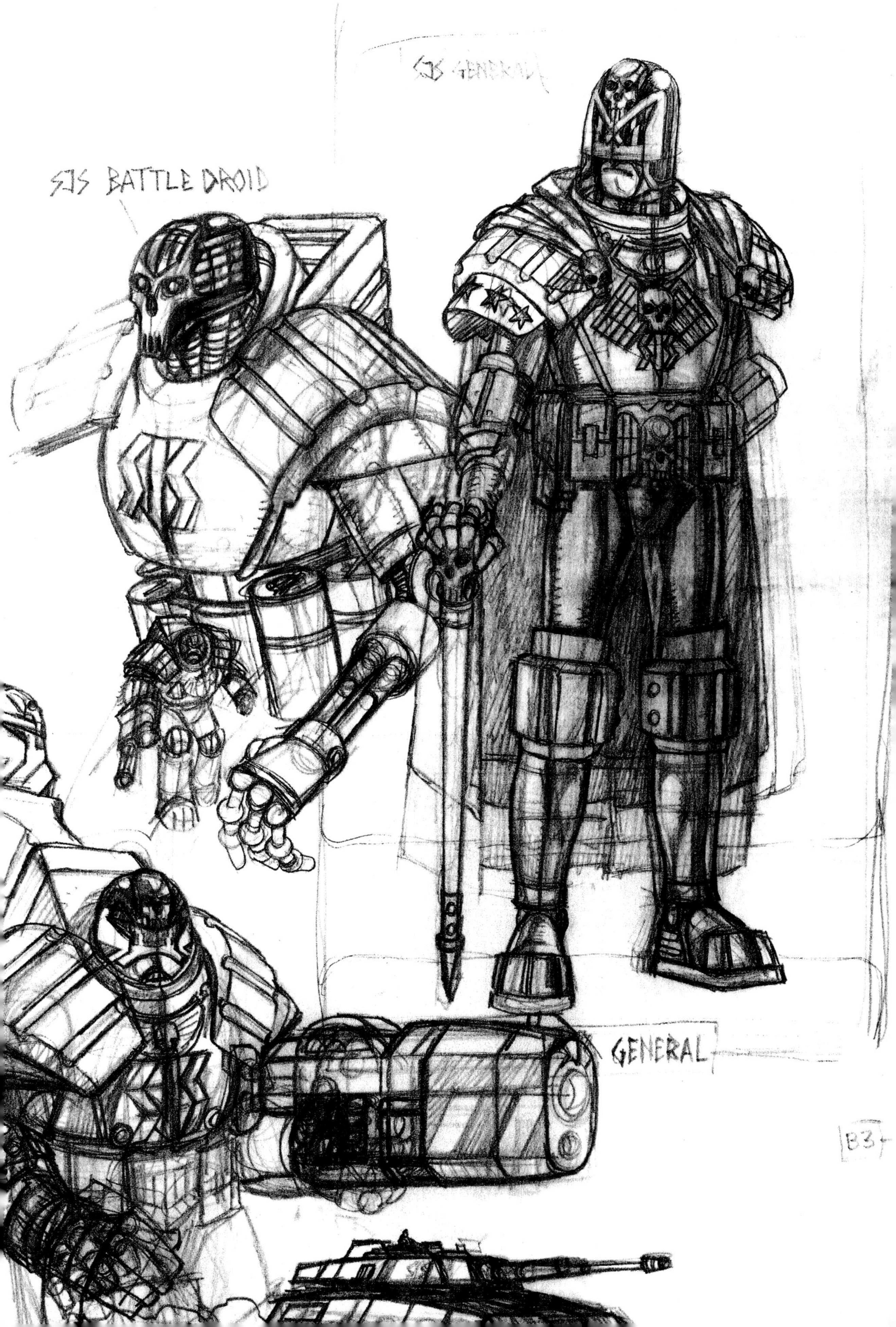
SJS GENERAL
SJS BATTLE DROID
GENERAL
B3

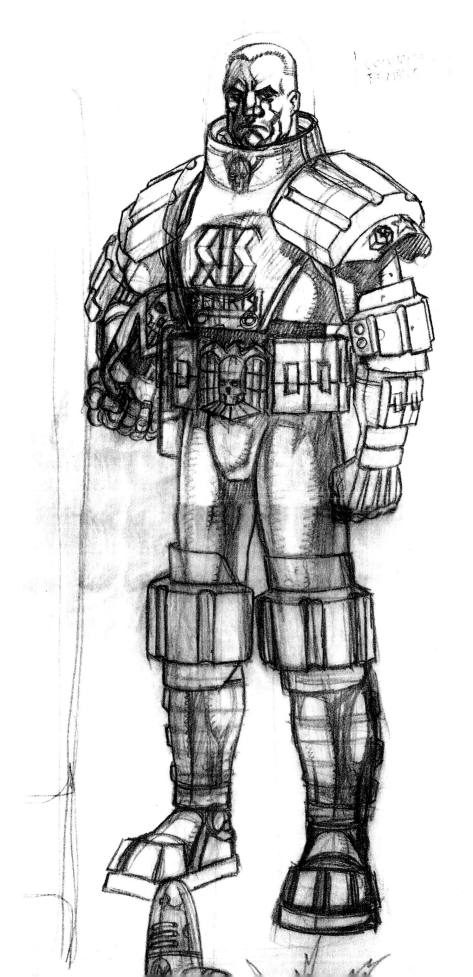

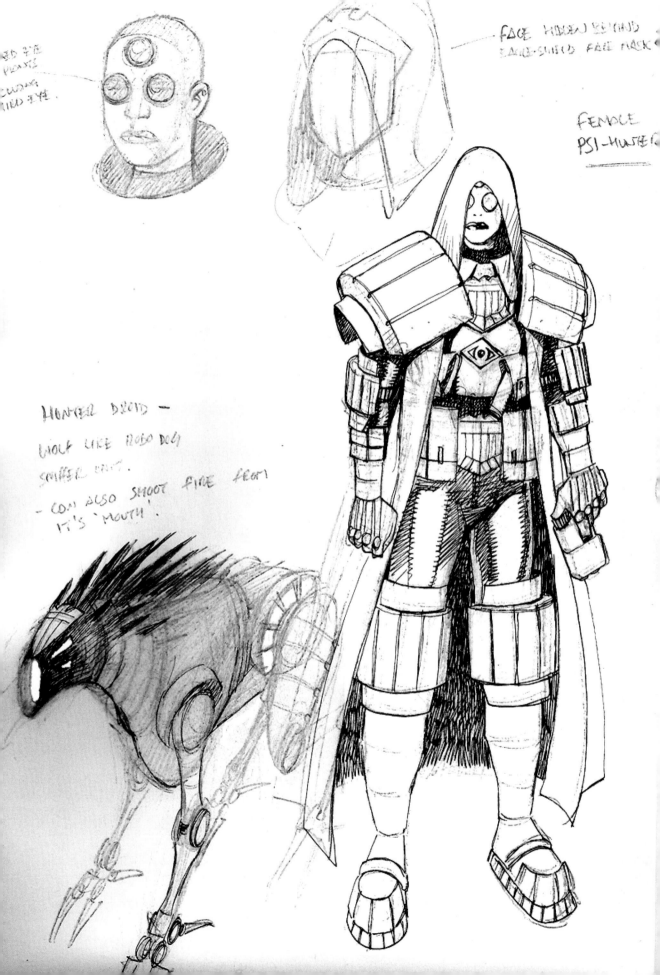

FACE HIDDEN BEHIND
SAND-SHIELD FACE MASK

FEMALE
PSI-HUNTER

HUNTER DROID —

WOLF LIKE ROBO DOG
SNIFFER UNIT.

— CAN ALSO SHOOT FIRE FROM
IT'S 'MOUTH'.

INSURRECTION PITCH

INSURRECTION
(or "Rebellion" tee hee)

working title
Megazine Judge epic, 6 x 9ppgs

Matt, here's the big idea. Please refer to Colin's glorious sketches to get a flavour of what we're about.

Basically, we feared that an epic space war story featuring the heavy duty Judge troopers inevitably means a nasty alien menace ("Return of the Kleggs"), and all the readers will therefore know what the outcome is going to be. It would also be one sided, in terms of reader sympathy and indentification. Soooo... how about this? It's much more ambiguous and 'grey', rather more political (in the true spirit of Wagner's stories), and fairly unswerving in its criticism of the fascist Judge regime (again, true to Wagner).

A colony world, let's call it Liberty, part of the human alliance (Matt - what is the 'world authority' actually called in *Dredd*? If this colony world is a Mega City colony, what does it call itself? What is it 'part of'?). It's a fringe world, maybe heavily industrial (a vital source of minerals for Mega City One). The population includes mutants, droids and genetically uplifted gorillas, all used as brute labour in the mines (and none with citizen status). The world is ruled by Judges, though we might want to call them Marshals out here, because there are fewer of them, more autonomous, forced to make their own laws and rules out on the high frontier.

In the years preceding the story, Liberty was caught up in a border war with some neighbouring alien race (could even be the Kleggs, if you like). Liberty mobilised, and fought the aliens off, winning the war (and protecting the flanks of Terran space territory). One of the reasons Liberty won is that the Marshals got permission from the Hall of Justice to enfranchise the workforce as soldiers: muties, droids and apes, a hell of a shock-troop force. All of them, especially the great apes, proved to be loyal, couragous and selfless. For the duration of the war, they were granted citizen status.

When the war was over, this status was withdrawn, despite the outrage of Liberty's Marshals, especially the war hero (our hero) Marshal Luther. The dispute dragged on, but eventually resulted in Liberty declaring independence from the human alliance, championing the civil rights of the sub-human underclasses.

And that just won't do. As the insurrection involves turncoat marshals, it becomes a matter for the SJS, which launches a huge assault force to bring Liberty to order.

Luther, with his marshals, his muties, his droids and, especially, his great apes, along with the population of Liberty (except for a few dissenters who cause problems along the way), lead the fight back.

So the reader should be rooting for the rebels, and hissing the Judges, which will get them going, because they will be aware that this is the Megazine, and fascist or not, the Judges always win.

Or do they? We think the climax of the story could be the SJS winning the physical war by sheer numbers, but the rebels (going underground at the end) winning the war of ideas which, after all, is what this is really about.

Room for a sequel, of course, and for what it's worth, here's how that goes: as the guerilla war rages on Liberty, the SJS trying to smoke out Luther's underground, Luther is contacted by representatives of the alien race that Liberty beat during the earlier war. The sneaky aliens offer to help the Liberty rebels against the 'common foe'. Realising, though he detests the SJS and the fascist rule of the Judges, that he's actually being asked to go to war with the human race, Luther courageously sides his forces with the SJS AGAINST the aliens. Victorious thanks to Luther, the SJS finally compromise, and allow Luther's sub-humans to keep citizen status, though this fact is suppressed so that no one in Mega City ever finds out about it.

Or... in true, bleak, typical Dredd terms, it could all end in poignant tragedy, in either the first of second story, ie:

1. Luther wins the war, but all his apes die in the process, and it is therefore a pyrrhic victory when the SJS disdainfully grants the apes citizen status.

2. The SJS simply crushes Luther and his insurrection, despite the fact the Luther has come close to victory and we're all rooting for him.

3. Dredd shoots everyone in the face and tells them to behave (kidding).

Or... we end up creating Liberty as, literally, the one outpost of lefty freedom in the entire Dredd-i-verse, a Shangri-La sanctuary for all the oppressed muties, crims, droids, runaways and dissenters in Mega City One.

Thoughts?

Dan and Colin.

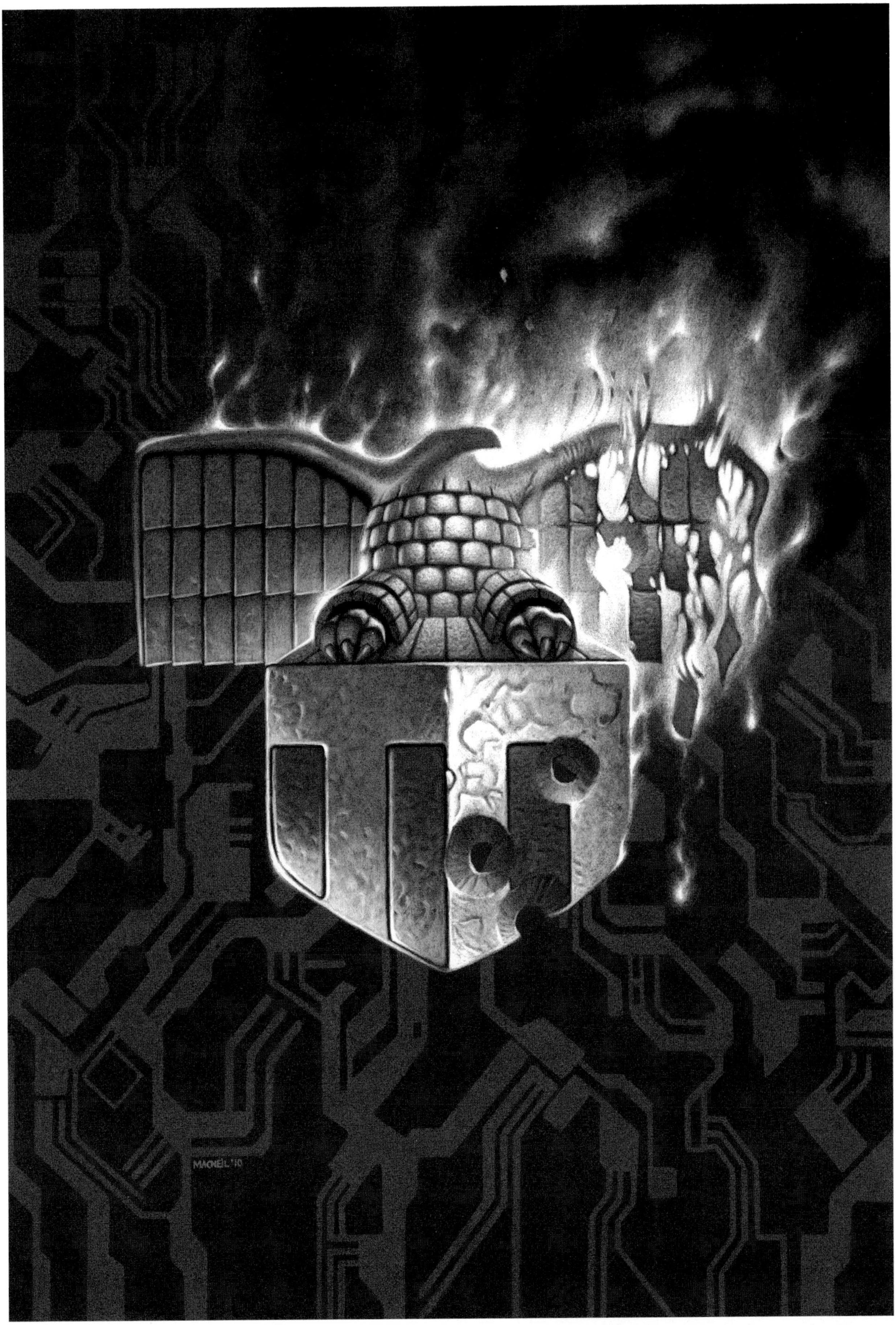
MACNEIL '10

*Judge Dredd Megazine* issue 305: Cover by **Colin MacNeil**

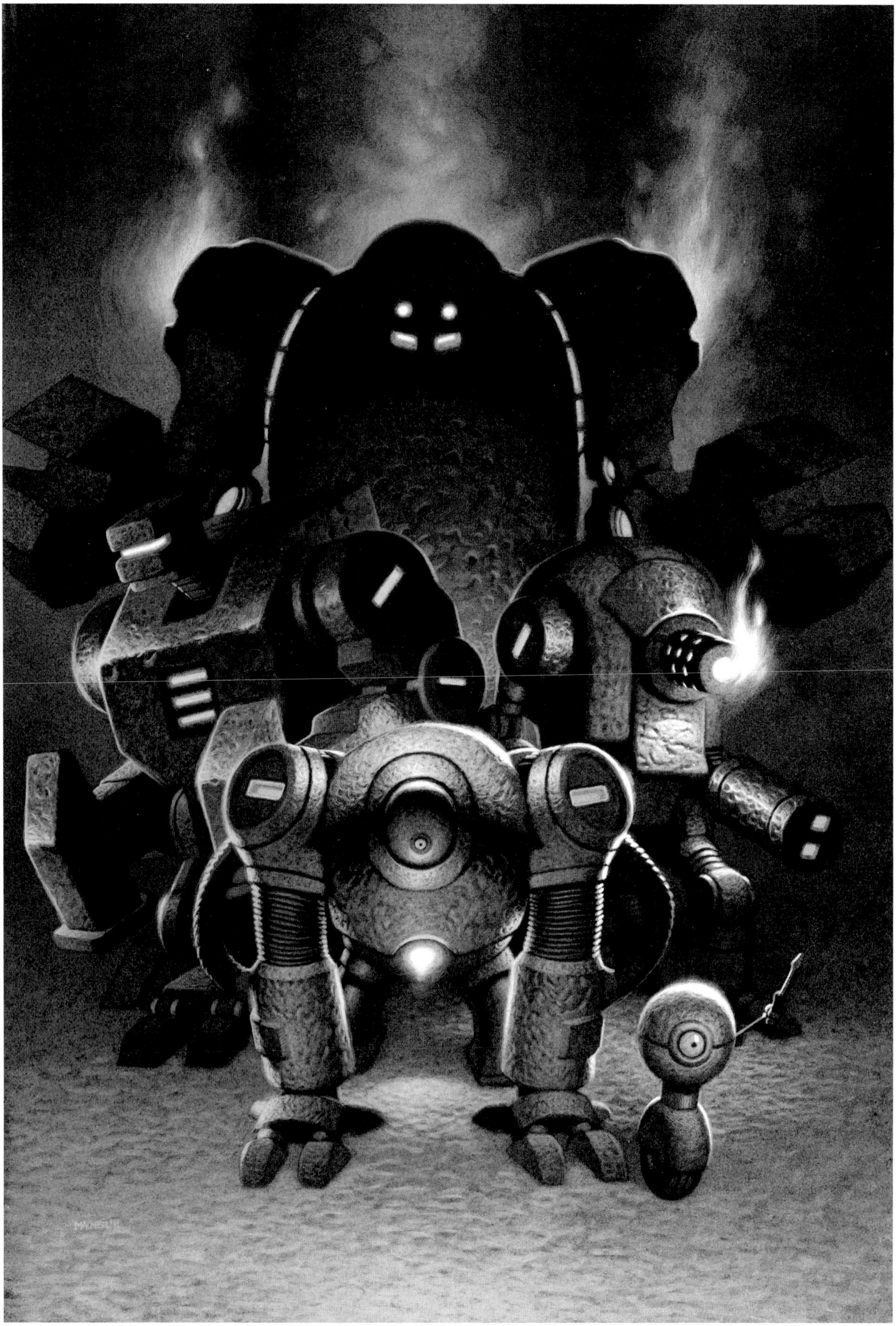

*Judge Dredd Megazine* issue 310: Cover by **Colin MacNeil**

# DAN ABNETT

**Dan Abnett** is the co-creator of *2000 AD* series *Atavar, Badlands, Sancho Panzer* and *Sinister Dexter*. He has also written *Black Light, Downlode Tales, Durham Red, Flesh, Future Shocks, Judge Dredd, Pulp Sci-Fi, Roadkill, Rogue Trooper, The VCs, Vector 13* and *Venus Bluegenes*, as well as *The Scarlet Apocrypha* and *Wardog* for the *Megazine*. A prolific creator, Abnett has also written for Marvel, Dark Horse and DC Comics. He is the author of twenty novels for the Black Library, including the bestselling *Gaunt's Ghosts* series. His most recent work outside the Galaxy's Greatest Comic is 'The New 52's' *Resurrection Man* from DC Comics. Dan Abnett was voted Best Writer at the 2003 National Comic Awards.

# COLIN MACNEIL

Since joining *2000 AD* in 1986 **Colin MacNeil** has worked on many strips, including *Chopper: Song of the Surfer* and the infamous death of Johnny Alpha in *Strontium Dog: The Final Solution*. He went on to collaborate with John Wagner on the award-winning *America* for the *Judge Dredd Megazine*. He has also worked on *Shimura*, *Maelstrom* and *Fiends of the Eastern Front: Stalingrad*, and, outside of the Galaxy's Greatest Comic, provided the atmospheric artwork on *Bloodquest* for Games Workshop. He also enjoys creating large abstract paintings. He says it's art therapy!